Looks like you have a winner — I haven't seen anything like it on the market. Could be the "*Self-Publishing Manual*" (Poynter) for the audio world!

(I) Had "Xerox impulses" (Kinko moments?) all the way through.

For anyone considering putting their book on tape, this is essential reading. . . And for those of us that are just a part of the process, this paints the big picture, putting our work in context.

I know that despite the fact that I've produced over 20 audio cassette albums I will be able to do a better job next time because of your book. . .You have studied the best of the best and condensed their wisdom into one book that makes it all manageable . . . .a fine piece of work.

This one goes into my infopreneurs' library, right next to Jeffrey Lant and Mark Hansen and Jack Canfield's How To Build Your Speaking Empire.

This book is VERY COMPREHENSIVE. Congratulations on a job well done!

It's about time somebody came out with a book like this! Excellent resource . . . all encompassing.

Stories on audio make powerful connections. I know people want tapes and CDs. They've bought mine for years. *Words On Tape* shows you how to bring stories to life in products you'll be proud to sell.

"This extensively researched, intelligently written book covers virtually every aspect of audio production....an invaluable resource for anyone contemplating entering the audiobook industry..."

Trudi Rosenblum, Audio column, Publishers Weekly, 12/1/97

"...stresses the importance of high quality audio production and manufacturing in order to succeed in today's booming audio market...Checklists, editing logs and various forms add value.."

Small Press, November/December 1997

"..Has it been helpful? It's the Bible of the audio world!"

Gail Golomb, The Kidney Stones Handbook, Four Geez Press, Roseville, CA

"Holy Smokes! I'm amazed at just how much information is packed into this book. With it by your side you can avoid all the common mistakes and instead create hot audio products...Excellent!"

Joe Vitale, The AMA Complete Guide to Small Business Advertising, Houston, TX

"I wish I'd had this book months ago. It would have saved me so much money. I've spent over $16,000 recording and editing. How to plan so that won't happen next time is summed up in one sentence in your book."

Mary T., first time audio publisher, New Orleans, LA

"There's lots in this book to help you, so if you decide to make audio tapes you won't feel stupid!"

Valerie Spivic, Junior High Teacher, Denver, CO

"Byers provides much needed advice in this one-of-a-kind reference. If you're doing audio you've absolutely got to get this book!"

Marilyn Ross, co-author, The Complete Guide To Self Publishing and co-founder of SPAN, Buena Vista, CO

Words On Tape

How to Create Profitable
Spoken Word Audio on Cassettes and CDs

Copyright ©1997 by Judith A. Byers.

All rights reserved. No part of this book may be reproduced or transmitted in any form or by any means, electronic or mechanical, including photocopying, recording or by any information storage and retrieval system without written permission from the author, except for the inclusion of brief quotations in a review.

Audio CP Publishing
1660 South Albion, Ste. 309
Denver, CO 80222

The title and trade dress of *Words On Tape: How to Create Profitable Spoken Word Audio on Cassettes and CDs* are trademarks of the author.

First Edition.

Publisher's Cataloging in Publication
Quality Books P-CIP

Byers, Judy.
    Words on tape: how to create a profitable spoken word audio on cassettes and CDs / Judy Byers.
    p. cm.
    Includes bibliographical references and index.
    ISBN 0-09655721-4-5

    1. Sound recording industry—Management. 2. Sound recordings—Production and direction. 3. Audiotapes. 4. Compact discs. I. Title.

HD9697.P562.B94 1997   621.38932
                                  QBI96-40838

Words On Tape

How to Create Profitable
Spoken Word Audio on Cassettes and CDs

Judy Byers

Audio CP Publishing
Denver, CO

ACKNOWLEDGMENTS

Many people contributed to the creation of *Words On Tape, How to Create Profitable Spoken Word Audio* on Cassettes and CDs. I am grateful for their professional contributions, encouragement and unfailing good cheer.

First and foremost, Dan Poynter has been a mentor, friend, nag, and generous font of knowledge during the months of preparation. Terri Lonier, author of the *Working Solo* series, has been a cheerleader, sounding board, and friend. Terri taught me the joys of e-mail, and provides an ongoing education in office technology and marketing. Jan Nathan, and many members of the Audio Publishers Association, have been accessible and gracious in sharing their knowledge of the audio publishing industry.

Toni Boyle, Tami Simon, Steve Sundberg, Rick Dasher, Linda Cano Rodriguez, and Marilyn Ross provided insights and knowledge on many aspects of the book and audio business. I couldn't have written this book without their support. I also want to thank Helen Downs, audio buyer, and Gordon Pierce from the business section at The Tattered Cover Bookstore in Denver, CO for suggestions on how to make the book more useful for readers. The Tattered Cover Bookstore is heaven on earth for book lovers.

Along the way editors Justin Mitchell and Linda Lawson have worked valiantly to make my writing clearer and grammatically correct. Paul Keebler, Brenda Ohlschwager, Marie Prokuski and Rob Wehner helped with page layout and interior design. Jill Spivey has checked in regularly, and been a wonderful problem-solving friend. I am especially happy to have met Jan Lierl, whose wit has provided many laughs during development of the cover and promotional pieces. Rodney Hawk has made this book a reality with his wizardry and speed at page layout.

Finally, I'd like to thank friends and family who encouraged my efforts and nourished my spirit: Lois Ripley, Barney Rouse, JT, Dick Duff, Elaine Floyd, Julia Byers, Barbara and Don Coloroso.

Judy Byers, 1997

For Teresa, Steve and Morgan

Table of Contents

The Exciting Growth of Audio Publishing

Every year, millions of people around the world enjoy spine-tingling mysteries, heart-fluttering romances, and action-filled dramas in their cars, trucks, tractors, homes, and health clubs. They invest in tapes to entertain and educate their children. They learn about self-development, financial success, spiritual growth, losing weight — and much more.

The common denominator: listeners value their time. In 1996 they spent over four *billion* dollars on spoken audio products.

Your audio tape or CD could be one of them.

Welcome to the exciting world of spoken audio — the most dynamic and fastest-growing segment of publishing. The 1996 growth rate for the audiobooks category was 11 percent. Early 1997 figures indicate a growth of over 20 percent for the year could happen. Today, more than ever, newcomers to publishing must understand how commercial products are created and sold.

Fifteen years ago consumers would accept lower quality products. Today productions from Simon & Schuster

Audio, Dove Audio, Books On Tape™, Recorded Books Inc. and dozens of other audio publishers of all sizes have raised the entry level. Consumers expect professional editing and sound quality. Fortunately quality production does not have to be much more expensive than second rate recording and editing.

This book is designed for readers who:

- Are thinking about audio products and how to sell them.
- Have made a tape(s), and want to move to the next level.
- Prefer a non-technical explanation of recording and editing.
- Are seeking information about duplicating, packaging and marketing.

What Does Spoken Word Encompass?

Audiobooks: The Audio Publishers Association (APA), founded in 1986, is comprised of members who publish primarily words, or spoken material. APA members range from Bantam Dell Doubleday Audio, Dove Audio, Random House Audio, Simon and Schuster Audio, Time Warner AudioBooks and other large companies to single-person shops. The common link is all the members' products rely primarily on the human voice. Music and sound effects, when used, are enhancements.

The major publishing houses in New York and California base most of their audio products on books. In 1996, after much discussion, the APA adopted the word *audiobook* to describe all products in this category, regardless of origin. The APA tracks sales of audiobooks and releases annual estimates to the media, explains Jan Nathan, executive director of the APA.

"Those figures represent retail sales through the traditional book selling pipeline. The APA has no way of gauging actual total sales," says Nathan.

(Contact information for all resources, including the APA, are at the end of the chapter where they are first mentioned, and repeated in an alphabetical appendix of resources in the back of the book.)

Non-book based audios: There are thousands of non-book based cassettes produced every year. Many are listed in *Words On Cassette,* a reference book similar to *Books In Print,* from R.R. Bowker. Thousands more new titles are produced each year and never appear in reference books. *Words On Cassette* (expanded onto CD in late 1997) is a dependable resource for audiobooks from major publishers. To my knowledge there's no reference or guidebook for the tens of thousands of tapes produced yearly by professional groups, churches, and to promote goods and services.

The Size of the Marketplace

Terence O'Kelly, former director of sales and marketing for BASF Corporation, and now director of new business development for Kodak Recording Products, has tracked audio cassette trends for 20 years. He estimates the spoken word audio market was $3.925 billion in retail sales in 1996, or more than double what the Audio Publishers Association reported. Newer figures from some industry experts are slightly higher.

Why the discrepancy in figures? The audio industry includes many small, independent tape publishers whose sales figures go unreported. While O'Kelly's figures are substantially higher than those from The Audio Publishers Association, they seem to represent a truer picture of the total market for spoken audio because O'Kelly arrives at his figures from three sources:

1. Consultants who research and advise bulk tape manufacturers/ suppliers (such as BASF).

2. Trade/professional association member-supplied sales figures (such as the APA, the Recording Industry Association of America, and Knowledge Industries Publications).

3. The footage of voice grade tape stock sold in a year, divided by average program length, and multiplied by an average retail price per unit.

Leaders of trade associations involved in cassette duplication recommended O'Kelly over and over as the individual with the widest perspective on the industry.

The Audience

A typical audiobook buyer is 30-55 years old with a college education and annual household income over $40,000. Bestseller fiction, spiritual and inspirational titles, self-help, professional development, biographies, language instruction and classics are all popular. Children's titles sell well.

Research shows that women use spoken audio more than men, although certain publishers' sales vary because their content is targeted to male audiences. In general, the market is filled with busy Baby Boomers who have a desire to read and grow, but not enough time to pursue all their interests. They find it difficult to cope with all their responsibilities, and still keep up with their reading. Most listening takes place in vehicles. Audio tapes and CDs help ease the frustration of commutes, hours of boredom on long road trips, and the restlessness of children in the back seat.

Bradshaw Cassettes, publishers of John Bradshaw Audio and Video Self Help Programs, is an example of a thriving smaller publisher. Bradshaw Cassettes sell evenly to men and women, however male customers tend to be around 40, females a few years younger. 65 percent of sales to individuals through their catalog are audio products, the remaining 35 percent are video. Matthew Fox, sales manager, knows why. "People say they don't have time to watch video, so they want audio to listen in their cars. It's kind of a cultural problem because people are rushing, trying to get everything packed into their life."

The Scene Today

We're in the midst of an economic revolution causing major shifts in the workplace. The U.S. is already an information society, according to the U.S. Census Bureau, based on the fact that most job classifications today involve handling and transmitting information.

People are struggling, with changes coming faster than we can absorb them. For most of us, time is our most precious commodity. Many women have a full time paid job, plus a home and family "job." Reading through their ears is an attractive alternative way to continue reading for pleasure.

Fueling the audio trend is the fact that the under-40 crowd is electronically literate. Children raised with computers and TV use electronic sources for entertainment and information. They're already habitual users of portable audio, though mainly for music. Their parents use computers, and the Internet at work, and increasingly at home too.

The over-40 crowd is turning to audio as an alternative to hunting for their reading glasses as the "*&%^#!" small print gets harder to read every year. Avid readers frequently developed their love of books because loved ones read to them. Audiobooks plug into those familiar, happy memory banks of books or radio dramas enjoyed with family and friends. I believe this is why it's so easy to become "hooked" on audiobooks.

Spoken word audio has a bright future. Baby Boomers are in their highest spending and earning years, and will continue to feel work, family, and time pressures until at least 2008, when the oldest boomers reach age 62. Even then, habits are unlikely to change as most people continue energetic, active lives either in careers or leisure activities.

In 1996, as the oldest Boomers began turning 50, the APA launched a small but effective campaign to increase public awareness of audiobooks. Their conservative estimate (as of 1996) was that less than 20% of the population has ever listened to an audiobook. Although some estimate the percentage is higher, there is general concurrence that once people try spoken audio, the majority will buy, borrow, or rent again.

265 million Americans + 26 million Canadians x 20 percent = 58.2 million people (conservatively) exposed to audiobooks by the mid 1990's. Over one million of them bought a copy of Stephen Covey's *7 Habits Of Highly Effective People*, from Simon & Schuster. You can read about 30 audiobooks that sold over 175,000 each in the September 2, 1996 edition of *Publishers Weekly*. *PW* covers audio publishing regularly in columns and feature stories. An increasing number of newspapers run feature stories and bestseller lists of audiobooks.

On a regional basis audiobooks sell best in southern California. They're also "hot" in Texas, Colorado, and certain urban areas of other states. California and Colorado are two "bellweather" states cited in *Megatrends,* an early 1980's bestseller, by John Naisbitt.

Predicting the Future Market

Charles Van Horn, executive vice president of The International Recording Media Association (ITA), says "Pundits have been declaring the demise of the audio analog cassette for years. The pre-recorded audio cassette is still doing well more than 12 years after the introduction of the CD. It took until 1995 for music cassette and cassette single sales numbers to start dropping," as music CDs began to supplant cassettes.

In other words, expect the cassette to be around for awhile yet. It may be low tech but it's inexpensive, "good enough" for most consumers, and it can be played worldwide without special adapters or conversion.

Spoken audio market expansion internationally is due in part to the Internet. The United Kingdom spoken audio industry is very active. Foreign rights buyers from many countries comb the aisles at international publishing fairs and Net booksites, seeking books to translate and record in their own language and style. Individuals post online requests for help finding specific authors or titles.

For example, a man in Africa recently queried publishers on an Audio Publishers Association listserv open to consumers. He was seeking books on cassette for his ailing father who can no longer see. Four members responded via the list, and more answered privately. Long distance calling charges for communicating swiftly with the African customer Zero. Time zone considerations? None. Did he get the books he wanted? Yes.

This market globalization via the Internet will continue at a rapid pace, and brings great advantages for new and small audio publishers seeking wider markets for their products.

People who still believe the Net is a passing fad might consider the U.S. presidential election night in November, 1996. The CNN news anchor reported their Website was getting 5 million "hits" an hour, and they projected 50 million attempts to access CNN news pages for specific election results before the evening was over. (Internet surveyors guesstimate 1 million "hits" is equivalent to 50,000 individuals by 1996 measurement methods.) Other news media web sites also were overloaded.

Sites like BookZone, Amazon.com, Audiobooks.com, Bookwire and ReadersIndex are all seeing a growing number of "hits." Some sites are informational, some more entertaining, and some World Wide Web sites are clearly designed for shopping. BookZone is an online catalog welcoming **24,000** visitors a week as of press time. It's the best starting place for spoken audio publishers and industry members.

Even Bill Gates admits to being surprised by how fast people are embracing E-mail and the World Wide Web. As electronically literate individuals reach out to access information online, publishers of all kinds will have an instant worldwide market and can fill and ship orders immediately — all thanks to technology.

What's Already Out There?

The quality of today's spoken word audio products is a reflection of how the industry has matured over the past 20 years. Jeff Baker, CEO of the audio duplication firm CPU, Inc., recalls, "Spoken word has come a long way since our company began in 1978. The clients we serve today are much more sophisticated. They benefit from the more organized and established channels of distribution. The audiobook publishers (primarily the large publishers on both coasts) have given the market a level of credibility. At the same time they've increased the level of quality and competition for smaller, newer publishers who want to join the audiobook marketplace."

Baker explains that the industry's most visible segment is the audiobook publishing component, followed by the children's category. According to Baker, other market segments in no particular order include:

• Direct response and direct marketing
• Multilevel marketing and other direct selling organizations
• Professional speakers and trainers
• Advertising agencies
• Promotional agencies
• Insurance companies
• Ministries
• Financial service companies

- Catalog companies
- Pharmaceuticals
- Schools, universities and educators
- Political campaigns

"My list is by no means exclusive," Baker says, "because new and innovative ways to use audio cassettes occur every day. All of us in the duplicating business see it, and this flexibility insures long-term opportunities for the medium."

How an Audiobook Differs from Print

Seth Gershel, senior vice president and publisher, Simon & Schuster, is a vocal, persistent crusader for the medium. Gershel served as president of the APA for its first six years. He knows audiobooks can create a special author-to-listener bond. "When we choose a work for audio we seek to create an informative, entertaining experience not equaled in print. The use of sound effects, music and a well-matched reader are just as important as the story line in contributing to the enhancement of the listener's imagination or stimulating their thoughts through inspirational works. The listener receives the same benefits, if not more in some cases, as they would have had they read the book . . . "

Frank Muller, narrator of over 130 audiobooks, has a huge listener/reader following with good reason. Comments from reviewers and fans help pinpoint that "author-to-listener bond" even further, as these quotes show:

- Author Stephen King said, "(When Frank reads) the blind will see, the lame will walk, and the deaf will hear." (Ed. note: Muller recorded King's *Green Mile* series for Penguin Audiobooks.)
- *AudioFile* Magazine says ". . . a perfect interpreter, the medium through which an author's words resonate to the listener. His voice is distinct, yet it yields a thousand characters. He can be transparent, offering the very essence of a character baring his soul or his teeth, or speaking elegantly as he spins out a descriptive passage. He makes the listener believe the characters no matter how wacky and makes classic characters live and breathe for a contemporary audience."

- *The Philadelphia Enquirer* says "Nobody can set you trolling the depths of the soul like Frank Muller can. . . . A veteran actor, and the darkly superb voice of some of Recorded Books' most challenging works. . . He has a voice and delivery that speak of distant, if darker places where life somehow takes on a greater significance . . . . "
- *The Chicago Tribune* wrote ". . . Muller has established himself as . . . the Laurence Olivier of the medium."

Frank Muller says simply, "In my humble opinion the objective should be to illuminate the text for the listener – not to alter its essential nature or the author's intent. If that standard is adhered to, the experience will indeed be changed, but not the book itself."

Is There Room for More?

Is there room in the marketplace for *your* audio? Yes, if you create and market skillfully, if you're persistent, and the timing is right. Many existing companies had humble beginnings.

Grady Hesters (1996-98 president of the APA) has been in the industry longer than most. He started with Newman Publishing shortly after college. Hesters and Seth Gershel, then with Caedmon, met George Hodgkins and his assistant, Jim Brannigan, when Hesters and Gershel were cooling their heels in the waiting room of Waldenbooks offices. For over a year Gershel and Hesters pitched their new products to George Hodgkins, the Waldenbook's buyer. Finally, in 1983, Hodgkins took a chance. From then on audiobooks moved steadily into traditional bookseller venues, and beyond.

These pioneers had persistence, belief in their products, and vision. Their companies flourished, and hundreds more have followed their path. All four are active leaders today in audio publishing. Grady Hesters and his wife, Linda Olsen, founded Audio Partners Publishing Corporation and Audio Editions, a catalog. Hodgkins eventually moved to the publisher side and at press time he was overseeing web pages and the APA online presence at BookZone.com. Jim Brannigan is vice president of HighBridge Company. Gershel, quoted earlier in the chapter, heads Simon and Schuster Audio.

Other early trends that have come to dominate spoken audio began outside traditional book publishing circles.

In Chicago, Earl Nightingale was a radio favorite recording commentaries on WGN and playing Sky King on radio and TV. Nightingale owned an insurance agency on the side, and used his radio skills to give pep talks to the salesmen every week. When time came for a vacation in 1956, he acceded to his panicky sales manager's request, and recorded some extra inspirational talks. One of them, *The Strangest Secret*, was written in less than three hours, after Nightingale had ruminated about it for a couple of weeks. He awoke at four in the morning, went to his typewriter at home, and then to the station to record the program. He finished before noon, delivered it to his sales manager, and went fishing.

When he returned from vacation Nightingale was unprepared for what greeted him. Dozens of people had heard *The Strangest Secret,* and all wanted their own copies. Before long Nightingale was selling 10 inch records at the rate of 2,000 a week for $5.00 each. Enter Lloyd Conant, a businessman, whose skills complemented Nightingale's. They formed Nightingale-Conant Corporation and collaborated to market *Lead the Field and Great Ideas in Selling*. Conant built the company as a mail order business. Nightingale wrote and recorded winners. Eventually, in the late 1970's, the company expanded to include tape album with other motivators and business leaders like Brian Tracy, Lee Iacocca, and Denis Waitley. Today Nightingale-Conant is always on the lookout for new authors in personal or professional development who've already sold lots of audio.

What You'll Find in This Book

Words On Tape is your guide to joining the ranks of successful audio publishing. In the following pages you'll go behind the scenes and discover what it takes to create a first-rate, profitable audio product. You'll find detailed information and examples to help you:

• Plan your marketing before you step to the microphone.
• Save energy, time and money.
• Keep your sanity and sense of humor.

- Create a product you'll be proud of.
- Increase your income and opportunities.

Chapter 1 introduces the industry and contents of this book. **Chapter 2** give you an overview of creating and duplicating an audio product. **Chapter 3** deals with the questions and preliminary analyses you'll make to determine the best timing and customers for your product. You'll learn how to create your marketing plan and establish your selling price. **Chapter 4** covers copyrights, contracts and other legal matters.

How much will it cost? **Chapter 5** includes the tools to draw up a budget, so you can make intelligent decisions about allocating resources. **Chapter 6** walks you through designing and writing a script. This is where you'll find information on narrating audiobooks, and when to hire a professional voice to read your script.

Chapter 7 shows different packaging options, with recommendations and resources. Decisions on packaging and covers are made *before* you head for the studio, since artwork and printing takes longer than recording, editing and reproducing cassettes or CDs.

If you choose to act as your own producer you'll find **Chapters 8, 9** and **10** are an indispensable guide. You'll learn about professional audio recording, and how recordings are later improved in the editing room. **Chapter 11** covers duplicating and labeling, including whether you should make copies of your master tape on cassettes or CDs.

Sales can happen in many ways. **Chapters 12 and 13** are about marketing and selling. Chapter 12 concentrates on non-bookseller avenues for your title, offering a wide variety of tips and techniques to get your audio product into the hands of buyers. Chapter 13 is where to look for bookstore and catalog selling information.

While the future cannot be foretold, in **Chapter 14** we've gathered experts and asked them to peer into their crystal balls. They tell us what important trends and opportunities they see coming that will shape the audio industry.

Throughout the book you'll find references for further study. You are encouraged to pursue the vast array of resources, and opinions, about recording, publishing and marketing. I've concentrated on the most common concerns: how to create tapes, how much it costs, how long it takes and how most companies sell. Callers rarely ask for equipment lists. Even if they did, any list would be outdated by better/cheaper/more user- friendly/way-cool new stuff before the ink dried on the pages of this book. Now let's look at how *you* can create spoken word audio tapes and CDs.

●●●●●●●●●
Resources:

Amazon.com, www.Amazon.com

Audiobooks.com, http://www.Audiobooks.com

AudioFile magazine, the annual *AudioFile Reference Guide,* and *AudioBooks On the Go,* Robin Whitten, editor and publisher, P.O. Box 109, Portland, ME, 04112, 207-775-3744, Fax: 207-775-3744, orders 1-800-506-1212

Audio Publishers Association, Jan Nathan, exec. dir., 627 Aviation Way, Manhattan Beach, CA 90266, 310-372-0546, Fax: 310-374-3342, e-mail: apaonline@aol.com, http/www.audiopub.org

Bantam Doubleday Dell Audio Publishing, Christine McNamara, Director of Marketing, 1540 Broadway, New York, NY, 10036, .212-354-6500, Fax: 212-782-9600, e-mail: McNamara C@BDD.com

BookWire, www.bookwire.com

BookZone, Mary Westheimer, P.O. Box 2228, Scottsdale, AZ 85252, 800-536-6162, Fax: 602-481-9712, mary@bookzone.com, www.bookzone.com

Bradshaw Cassettes, Matthew Fox, P.O. Box 720947, Houston, TX 77272, 800-627-2374 (1-800-6bradshaw), Fax: 713-771-1362, www.Bradshawcassettes.com

CPU, Inc., Jeff Baker, CEO, Commerce Way, Arden, NC 28704, 800-545-3828, Fax: 704-687-3558; western U.S. plant in Irvine, CA

Dove Audio, Dove Entertainment, 8955 Beverly Blvd., Los Angeles, CA 90048, 310-786-1600, Fax: 310-247-2924 or www.doveaudio.com/dove/

HighBridge Company, Jim Brannigan, 340 Woodhouse Avenue, Wallingford, CT, 06492, 203-269-0065, Fax: 203-269-3818, e-mail: JimBrannigan@Worldnet.att.net

ITA, The International Recording Media Assoc., Charles Van Horn, exec. dir., 152 Nassau St., Suite 204, Princeton, NJ 08542, 609-279-1700, Fax: 609-279-1999

Knowledge Products, Shirley Cantrell, P.O. Box 305151, Nashville, TN, 37230, orders 800-264-6441, 615-742-3852, Fax: 615-742-3270, crom@edge.net

Frank Muller, e-mail: WaveDancer@aol.com

Nightingale-Conant Corporation, 7300 Lehigh Ave., Niles, IL 60714, 800-525-9000, 847-647-0306, Fax: 847-647-7145, www.nightingale.com

Terence O'Kelly, KODAK Recording Products

Publishers Weekly, 249 W. 17th St., N.Y., NY 10011, 800-278-2991

R.R. Bowker, 121 Chanlon Road, New Providence, NJ 07974, Publishers of *Literary Market Place* and *Words on Cassette,* 800-521-8110, Fax: 908-665-6688

Random House AudioBooks, 201 East 50th Street, New York, NY, 10022, 800-726-0600, Fax: 800-659-2436, e-mail: audio@Randomhouse.com, randomhouse.com

ReadersIndex.com, www.ReadersIndex.com

Recorded Books, 270 Skipjack Road, Prince Frederick, MD, 20678, 410-535-5499, Fax: 410-535-5590, e-mail: www.recordedbooks.com

Simon & Schuster Audio, 1230 Avenue of the Americas, New York, NY 10020, 800-223-2348, 212-698-7184, Fax: 212-698-632-8091

Time Warner Audiobooks, Maya Thomas, producer, or Samantha Fahnestock, 1271 Avenue of the Americas, 11th Flr., New York, NY 10020, 212-522-7334, Fax: 212-522-7994, www.pathfinder/twar

One Size Fits Nobody

No two audio products are alike. That's why successful audio publishing is an industry that requires experience, or assistance from people who work full time in the industry. This chapter covers definitions and decisions you'll use as you proceed with your project.

The First Five Questions

Newcomers to this exciting publishing arena have dozens of questions. In my consulting with individuals and companies, these are the five most frequent questions:

1. "Should I make a tape?"
2. "How much will it cost?"
3. "What kind of packaging should I use?"
4. "What's the best way to market my tapes?"
5. "How long will it take from now until they ship?"

The answer to these questions is all the same: "It depends."

It depends, because one size doesn't fit all. If creating successful, hot-selling products were as simple as recording in a quiet spot at home and mailing a few hundred announcement flyers, success would be guaranteed. (There also wouldn't be any need for this book!)

Spoken audio products are all unique. Your topic may be similar to another publisher's, but your interpretation and presentation will reflect your own personality, style, views, and experience. Audio products are created for many purposes. Businesses use audio tapes as gifts, or perks, for clients. There are businesspeople who generate hundreds of thousands of dollars from tapes each year who don't even think of themselves as publishers. As one explains: "We're just makin' our stuff available because people asked for tapes, starting a few years back. It turned out to be a good deal for us. People tell their friends, and word spreads."

Tape production expenses range from a few hundred to thousands of dollars, with many variables in costs. A union voice talent (anyone at the microphone is referred to as "talent") will cost hundreds of dollars more than non-union. A studio in California charging $150/hour could have equivalent facilities and engineering at $55/hour in another state. One individual purchases duplication based entirely on cost per cassette, and states "I don't care if it's only played once and thrown away," while another wants "high enough quality so it can be played 400 times, and I want it in environmentally friendly packaging."

Your audio product will be as individual as the choices of three neighbors who purchase new vehicles. All will end up with transportation, but each chooses a different model, color, options, and payment method.

As the flow chart on the next page shows, the first step to success is planning and research. You'll find the answers to all five of the preliminary questions, and more, during planning and consultation.

Thanks to television and the movies, an aura of glamour surrounds recording sessions. Voices are captured perfectly, re-takes are infrequent, and everything runs smoothly. In reality, creating a quality audio product involves dozens, if not hundreds, of decisions. Experienced audio publishers will tell you real-life audio production isn't as simple as it looks from the outside. (What ever is?)

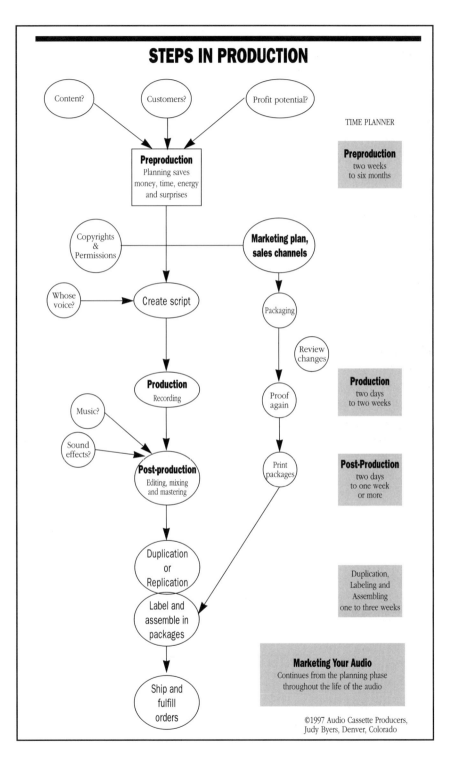

STEPS IN PRODUCTION

Content?

Customers?

Profit potential?

TIME PLANNER

Preproduction
Planning saves
money, time, energy
and surprises

Preproduction
two weeks
to six months

Copyrights
&
Permissions

**Marketing plan,
sales channels**

Whose
voice?

Create script

Packaging

Review
changes

Production
Recording

Production
two days
to two weeks

Music?

Proof
again

Sound
effects?

Post-production
Editing, mixing
and mastering

Print
packages

Post-Production
two days
to one week
or more

Duplication
or
Replication

Duplication,
Labeling and
Assembling
one to three weeks

Label and
assemble in
packages

Ship and
fulfill
orders

Marketing Your Audio
Continues from the planning phase
throughout the life of the audio

©1997 Audio Cassette Producers,
Judy Byers, Denver, Colorado

Most of all—success requires diligent, effective marketing, week after week. Shari Posey, co-founder of ExecAudio, puts it like this: "Probably the biggest lesson I've learned in the business so far is that producing a good, quality product is a snap compared to marketing it as an independent."

It's a good thing audio publishing is also lots of fun.

Some Working Definitions

The diagram on the previous page shows the process of creating an audio tape, from "concept to completion" as advertising agency folks would say. Therefore, throughout this book I refer to "publishers" to include all sizes, from giant companies like Simon & Schuster or Random House, to micro-companies with one person in a back bedroom or basement. My goal is for you to understand the process and jargon of the industry, whatever you ultimately decide.

Author: A person who creates intellectual property. Authors can sell the right to develop and distribute their work to book publishers, magazines, seminar companies, educational institutions, movie makers, or other electronic publishers. Some authors decide to develop, print or record, and fill orders themselves. They become self-publishers.

Distributor: This person, or company, acts on your behalf as a selling agent. Distribution companies fill orders from libraries and retailers. They also (in theory) show your title to potential buyers and work to increase your sales. Some distributors only handle books. Many specialize. One distributor represents business topics, another knows the gay and lesbian, or science fiction, or Christian markets and stores. Distributors who handle only audio are rare.

Media: Radio, newspapers, magazines, television. Increasingly the Internet has some attributes of traditional media as an avenue for sharing information, product promotion and sales.

Producer: An individual who oversees the creation of audio masters from concept (the idea stage) to the finished master tapes. Many producers also arrange duplication and packaging. Producers work for publishers, either on salary or as contractors. A producer's job is to make the best possible product within a given budget. Producers sell their time, knowledge and experience to publishers who understand how bringing in a specialist can save time, energy, and money.

Experienced spoken word producers are in short supply. Producers in broadcasting, video and audio do not finance projects.

Publisher: Publishers put up the money to develop creative works. Once a product is made they promote, advertise, distribute, receive the income, and pay the author royalties.

When publishers buy the "rights" to create products they pay an "advance" amount of money against estimated sales. Audio publishers can buy rights to create either abridged or unabridged products, and sell the same book for an audio performance, or narration. That's why there can be more than one audiobook of the same title. Readers who want to sell audio rights to intellectual property should seek advice from an agent or publishing attorney. (Chapter four includes some basics, and resources.)

Retailers: Stores where individuals can purchase audiobooks.

Title: Noun: The complete packaged unit, sold under one name. Audio products may be one tape, or 12 tapes long, just as a book title could be 75 pages, or 900 pages. 2. The product identity, or name. 3. Verb: To name a creative work.

Wholesaler: A company that warehouses products and fills orders for booksellers and libraries. Wholesalers maintain inventory, ship product, invoice, collect payment, and forward a percentage to publishers as agreed.

The Three Most Common Mistakes

The single biggest mistake new publishers make is rushing to create a tape without enough planning. That's why you'll find in-depth answers to all five questions at the top of this chapter, and much more, in the planning section, chapters 2-5. Careful research and preparation always takes time. Do it anyway. This first step will save you time and money later.

The second mistake is creating a sloppy, amateurish product, and expecting to succeed with distributors, retailers, and consumers. You won't appeal to sophisticated and discriminating buyers with a substandard product. It doesn't cost significantly more to create a good quality tape and packaging, instead of something that discredits you.

The third major mistake is a poor cover, especially in the wrong style of package. Covers are often an afterthought, instead of part of the original budget and plan. Your content, no matter how good, won't be heard, except for rare cases, unless your packaging sells your product. You'll never reach listeners on retailer shelves, or through catalogs and direct mail without a cover that "works." Four-color covers are standard for retail packaging. That's what consumers expect.

What Sells?

Audiobooks and non-book based products are either bought, borrowed, leased, or rented. Research indicates people choose based on the title or subject, then on the author if well known. Audiophiles are influenced by performers or readers, choosing abridged over unabridged based on sound and interpretation more than price points. Regardless of how titles are acquired, listener preferences are the same.

Fiction is the best-selling category. In fact, in England during the 1850's "penny dreadfuls" were cheap diversions relying heavily on sex and violence. The House of Commons debated whether the first public library in Manchester, England was in the the best interests of the country. The opposition fretted that people would stay off the land, curled up with their reading, neglecting their crops and herds. No one would go to pubs and support local establishments! The lobbyists lost.

After awhile the Manchester library officials reported patrons' interests. The two most popular categories then, as now, were fiction and practical instruction. Today we call it "business/professional" or "personal" development, or simply self-help. If your title falls under fiction or non-fiction, you'll have plenty of competition — and potential customers.

A recent breakdown on the Audio Publishers Association Web pages under "What Is Spoken Audio?" reflects categories of publisher members as of this writing. The page can be reached easily from http://www.BookZone.com. It looks like this, in part:

". . . it's safe to say any subject you can think of is probably available as a Spoken Audio production. Here's a sampling of the kinds of programs APA members produce:

Autobiography	Bestsellers	Biography	Business
Children's	Classics	Drama	Erotica	Fiction	History	Humor
Language	Lectures	Motivation	Mystery	Mythology	Nature
New Age	Non-Fiction	Parenting	Philosophy	Poetry
Psychology	Religious	Romance	Science Fiction	Self-Help
Sports	Storytelling	Westerns	Young Adult
and more...more than you can imagine."

APA pages include links to dozens of audio publishers and publishing related websites. You can learn much about industry players in a short time online. Web pages can be updated faster than printed catalogs.

Pricing Your Products

Audio program prices depend on what the market will bear, and how competitive products are priced. If you're soliciting new business, your tape will be free. In contrast, when you're a highly respected expert in a narrow specialty you might be able to charge $40 per cassette. Customers will thank you for sharing your knowledge and gladly pay top dollar for information they'll use.

Let's look at three examples:

1. Kenneth is a plastic surgeon known for his presentations at medical association conferences. He speaks about reducing malpractice lawsuits, stressing good communication skills. Other plastic surgeons are eager to learn how he explains delicate

surgery and post-op care to lay people. Kenneth has a small but highly motivated pool of potential customers. Other physicians ask for a tape. Lately they've been calling his office for advice.

Kenneth decides to modify an article and notes from a presentation, and create a detailed outline script. He takes half a day off to do the recording, and delegates the details to a producer recommended by friends. Physicians willingly pay $39 for 45 minutes of Kenneth's explanation and role playing. They know body image and health are highly emotional subjects for many patients, and emotion fuels lawsuits. Kenneth's audio program sells very well to a small, select audience.

2. A multimillion-dollar insurance salesperson with a knack for public speaking sells a lot of tapes on sales techniques. Industry specific tapes are frequently sold in the back of the room at presentations. $50-$100 for a set of six tapes in a vinyl album is the typical price range. Some products are priced higher, and sell when customers perceive a high potential payback.

3. A best-selling author in pop psychology records an abridged version of her book. Sales are through bookstores and online book malls. The product must conform to the price range bookstore buyers expect for a single tape product. Similar items sell for $10-$16. Two-tape packages are half again the retail price of single tape products, averaging $15-$20 for abridged books. Look for unabridged popular fiction to be priced between $25 and $40, depending on the number of cassettes. Pricing for unabridged books is very competitive titles are usually limited to best-selling authors.

A few publishers specialize in recording unabridged audiobooks. They have reputations for consistently high quality, a wide selection and good service, and command higher retail prices. Companies like Recorded Books and Books On Tape® take rental orders over toll-free lines. Audiobooks are shipped in postage paid, mail-back boxes. Most of their consumer business is on the rental side. Libraries purchase the majority of their unabridged books.

Many small audio-only stores around the country rent audiobooks from the major houses and from dozens of smaller audio publishers.

Stores devoted to audiobooks offer personalized service, and convenience. While you can rent from the grocery store or video store, the clerks won't know the books, nor can they let you listen to a program before you decide to buy or rent. Audio booksellers are more accommodating. Many have frequent listener programs. Audio specialty stores are also good places to find regional subjects.

What Can You Make?

In the three examples earlier, the most profitable audio, per unit, is the plastic surgeon's tape. Kenneth can expect to net over $35 of each sale. Second most profitable are the business and professional development titles. These are sold "BOR," or back of the room, eliminating middlemen. They net 35-85%, depending on various arrangements with publishers, freight, taxes and overhead. (Catalog and bulk sales will fall within the middle range — around 40-65% net.)

Traditional retail bookstore channels are the least profitable per unit, because everyone involved in getting your title into customers' hands earns part of the sale. For example, 30-40% goes to the retailer. Another chunk goes to distributors or wholesalers. Each provides a necessary service within the established distribution system. This is the hardest market to crack for small publishers.

First-time publishers are usually taken aback to learn most books and many tapes on booksellers' shelves are on consignment. Products are ordered, displayed, and sent back to the wholesaler or distributor for credit if not sold in 90 days or less. If you supply 1,000 copies and sell only 350 in 6 months, you won't cover your expenses if you rely solely on booksellers to move your product.

If the bookstore route is how you plan to sell your title, ask yourself — does your book already have a good track in stores? Titles with the best sales stand a chance. The second qualification is timeliness. An almanac, or even a best-seller on a topical subject is a poor choice for audio tapes, since it will be out-of-date or no longer trendy in a few months. Other titles are problematic because of competition or an already saturated marketplace.

At the other end of the spectrum, if you're fortunate enough to be Sue Grafton's, John Grisham's or Dean Koontz's publisher there's no debate. You can safely add their audiobooks to your product line and be confident. You'll make money — a lot of money, as articles in *Publishers Weekly* attest. Many popular best-sellers sell tens of thousands of units for a few months, and continue selling for years as "backlist" titles that remain "in print."

Do non-bookstore books have a good chance of selling in audio? If you've sold a minimum of 15,000 print copies of a title and it continues to sell well through direct sales, audio publishing probably makes sense. Keep in mind that a specialty audiobook can yield the same results as books sold directly to tightly targeted markets. As a "rule of thumb" expect to sell one audiobook for each 10 books sold. Ten percent. Assume the conservative figure of 10% to begin with, and if the numbers work you may well have a profitable spin-off audio.

●●●●●●●●●
Resources:

BookZone, Mary Westheimer, P.O. Box 2228, Scottsdale, AZ 85252, 800-536-6162, Fax: 602-481-9712, mary@bookzone.com, www.bookzone.com

Executive Insights, Shari Posey, Long Beach, CA

Publishers Weekly, 249 W. 17th St., N.Y., NY 10011, 800-278-2991

Random House AudioBooks, 201 East 50th Street, New York, NY, 10022, 800-726-0600, Fax: 800-659-2436, e-mail: audio@Randomhouse.com, randomhouse.com

Recorded Books, 270 Skipjack Road, Prince Frederick, MD, 20678, 410-535-5499, Fax: 410-535-5590, e-mail: www.recordedbooks.com

Simon & Schuster Audio, 1230 Avenue of the Americas, New York, NY 10020, 800-223-2348, 212-698-7184, Fax: 212-698-632-8091

Terry's Audiobooks, Terry Pogue, www.idsonline.com/terraflora/audio

Planning Your
Project

Audio publishing is a dynamic growth industry. Like all publishing, this subcategory requires a commitment of resources to be successful. Savvy business owners think about how they'll spend their time, money and human resources *marketing* a title before they ever write checks to studios, a producer or duplicator.

The purpose of this chapter is to help you develop your plan while the risk and dollars invested are still low. If there's nothing new here, and you already have marketing in place, great! If not, read on. You'll find this chapter has three subsections:

1. Clarifying your goals and customers.
2. Research.
3. Writing a marketing plan.

Does an Audio Tape Make Sense?

"Should I make a tape?" is often the first question people ask. The response, "Tell me a little about your book or topic," is an invitation to share some information about the project. Information such as:

- Do your customers ask for audio tapes?
- Who is interested in tapes? Describe a target customer(s). Be specific!
- Where will they buy it?
- What is your price point at retail? What about discounts?
- How will they buy? In bookstores, by mail order, by phone, online?
- What middlemen will be needed on the way to the sale?
- How many units can you sell in the first six months?
- What type of packaging will you use?
- What are you, yourself, prepared to invest? How much in time, energy, and money to publicize, distribute and promote sales?
- What rewards do you want from your investment?

These questions are only important if you wish to be profitable. Entrepreneurs who succeed and stay in business look at what the marketplace will buy. They can be annoying questions when you're ready to charge full-steam ahead. So frustrating that occasionally people react angrily, brushing off any suggestions that they do their homework.

Publishing is a tough business, and many newcomers make three common mistakes. Lack of planning is the most common mistake of all. Other incorrect assumptions that lead to failure include believing your marketplace is wider than it is. "Everyone" will not want to buy your tape, or what it promotes. Packaging that doesn't appeal to customers can undermine sales. Poor, or inappropriate, packaging is the third way a good product can languish in storage.

Whatever level of preparation and planning you decide on, the following comments should help you think as a marketer. The exercises later in the chapter are fun for most people, and will help you focus faster on answers.

Market Sense: Start from the sale to a customer and work backwards. It's easier to devise a good marketing plan this way because you'll include all the steps between the purchaser and your company. Platform presenters who expect to sell their audio learning products in conjunction with training first must know which segment of the $75 billion meetings market they can serve effectively. "I'll sell to trade associations" is too vague. By the same logic, saying "I'll sell to bookstores" or "Through catalogs, like Nightingale-Conant's" is a starting place, not a plan.

Audiobook distributors, catalogs, and booksellers know the steps in the distribution system, and they'll expect you to understand them, too. Anyone hoping to interest retailers (or libraries) needs a marketing plan *before they pitch their product.* There are dozens of publishers vying for attention and shelf space. Because of time constraints most retailers and libraries order through wholesalers or distributors, who make it easy to order many titles on one form, and later pay with one check.

Do you know your best options for moving product to end customers?

Customer Sense: My favorite definition of a target customer comes from Cliff Ennico, author of numerous books and articles for lawyers, and co-host of "The Money Hunt" television program. Ennico tells business audiences, "Imagine a room of 100 people who are *exactly the kind of customer* you believe will buy your product or service. Now imagine yourself telling them about your product or service. If at least 50% of them buy, you understand your target market. You've gotten inside their heads and their lives. You empathize with them, and you understand what will motivate them to buy what you're selling."

You could have several targets for your audio. Ranking them will indicate where to concentrate your early marketing efforts.

Financial Sense: How will your proposed audio increase your income? Money might flow in as direct income (product sales) or indirectly, by capturing the attention of someone who'll do business with you. Many people create books and audio products partly to position themselves as experts in their field. Their products are valuable in themselves, but can make their consulting services or presentations even more valuable.

Experts often attract media attention. You might get 10 calls from reporters or producers "checking out something for a story," over many months. Your name or product is never mentioned. Then, bingo! A TV network calls, sends you airline tickets, makes hotel and meal arrangements, picks you up in a limo at the airport, and you're interviewed for an hour in their New York, Toronto or Los Angeles studios. That night, four minutes of your hour-long session appears on a national show. The next day your phone is ringing off the hook. All this due in part to your audio product, even though direct tape sales were modest.

The right person heard your message, at the right time. You got lucky.

That's indirect income.

Promotional Sense: Your audio business card, or promotional tape, gets past a prospect's junk mail (round) file. A freebie — coupled with natural curiosity — means your tape goes into the car player, giving your message a chance. Busy individuals can listen while driving, qualify themselves, and request more information. The same people would refuse appointments to sit through a sales pitch.

Effectiveness is measured in how much new business your tape campaign generates vs. how much it cost you to generate the same amount of new business by traditional "call, mail, call, visit" methods. Tapes are very inexpensive compared to personal sales calls. Brokerage firms, insurance sales people, multilevel marketing organizations, and trade/ professional association membership campaigns all use audio tapes to reach hundreds of people simultaneously. Can this sort of initial contact work for you, too?

Service Sense: How do your prospective clients or customers live? For example, a trade group sends farmers a tape because they're in their trucks and tractor cabs most of the day — habitual listeners to tapes or radio. A newstape about pending legislation can generate a quick response whereas a story included in printed newsletters is often parked on a desk or kitchen table. Two months later, when the stack is about to topple over, the paper version is thrown out. But, if Farmer Finley gets the tape in Thursday's mail, everyone for miles around will know about a proposed tax increase within 24 hours. Why? Well, farming can be a solitary life, so farmers talk on the phone with neighbors, or go to town for supplies or socializing. Finley shares his opinions about the proposed legislation with the tractor dealer, gas station attendant, feed store clerk, and his sister and brother-in-law, all before supper. Tapes used this way stimulate the "grapevine."

Newstapes, executive summaries, and briefings about industry-specific issues are a convenience and service for workers with lots of "windshield time" associated with daily tasks.

What if your assignment is to provide training for top-level health care managers? Do they have time to keep up with *The Harvard Business Review?* With journals in all the various specialties? What about the latest spiritual books and thinking? Probably not, but they might have time to listen on the commuter train, bus or on the expressway, if you provided convenient access through a lending library, or discount purchase plan. Alliances or special arrangements between publishers and blocks of customers can work to everyone's benefit.

On the publisher side, can your original concept expand to offering more options for narrow niche markets? Could you link with colleagues, and share expenses and profits?

Personal Sense: Every choice you make means you cannot follow other paths. What do you want to achieve, and what are you willing to give up to get it?

Occasionally I hear from people who, in truth, want the "experience" of recording an audio tape, and don't care about a financial return on investment. That's fine, so long as you know that's your motivation going in. You can enjoy pride of creation, and learn from the adventure. You'll do yourself a favor though if you approach it as a personal project, not for profit.

Experience Sense: Should you learn the business side elsewhere, before you begin marketing your own product? The biggest mistake I made as an independent producer was assuming experience in broadcasting, a love of audio learning and production, and growing up with entrepreneurs was enough. Running a business is harder than it looks. It would have been smarter to learn from someone else's mistakes, and draw a paycheck. Why not cut your learning curve way down, before you risk your own assets? Read the books, surf the Web, look at the publications mentioned in this chapter, and pick the brains of other publishers. If at all possible work within the industry before going on your own. Audio publishing is a wonderful growth industry, and it takes many skills to succeed.

To get a running start, try one or all of the following three methods. These are techniques "for your eyes only," so you can get on to the "fun stuff" faster. Your most useful answers will come if they're uncensored. Rephrase them in socially acceptable terms later, if necessary.

Method 1: The Commentator's Quick Test

A wise radio producer at the Canadian Broadcasting Corporation taught me this technique over 20 years ago. It doesn't address financing a new product, but it clarifies your message, market, and motivation. Sometimes this exercise exposes a weak premise or too narrow a market. In that case, you'll save yourself from taking a wrong step.

First, take a sheet of blank paper, divided horizontally into thirds. At the top of the paper write: "What do I want to say?" One third of the way down the paper put: "Who do I want to tell?" In the last third, write: "Why do I want to tell it?" *Sample exercise pages are included in the appendix.* Your answers could change as you learn more. Copy the appendix pages as needed rather than write your answers here.

Create a sheet for each target market, and use this format in the preliminary development of your new product. For example, a prize-winning rose gardener might write the following:

What do I want to say?
Roses can be grown successfully all across the continent.
Satisfying hobby or business.
How I do it and win prizes.

Who do I want to tell?
Amateur gardeners and hobbyists.
Nursery workers, horticulturists, landscapers.

Why do I want to say it?
Share my knowledge and experience. Help others.
Add to retirement income.

Another version of this exercise is from your customer's side of the transaction. You evaluate your tape from the end user's point of view. In the three areas, fill in what your customer would think or say.

What is the tape about?

Why should I buy/borrow it?

How much $$ is it worth to me?

You could take each component and go even deeper into the motivations, circumstances and lives of prospective customers.

Save your answers. It'll be interesting to review them, especially after market testing your products.

Method 2: Mindmapping®

This is a favorite technique for pulling together a presentation, article, speech, or strategy. It's fast, easy, and comprehensive. What if you had a search engine for your own knowledge banks? Pretty slick, you say? That's how I think of Mindmapping®. It's a quick brain scanning technique that helps you get your best potential solutions and ideas on paper. Neatness, spelling, logic, and structure don't count. You can be organized and neat later — after your mental sprint.

Use a timer, watch alarm, or similar device to be sure you work fast. I like three minutes, some people do five. Write your word or question in the center of a page. Write *everything* that comes to mind about the word or question, *as fast as you can.* Add anything your thoughts trigger. *Don't edit anything at this stage. Neatness doesn't matter.* Here's an example of what it might look like.

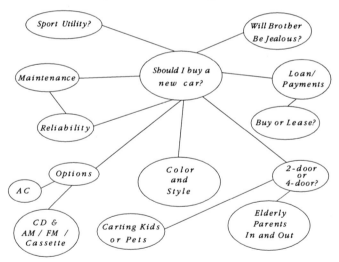

Once your ideas are on paper, you can highlight, color code or prioritize. People who balk at Mindmapping® as an access technique are usually linear, analytical thinkers.who say Mindmapping® is too random for comfort. If this sounds like you, try hard to push past any discomfort. Over time, the benefits will be worth it. With practice you'll find yourself saying, "Of course! Why didn't I see these connections before?"

Find out more about Mindmapping® from books and tapes by Tony Buzan, Joyce Wycoff and Bob Pike on the resource list.

Method 3: A Check-Off & Fill-in-the-Blanks Quiz

- Are people asking for tapes of your book or information?
- What return on investment will make this project worthwhile?
    What will start-up costs be?
    How much for marketing?
    What is the break-even point? (investment=net income)
    Is this the best use of your resources?
    What has to happen to make this audio project yield a better return?
- How do you plan to publish?
    With a large, mid sized, or small audio publisher?
    An established book publisher expanding into audio?
    Self-publish?
    Why, or why not?
    Have you reviewed any contract with a publishing attorney?
    Can you depend on the your publisher to develop and market your work as promised?
    How will royalties and advances be calculated?
    How often will you be paid?
    Have you talked with other authors who work with the publisher?
    What has their experience been?
- Where will customers see your product(s) or services?
    Truck stops? Roadside restaurants?
    At speeches or seminars?
    Post cards? Card decks?
    Newsletters?
    Through catalogs or mail order audiobook clubs?
    In audiobook stores? Video stores?
    In trade show or convention booths?
    At your office or store?
    On the Internet via the WWW?
    In magazines? If so, which ones?
    Discount warehouses?
    Booksellers? Chains, independents or specialty booksellers?
    From their employers?
    TV infomercials or TV shopping networks?
    Radio or TV interviews and guest appearances?
    Libraries?
    Other?
- Describe your customers. Do this for each target market.
    Listening habits?
    Lifestyle?

Age?

Sex?

Income level?

Education?

Region of the country, or world?

All other pertinent information.

- How will they buy?

    Using cash, money orders, or checks?

    With purchase orders?

    By postal mail?

    By fax?

    Online, by e-mail, from a book mall or your own website?

    Are there changes or trends in how they're buying that could affect your sales?

- Are you prepared to take and fill orders?

    Do you have an 800/888 number?

    Should you use a fulfillment service or pack/ship in house?

- What will a listener tell a friend after listening to your tape?

- Describe your title's direct competitors. Include author reputation, publisher, packaging, price point, content, distribution channels and estimated sales volume.

- Are there indirect competitors for your target customer's time and money? For example, if you make an audio tape on weight loss, will customers see an exercise video as solving the same problem, or offering the same hope?

- What makes your book, speech, service, or product unique?

- How will you price your product?

- Could your audio title be duplicated on tape now, then become part of a CD-ROM or computer-based training in the future?

- What's in it for you, personally? Do you have a passion for your subject, and a driving desire to tell your story? Or something else?

- Can you delegate? Should you? How involved do you want to be in details?

- What do you want your listener to *do* after hearing your tape? To think or feel?

- How do you feel about media interviews?

- Can you handle the stress and demands of brief fame?

- How do audio products fit into your long term goals?

All three of these methods clarify your thinking and feelings so you can make decisions and communicate more clearly. Use any or all of them to begin pulling together a realistic marketing plan

Making a Plan that Works for You

Your marketing plan will be a working document to refer to and modify, depending on the opportunities that open to you. If you use the marketing plan to show lenders, it's a good practice to begin with an executive summary, describing an overview, and what steps you'll take to your goal.

The body includes details about what the product is, how it fits into your product line, and why the market exists for the product. You'll explain how you'll finance the production, and how much it will cost to market the titles. Explain why you believe it will sell. Name names of who will distribute your product, and where they will sell. Will you be paid within 60-90 days, or will you need to finance thousands of dollars of product, before any income is returned?

This is where good ideas are separated from those that are marginal or insupportable. Any financial backer will want to know what you plan to do with the money, and how their investment will yield an attractive return.

Motivational speakers and authors are right. Writing something down influences your odds of successful achievement. Many successful new publishers also use visualization. Mark Victor Hansen and Jack Canfield visualized themselves on the *New York Times* bestseller list. "*Chicken Soup*" books have been constant residents on bestseller lists now for over a year. Scott Adams visualized himself quitting his job at the phone company to become a full time cartoonist. His *Dilbert* books, tapes and products are partly the result, he says, of affirmations. Adams wrote "I will be a syndicated cartoonist" over and over, every day. Next, he visualizes Gary Larson (*The Far Side*) and Bill Watterson (*Calvin & Hobbs*) retiring. They did.

Thinking through what you want to do, when, and how helps you avoid feeling blindsided by problems later. Some of those problems arise when you either don't know, or can't articulate, just what you want to achieve, and why. Clear communication saves you money. If you keep a silent agenda you could inadvertently send your team in the wrong direction. They could do everything right, yet you'll feel dissatisfied. I belabor this point because many good audio products never achieve their potential for the makers. There are a dozen reasons why tapes sit in storage. Marketing is difficult and a constant challenge, so market realities are a big part of disappointing sales. Self-sabotage is another result when our true feelings and our stated goals are incompatible. In the following examples, each publisher achieved important goals, but only one sold enough tapes to see a profit.

Two Stories

1. John's Reluctance. Trevor, a producer in Atlanta, GA., took his new client at his word. John insisted his goal was to be on the cover of *Publisher's Weekly,* and in the windows of Barnes & Noble nationwide. He was gung-ho for a media tour, and had the financial backing to succeed. During the editing phase of production, John bought two expensive custom-made suits and had an eye lift, so he'd look younger on TV. He repeatedly said he wanted to "sell lots of tapes and change lives for the better all over the country."

Trevor noticed, however, that as the production phase ended John persistently ignored his publicist's recommendations, and didn't return calls. He procrastinated and wouldn't hire a full-time staff person or authorize his publicist to work out distributor and TV booking arrangements. John's "language of behavior" spoke loudly. Anything connected with marketing and selling was too uncomfortable.

Six months later, Trevor ran into John at a reception. John said he'd stored the finished tapes and still had done almost no marketing. Instead, free copies went to all his friends. He had the cover framed and sent to his mother. As they talked amiably Trevor realized that although making money and sharing his message were important motivations, John's belief system got in his way. Trevor wished John had understood and conveyed his own true agenda when they first met. True, he'd been paid in full for his part, but it was unsatisfying work. He knew John's contributions wouldn't make an impact unless enough people heard his message.

2. Twins with a Successful Strategy. Mary, co-owner of a studio in San Jose, CA. tells of a production her firm did for twin brothers. The men had a clear business strategy. Once again, the production was influenced by personalities, values, and experience — an audio product was a means to an end for the brothers.

Barney and Brad outlined a four-tape series about managing a biotech business for Mary. The two had compiled a well-organized mailing list and set aside an adequate promotion budget for a year. They deliberately kept their series priced low, at $30. They wanted volume sales, to prime the pump of "word of mouth" advertising within their industry.

Using a carefully crafted scripts the brothers presented themselves as understanding experts. They'd started as innovative nerds, and made enough right decisions to guide their company to $60 million in sales. Their audiotapes showed their senses of humor, depth of experience, and non-traditional approaches to solving problems. Within six weeks of their first meeting with Mary and her engineer, the twins were selling their series.

Response was slow at first. They'd expected that, so they didn't give up. They kept working their marketing plan. Within six months, the full costs for launching the marketing tape series were repaid. Within eighteen months not only had the tapes helped increase their company revenue, but two copies were passed along to scientists working on similar technical challenges in Europe. A scientist-to-scientist connection was established via e-mail. It led to collaboration on an important leap ahead in their field. Four of the collaborating researchers reported their results in professional journals on both continents, sharing credit for their discovery.

What was the unspoken goal of each of the twins? Brad wanted to conduct seminars and write a book for other high-tech business people. Barney hoped, in addition, to make bi-monthly planned "escapes" for vacations with his family. He yearned to break out of a rut, and explore new trails with his kids on their mountain bikes — something he couldn't find time for at home in Silicon Valley.

Barney and Brad used audio tapes strategically. Their primary purpose was to increase awareness, and therefore new opportunities, to grow their company. Looking ahead personally, they wanted to open doors to travel and teaching within their field. All goals were met.

Research: Check Out the Competition

Books: Begin your search for competing titles in *Words on Cassette*. R.R. Bowker began publishing a spoken audio reference in 1985, with

11,500 records and 200 producers/publishers listed. *Words on Cassette* is a companion to *Books In Print.* (After September, 1997 *Words on Cassette* will merge with video titles and be available under a different name, and on CD, from Bowkers.) Look in library reference sections or large bookstores. Bowker also publishes *Literary Market Place,* a yearly update of the publishing industry. Ask a reference librarian for assistance if necessary with these and other directories to periodicals, CD titles, videos, catalogs, Internet addresses, and associations.

The 1996 11th edition *Words on Cassette* lists 71,000 titles (more than 7,000 new in 1996), and more than 1,800 companies producing titles. Information is submitted voluntarily. There is no charge. Many publishers outside the audiobook/bookseller trade either are unaware of, or ignore Bowker, so they never appear in databases.

Writer's Markets is another popular resource for authors. It lists publications that buy free-lance articles, including circulation figures, all the contact information and suggestions about the readership interests. Specialty magazines may be interested in articles, and may trade out for ad space. In terms of research, these magazines are a good source for phone and fax numbers as well as Web addresses of competitors.

Audios: Listen to at least half a dozen audiobooks, promo tapes, or learning products in your specialty. If you have no direct competition, ask yourself why there's nothing available. Is there a market for your tapes after all? If you believe there is an untapped market, look at titles on a similar subject. If your title is for antique car fans, for example, listen to *The Best of Car Talk,* from National Public Radio, because chances are good many members of your target market laugh along to the weekly hour of automotive advice and nonsense.

If you don't normally listen to audio, this is *essential* research. Select from different publishing houses. Jot down your own review notes. If you listened in a vehicle, how was the volume? What did you like and what would you have done differently? Tapes are free from libraries, and available from audio rental and retailers nationwide. Make sure some of your listening includes titles from the bestseller list. The most popular audio tapes mirror popular book sales. Although mysteries or personal development may not be direct competition. Your customers will compare your product to the standard of quality coming from the big audiobook publishers.

Lurk in the audio section of a well-stocked store. Stores are better lurking spots than libraries because the covers are all intact, as shipped from the publishers. (Rental stores and libraries often cut up covers to fit heavy duty or standardized packaging.) Watch how people choose titles. What covers draw the eye? Who is buying? Are they buying more than one title? How much time do they spend per audiobook before they make a decision? Do they purchase several audios at a time?

Truck stops sell and rent lots of audio cassettes. Next time you're on the interstate, look for the big rigs lined up. Chances are you'll see racks of tapes not far from the coffee, soda, cigarettes, and snacks. Or stop into Cracker Barrel restaurants, located near interstate interchanges, in many states. They cater to travelers. Their audio selection changes daily as some are dropped off and others rented. AAA automobile clubs offer a similar convenience for members, with selections for a variety of interests from classics to investments to spy novels.

Online research: Tony Alessandra, an author and professional speaker based in La Jolla, CA, has become a big fan of online research. Alessandra tells why, in *The Speaking Secrets of the Masters*.

"When I first began speaking in the early 1970s, I had to do all my research at the library. It was a tedious process. Today, things are very different. Now you can do most of your research, if not all of it, 'online' with a computer and a modem. One of the experts in this new field is Wally Bock, a consultant and the author of *Cyberpower.* He recommends the ABI/Inform database (see end of this chapter), a source that provides international coverage of more than 800 journals on banking, insurance, real estate, accounting and finance, marketing, data processing, and telecommunications. This database includes informative abstracts which summarize the contents of the original article."

Bock's Web pages include free and helpful articles. If you find searches on the Web frustrating (who doesn't at times?), Bock and others recommend trying a sequence of search engines since they search differently. Online phone directories and listserv indexes are also excellent places to narrow your search. You'll find more, and can explore your subject further, by following links from useful pages.

Read a Few Dozen Reviews

AudioBooks on the Go, by Robin Whitten, is a compilation of 400 (primarily fiction) reviews of *quality* releases, taken from 1992-1995 *Audio-File* issues. At *AudioFile* quality means:

- The original book is a good choice for audio. (Some books aren't.)
- The narrator is a dynamic component, reflecting the author's meaning and intent.
- The narrator makes the text come alive for the listener.
- The sound quality is excellent.

Nonfiction titles were added in 1995. Feature articles and Whitten's editorials are wonderful extras you won't find in her book. I recommend *AudioFile* to clients, and pore over it when it arrives.

AudioFile's yearly *Audiobook Reference Guide* is a MUST HAVE for new audio publishers. *Reference Guide* is the only practical, well-organized, up-to-date way to find suppliers, wholesalers, distributors, and others in the audio industry. It's your industry phone book. If you buy nothing else, get this for your desk because it'll be the best $20 you spend on research and marketing contacts if you have any dreams of bookstore, library, or specialty retail sales. Use the order form in the back of *Words On Tape* and order at a discount directly from *AudioFile.*

Audiobook reviews appear in more publications every quarter. *The Christian Science Monitor, USA Today, The New York Times* and *Small Press* feature audiobooks. You'll find them in many metropolitan daily papers and magazines. *The Washington Post* has added a section devoted to audiobooks. Expect to see more coverage in the years ahead.

Industry Publications, Meetings and Trade Shows

The American Booksellers Association trade show is held each Memorial Day weekend. It's been experiencing some changes, and is now officially called the *Book Expo America.* Many consider it the best place to assess trends — what's hot and what's not. You'll see first hand how hundreds of tapes and CDs are marketed and packaged, in a way no book or single store can possibly convey.

The Audio Publishers Association holds its annual meeting and seminars just before the Book Expo. Sessions are open to the public. Publishers Marketing Association (PMA) holds a Publishing University seminar series two or three days before the Book Expo, with the emphasis on marketing for micro- to medium-sized publishers. There's a wealth of information in these conferences, and from the session cassettes. Contact the APA for details about past and current conferences, including fees.

National trade shows are so big you'll spend a couple of days on the floor when you first go. If you prefer to start smaller, attend a regional author and book publishing group, or smaller regional and city shows. Most national associations and trade groups have regional or state/provincial affiliated groups.

The second major trade show is sponsored by the America Library Association (ALA). Libraries are actively building collections of audio titles because of patron interest. There are Public Library Association shows, college library groups and regional meetings.

You could have the perfect title for library collections, but you won't know until you familiarize yourself with publications like *Library Journal, Booklist, School Library Journal* and *Kliatt*. Look at all of these, and compare their coverage to what acquisitions librarians are reading in AudioFile reviews.

In addition to these, there are many for-profit meetings and conferences led by recognized industry experts. Contact the companies listed at the end of this chapter, and again in the resource appendix for the dates and details. Dan Poynter, Tom and Marilyn Ross, John Kremer and many other full-time authors, publishers and marketers sponsor meetings. Dozens of colleges and local adult education organizations offer beginner to advanced-level courses. Organizations like International Association of Business Communicators have regular meetings in most cities, as do affiliated members of the Direct Mail Marketing Association and many other groups specializing in business communication.

Whatever your topic, there's a publication, conference, trade show, convention, or meetings of people interested in the same thing. Spend a day at the library with plenty of change for the photocopy machines so you *know* what your target market is reading and thinking. Research like this can change the focus of your audio, and make it more marketable. Research librarians can point you toward the right online database searches in the library. Some will even conduct an extensive search for you, for a fee.

Books About Publishing

Books about publishing are most useful when they include extensive resource listings. An excellent book for newcomers is Judith Appelbaum's *How to Get Happily Published, 4th edition* (A fifth edition is due soon.) The resource section is 70 pages long, with notes. Appelbaum is a former columnist and reviewer for *The New York Time Book Review* and was managing editor of *Publishers Weekly.* She currently operates Sensible Solutions, Inc., a consulting and support company for publishers. Her book is especially useful for authors who want to sell to established publishing houses.

Another straightforward and easy-to-understand new book for non-fiction authors *Writing Successful Self-Help and How To Books,* by Jean Marie Stine, draws on the author's experience editing over 50 self-help titles, including several best sellers. Stine also geared her book for authors or would-be authors who want publishers to take notice of their work.

Your Unique Plan

There is no cookie cutter plan for marketing audio. You are the best expert about your subject, goals and customers. I urge you to take the time to identify your market, and then create a detailed plan for how you will make money with the project. Successful audio publishers stress the importance of the marketing aspect. Over and over they say "marketing is everything."

You certainly can be successful. It's a fine time to enter the business, as long as you are realistic about what it may take to reach your financial goals.

•••••••••
Resources:

ABI/Inform, www.library.upenn.edu/index

Scott Adams, Dilbert creator/author e-mail: scottadams@aol.com

Tony Alessandra, Ph.D., 7596 Eads Ave., #140, P.O. Box 2767, La Jolla, CA 92037, 619-459-4515, Fax: 619-459-0435, e-mail: Dr Tony A@alessandra.com

Amazon.com, www.Amazon.com

American Booksellers Association, Terrytown, NY, 914-591-2665

American Library Association, 312-944-6780

Judith Appelbaum, *How to Get Happily Published,* ISBN 0-06-273133-5

AudioFile magazine, the annual *AudioFile Reference Guide,* and *AudioBooks On the Go,* Robin Whitten, editor and publisher, P.O. Box 109, Portland, ME, 04112, 207-775-3744, Fax: 207-775-3744, orders 1-800-506-1212

BookExpo America, 203-840-5476, Fax: 203-840-9476, bookexpo, reedexpo.com

Booklist, 630-892-7465

Canadian Broadcasting Corporation, headquarters in Toronto, Canada

Jack Canfield, Self-Esteem Seminars, *Chicken Soup For The Soul*™, P.O. Box 30880, Santa Barbara, CA 93130, 805-563-2935, Fax: 805-563-2945, soup4soul@aol.com

Clifford R., Ennico, Biennix Corporation, *The Money Hunt Guide to Growing Your Business and Managing Your Legal Career,* 2490 Black Rock Turnpike, #407, Fairfield, CT 06432, 1-888-243-6649, Fax: 1-888-243-6649, http://moneyhunter.com

Mark Victor Hansen, *Chicken Soup For The Soul*™ co-author, P.O. Box 7665, Newport Beach, CA 92658-7665, 800-433-2314, 714-759-9304, Fax: 714-722-6912

Kliatt, phone/fax 617-237-7577

Library Journal, 245 West 17th Street, NY, NY 10011-5300, 212-463-6819

Midwest Book Review, James A. Cox, Editor-in-Chief, Diane C. Donovan, Editor, 278 Orchard Drive, Oregon, WI 53575, www.execpc.com/~mbr/bookwatch

National Public Radio, the *Best of Car Talk*®, www.NPR.org, shameless commerce division

Nightingale-Conant Corporation, 7300 Lehigh Ave., Niles, IL 60714, 800-525-9000, 847-647-0306, Fax: 847-647-7145, www.nightingale.com

R.R. Bowker, 121 Chanlon Road, New Providence, NJ 07974, Publishers of *Literary Market Place* and *Words on Cassette,* 800-521-8110, Fax: 908-665-6688

ReadersIndex.com, www.ReadersIndex.com

Resources for Organizations, Bob Pike, 7620 West 78th Street, Edina, MN 55439, 612-829-1954, Fax: 612-829-0260

School Library Journal, (Book review dept., or A/V review dept.) 249 W. 17th Street, N.Y. 10011, 212-463-6759, Fax: 212-463-6689, www.sljonline.com

Small Press Magazine, Jerrold Jenkins, co-author with Mardi Link, *Inside the Bestsellers,* 121 E. Front Street, 4th Floor, Traverse City, MI 49684

Jean Marie Stine, *Writing Successful Self-Help and How To Books,* ISBN 0-471-03739-7, John Wiley & Sons. Available from IFGE, Box 229, Waltham, MA 02254-0029, Orders 617-895-2212 or Fax: 617-899-5703

Writer's Market, Writer's Digest Books, F&W Publications, 1507 Dana Avenue, Cincinnati, OH 45207, 513-531-2222, Fax: 513-531-4744

Joyce Wycoff, Mindmapping®, www.mindlinks.com

Copyrights, Contracts, and "ISBNs"

As we begin this chapter, please note a disclaimer. This chapter is not intended to offer legal advice. Basic audio publishing questions are covered. *For advice on specific situations, consult appropriate legal counsel or professionals.*

Learn Some Basics Before Visiting an Attorney

This chapter contains information primarily of interest to self-publishers and authors who have retained the audio rights to their intellectual property. If you've signed a contract with an established publisher, you may no longer control the audio rights to your work. Skim the chapter anyway, as it will be useful for future reference.

Jonathan Kirsch is an attorney who specializes in publishing. His book, *Kirsch's Handbook of Publishing Law,* is a good source of clear information. The 1995 edition covers much more than audio publishing, and is a valuable reference for any publisher's bookshelf. *Kirsch's Publishing Law Update* is a quarterly briefing service covering all aspects of print, audio and electronic publishing.

The Self Publishing Manual, by Dan Poynter, now in its ninth edition, is available in most libraries and bookstores, or direct from the publisher. This complete guidebook offers all of the information most publishers need to get started. In addition to free documents, you'll find news, product information, and resources on Para Publishing's Web page, updated frequently.

Para Publishing offers many free documents, inexpensive special reports, contracts on disk, and other resources widely used by publishers. Call their fax-on-demand number at 805-968-8947 from the handset of a fax machine and follow the prompts. The documents you select will be delivered immediately to your fax machine. You pay for the phone call.

Publishers Marketing Association (PMA), a non-profit group, is a clearinghouse of information and provides co-op marketing opportunities for independent publishers. PMA publishes a monthly newsletter with frequent articles and resources about the business and legal concerns of publishers. Membership is inexpensive, starting at less than $100/year, and easily paid back using the co-op marketing programs. PMA sponsors the Publishing University prior to the annual publishing industry trade show, Book Expo America, in late May. Seminar sessions are based on member requests and feedback, and feature industry experts. For a free newsletter issue and membership information, contact PMA. PMA and the Audio Publishers Association share an executive director and address.

Tom and Marilyn Ross' *The Complete Guide to Self-Publishing, 1994 edition,* guides you through every phase of print publishing and marketing. Legal and listing details for launching a title are covered in chapter 6 of the Ross' book. This excellent guide is available in the publishing section of bookstores and libraries, or directly from the publisher, About Books Inc. Their company offers turnkey book production and marketing services for print books.

In 1996 the Rosses formed the Small Press Association of North America (SPAN), a non-profit organization for those involved in creating, distributing and selling books and related products. Order a complimentary copy of *SPAN Connection,* the monthly newsletter filled with valuable information on publishing from SPAN by fax, phone or online.

Additional general information about intellectual property rights and publishing law is available online through legal forums on major services, websites, and listservs (using e-mail individuals with shared interests post messages to a group of similar-interested people). Nolo, a California legal press, features many useful resources — along with a fine collection of lawyer jokes — on their Web site.

Or go to the source directly. The Library of Congress has numerous forms and information online. Copyright Office records of registrations and other related documents dating from 1978 are available over the Internet. The Copyright Public Information Office is open Monday-Friday, 8:30 AM to 5:00 PM, Eastern time.

Through state and provincial bar associations, you can find attorneys in every state or province that specialize in publishing and intellectual property rights. Some offices have free literature, and lists of members who specialize in copyrights, publishing law, and intellectual property. Many attorneys will consult with you for 15-30 minutes at no charge to allow you to assess their expertise, ask some questions, and to determine if the "chemistry" is right between you. Michael Raydon, a specialist in intellectual property at Kerstetter & Rillo, says some communities have low-cost legal advice from Volunteer Lawyers for the Arts or a similar nonprofit program.

What's an International Standard Book Number?

Retailers and libraries have been moving steadily to computer tracking, keeping minimal inventories of each title, and reordering by a title's International Standard Book Number, or ISBN. If you want your audio products in bookstores, discount clubs, and rental services, you must follow the rules of the road — and that includes having a standard ISBN on your packaging. It takes extra effort for resellers to order your title without an ISBN, and publishers without them have either lost sales or had to pay extra fees to have ISBN stickers applied to packages.

ISBN applications are available from R.R. Bowker in New Jersey. Order the forms from 800-526-4902, x6770 or 908-665-6770. You'll receive multiple numbers on a sheet. Instructions on how to use and assign the numbers come with the sheet. Prices have gone up over the last few years. Bowker is online, as part of Reed Reference Publishing.

An ISBN assignment triggers a request from R.R. Bowker for more information. Fill out and return the form so Bowker can include your title(s) in *Words on Cassette*. The listing is free and Bowker updates the reference book yearly.

Librarians, booksellers, and customers locate where to order titles by means of the ISBN. Each number is assigned to one, and only one, title. You'll need film made of the number with the Bookland/EAN bar-code, including the price. The Bookland/EAN code with price extension is what retail outlets scan for prices and inventory tracking. Check first with your graphic artist before requesting the ISBN on disk or via e-mail. The file must work on both ends. You can locate film suppliers in the Yellow Pages, or through one of the numerous publications for writers and publishers.

The following diagrams are reprinted courtesy of Ron and Celeste Lasky, owners of Write On Publications. The Laskys developed an instructive program and special report titled "*The Basics of Getting Started in Self-Publishing*" for independent publishers.

Copyright Your Work

Since March 1, 1989, once your product is completed and a copy is in hand, you are entitled to copyright protection under United States law. To protect your rights, you should use the copyright symbol or the word "Copyright," the year, and the name of the copyright holder on all cassette labels and packaging. In addition, most audio cassettes carry a P in a circle, copyrighting the *performance* of a work. You'll find several label examples in the chapter on duplicating and packaging.

© for the content   ℗ for the audio performance

Registering a copyright with the United States Copyright Office is simple and inexpensive, and adds strength to your case if someone later appropriates your property. The forms take a little time to read and complete, but are not difficult.

When you find a book or other material you wish to record and publish, you're required by law to have permission from the copyright

Bookland EAN Bar Code (European Article Number)

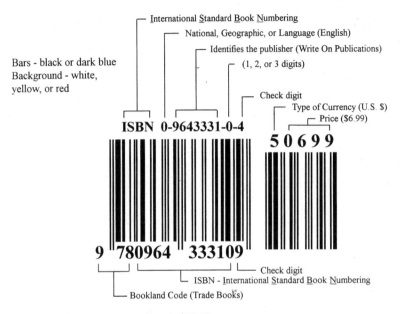

International Standard Book Numbering

National, Geographic, or Language (English)

Identifies the publisher (Write On Publications)

(1, 2, or 3 digits)

Bars - black or dark blue
Background - white,
yellow, or red

Check digit

Type of Currency (U.S. $)

Price ($6.99)

ISBN 0-9643331-0-4

5 0 6 9 9

9 780964 333109

Check digit

ISBN - International Standard Book Numbering

Bookland Code (Trade Books)

EAN Bar code   => approximately $30.00

All ISBN Numbers are 10 digits long

Examples:

0-9643331-0-9	10 number series
0-940217-34-8	100 number series
0-87503-576-5	1000 number series

Bookland EAN check digit:

Multiplying Factor:	1	3	1	3	1	3	1	3	1	3	1	3
Bookland EAN:	9	7	8	0	9	6	4	3	3	3	1	0
Value:	9	+21	+8	+0	+9	+18	+4	+9	+3	+9	+1	+0	= 91 + 9 = 100

Check digit ⅃

Multiple of 10 ⎦

holder. Get permission before you invest in a script, packaging and any production. Copyright laws may apply to a translation or edited version of a title you believe is in public domain (either never copyrighted or the copyright has expired). Don't infringe on someone else's right to profit from their intellectual property. Besides being unethical, it could cause you complicated and expensive legal difficulties later. *Kirsch's Handbook of Publishing Law* and many other sources explain copyright in much greater detail.

After you learn who holds the copyright, you'll want to see if subsidiary rights are available. Do this by talking to the publisher or author's agent. They may not plan to develop the audio, and if rights are for sale you can negotiate. Rights to record and publish a title on audio are often sold more than one way. You might buy the rights to an abridged version, while another publisher is bargaining for the rights to make an unabridged audiobook. Both publishers will pay for the "right" to create their audio performance of the book.

Only a small fraction of the books published every year make it to audio. Nevertheless, most publishing contracts include electronic rights. Nearly all bestselling fiction authors with titles on the *Publishers Weekly, New York Times and Los Angeles Times* bestseller lists are produced for simultaneous release on audio, and an increasing percentage are on CD.

Audio or recording rights can be sold separately for audiotapes, records and compact discs. The term of such recording rights is usually two years with automatic renewals until one or the other party serves notice.

Jessica Kaye, president of The Publishing Mills, confirms that royalties for audio rights are typically in the five to ten percent range, based on net sales. Kaye was with Dove Audio before founding The Publishing Mills. She is also an attorney.

Dianna Booher has written and published a number of successful books, audios and videos. Most are through major publishers. She advises negotiating electronic rights carefully, even if the publisher says you have to sign, or no deal. The representative may tell you all contracts are this way, etc. It's in the publisher's interest to get as much as possible, with the least restrictions. It's in your interests to do the best deal for your side. Keep in mind that audio is just one electronic delivery method. The Internet and other fast-developing uses of digital technology mean the greatest profits in the future may be generated by electronic means.

If you agree to sign away electronic rights, include a time limit so they expire within a certain number of months or years, *without* requiring written notification. Then, if the publisher does not develop the audio rights they revert to the author, without hassles. Nobody has to remember, follow up, or research a paper trail. Your publisher buys rights until X date, period. Be prepared for resistance, and remember — the person you negotiate with may well move on in a few months. The publisher may be taken over. You are making a deal with a company. No matter how nice people are, or what they say, get it in writing.

It pays to consult an experienced attorney or agent so you can obtain the best advice and contractual arrangement in the fast-developing electronic arena.

The Internet

As Internet use explodes with worldwide access, there are many unresolved issues of ethics and property rights. The Internet will remain a frontier of many cultures for years into the future. The very freedom of the Net is a Catch-22.

Online piracy and reuse of audio samples are concerns. Many publishers believe posting samples of their products is an acceptable risk. It helps sales by allowing potential customers to preview content and style. After all, the argument goes, if someone is determined to make illegal copies, they'll buy your tape and use that to create duplicates. It happens already with music CDs.

There is no simple answer.

Permission to Use Copyrighted Work

When you research a subject and explain it in your own words, with your own examples, you're fine. If you use material, including music, that is in the public domain, you're also home free. If you plan to tell someone else's story, poem, use their example or method, however, and it is copyrighted, you will need permission.

A simple letter requesting permission is often sufficient. I like the example on page 152 of an excellent new book, *Writing Successful Self-Help and How-To Books* by Jean Marie Stine. After walking readers through the permissions process in clear and simple language she says, "After years of gathering clearances for my own books, I've learned three rules that may help smooth your own permissions process:

- Start early.
- Look on the label.
- Ask your publisher for help."

Non-fiction works often mention research. Fact checking is standard practice in news organizations. Make every attempt to be accurate and understand the basis for another's conclusions when you quote research. Don't assume your use of someone else's work will go unnoticed or unreported. The North American population density may be more than double what it was at the turn of the century, but it's still a small world.

Occasionally, as producers, we're faced with an ethical and legal dilemma. Speaker A decides to include a story we know is a "signature story" or long-developed staple of Speaker B's presentation. Speaker A may have been using it for so long she forgot the source, and the staff believes it is A's original material. "A" is on dangerous ground, infringing someone else's right to sole profit from copyrighted material. Publishers can struggle through years of court battles over copyright infringement with high financial and emotional costs. This is why you're better off getting written permission up front. In the end, you may decide it's easier to leave out copyrighted material.

If you are in a segment of audio publishing outside the traditional "publishing world" — for example, a seminar leader — consult an industry expert qualified to understand your unique situation. One such specialist is John Patrick Dolan of Brea, CA. Dolan is an attorney, specializing in mediation and negotiation. He offers speakers and other information professionals services under the banner, LawTalk. Dolan is an author, audio and video publisher, and worked for CareerTrack as a seminar presenter earlier in his career. He's lived the life.

Contracts

Creating new audio products frequently requires outside talent and independent contractors. While an agreement for services may take many forms, most have similar purposes. I recommend publishers clarify what they are buying, and the terms of the agreement, before proceeding with a producer, studio, duplicator, or graphic artist.

For years, we did many jobs on a handshake — and such informal arrangements work well much of the time. These days, however, we use a written agreement. Why? Because when things get hectic, delayed, or complicated, a written agreement lets both parties be clear about what each agreed to be responsible for, the scope of the work, payment terms, and deadlines. We customize the agreement, based on what the client wants to accomplish.

In 12 years of independent production work, I've found that people collaborate better when they aren't wondering about surprises.

Work for Hire

When you hire a voice talent, script writer, or any other professional who contributes to your production, you will need a clear understanding about who owns the copyright and what you're paying for. Some union contracts grant residuals based on usage. Others are a buy-out for services. Many audio publishers are unsure about potential sales, so they need a clean and simple agreement. They pay once, and they're done.

Here's the agreement we use with non-union talent. Adapt or modify the following to suit your needs, based on your legal counsel's input.

AGREEMENT

I, _____, do hereby agree to allow my voice to be used for the recording of narration and transition passages for the audio programs **TITLE, ISBN** _____.

In return for my services, I accept a buy-out payment of $_____. This payment gives **your Company** and their above-named client all rights to the use of my recorded voice, in perpetuity. My signature below holds **your Company** and their subsidiaries and clients free from all demands that might be made in the future by any agents, talent agents, unions or others who may represent me.

Signed by: _____

Address: _____

_____

Phone: _____

S.S.#: _____

Date: _____

Publisher Sig. _____

Date: _____

One copy goes to each party involved. As a precaution, make copies of the signed agreement and the canceled check and file them together. Later, if any questions arise, you will have paperwork to verify the individual was paid in full at the time the work was completed.

Don't Go It Alone

You'll invest time and money in your audio venture. Use the resources listed at the beginning of this chapter, and any other individuals or sources you deem appropriate to protect your rights and profit potential. Do not rely on just one source. Publishing has become too complex for anyone to go it alone.

•••••••••
Resources

About Books, Inc., Tom and Marilyn Rosses' *The Complete Guide to Self-Publishing*, 3rd edition, P.O. Box 1306, 425 Cedar St., Buena Vista, CO 81211, 719-395-4790, Fax: 719-395-8374, e-mail: abi@about-books.com, www.SPANnet.org

Booher Consultants, Inc., Diana Booher, 4001 Gateway Dr., Colleyville, TX 76034, 817-318-6000, Fax: 817-318-6521, e-mail: Booher@Compuserve.com

John Patrick Dolan, attorney, 3 Pointe Dr., Suite 302, Brea, CA 92621, 714-257-3414, Fax: 714-257-3424

Kerstetter & Rillo, San Francisco, CA, 415-399-8330

Kirsch's Handbook of Publishing Law, ISBN 0-918226-33-3, Acrobat Books, P.O. Box 870, Venice, CA; Jonathan Kirsch, 310-785-1200

Ron and Celeste Lasky, *The Basics of Getting Started in Self-Publishing*, Write on Publications, 2441 Long View Drive, Estes Park, CO 80517, 970-586-8374, Fax: 970-577-0351, e-mail: writeon-pub@aol.com

Library of Congress, Madison Building, Room 401, at 101 Independence Ave., S.E., Washington, DC, www.lcweb.loc.gov

William Morris Agency, Inc., 1325 Avenue of the Americas, New York, NY 10019

The National Association of Independent Publishers Representatives, 111 E. 14th St., Ste. 157, New York, NY 10003, 508-877-5328 or fax 508-788-0208, e-mail: naipr@aol.com

Para Publishing, *The Self Publishing Manual*, ISBN 1-56860-018-6, Daniel F. Poynter, ninth edition, P.O. Box 8206, Santa Barbara, CA 93118-8206, Order line: 1-800-PARAPUB, Free info kit: 805-968-7277, Fax: 805-968-1379, Fax-on-demand: 805-968-8947 (some free documents), www.para-publishing.com

Publishers Marketing Association (PMA), Jan Nathan, 627 Aviation Way, Manhattan Beach, CA 90266, 310-372-2732, Fax: 310-374-3342, www.pma-online.org

Publishers Weekly, 249 W. 17th St., N.Y., NY 10011, 800-278-2991

The Publishing Mills, Jessica Kaye, President, 9220 Sunset Blvd., Suite 302, Los Angeles, CA, 90069, 310-858-5385, Fax: 310-858-5391, e-mail: editor@pubmills.com

R.R. Bowker, 121 Chanlon Road, New Providence, NJ 07974, Publishers of *Literary Market Place* and *Words on Cassette*, 800-521-8110, Fax: 908-665-6688

Small Press Association of North America, SPAN, See About Books, Inc., e-mail: abi@about-books.com, www.SPANnet.org

Jean Marie Stine, *Writing Successful Self-Help and How To Books*, ISBN 0-471-03739-7, John Wiley & Sons. Available from IFGE, Box 229, Waltham, MA 02254-0029, Orders 617-895-2212 or Fax: 617-899-5703

The Budget: Time and Money

When people ask about cost, they usually specify "how much money?" The real question may be "How much value will I get for my expenditure?" Let's assume for purposes of this chapter that you already know how you'll benefit from having an audio tape. You're ready, and you want numbers to plug into projections.

Your budget will, in the most simplified form, have three expense components, and a revenue line:

Sales	+	_____
Production of master tape	–	_____
Duplicating and packaging	–	_____
Marketing and sales	–	_____
Total	=	_____

You'll look at the expenses, how many tapes you sold, and see if you came out with a positive or negative number. This quick-and-dirty method won't be enough for planning. To be useful, your budget must also be more carefully drawn. As you work with the budget forms in this chapter, adapt it to suit your needs.

The generic budget covers the expenses of making master tapes, and duplicating and packaging an audio product. (This is a good time to revisit the flow chart from Chapter Two.)

PROJECTED TWO-YEAR BUDGET		
PROJECTED REVENUE		
INCOME SOURCES	*FIRST YEAR*	*SECOND YEAR*
PERSONAL FUNDS (SEED MONEY)		
SPONSORSHIPS		
REVENUE from RETAIL SALES		
REVENUE from DIRECT SALES		
REVENUE from OTHER SALES		
REVENUE from RELATED PRODUCTS		
INDIRECT REVENUE		
MISCELLANEOUS INCOME		
FIRST YEAR TOTAL REVENUE		
SECOND YEAR TOTAL REVENUE		
PROJECTED EXPENSES		
PLANNING (PRE-PRODUCTION) - CHAPTER 3	*FIRST YEAR*	*SECOND YEAR*
RESEARCH		
PAID DATABASE SEARCHES		
BOOKS, MAGAZINES		
AUDIO PRODUCTS/COMPETITOR TAPES		
ON-LINE SERVICE PROVIDERS		
LONG DISTANCE TELEPHONE AND FAX		
COPYING		
CONSULTANT		
TRAVEL / MEETINGS		
MARKETING PLAN (refer to Chapter 13)		
CHAPTER 3 SUB-TOTAL		
COPYRIGHTS, CONTRACTS - CHAPTER 4		
AUDIO RIGHTS		
PROFESSIONAL ACCOUNTANT FEES		
PROFESSIONAL ATTORNEY FEES		
PRODUCER FEES		
DIRECTOR FEES		
CHAPTER 4 SUB-TOTAL		
DESIGN & SCRIPT - CHAPTER 5		
SCRIPT WRITER		
ABRIDGER		
FIRST DRAFT OF SCRIPT		
SECOND DRAFT OF SCRIPT		
FINAL SCRIPT, PLUS COPYING/PRINTING		
VOICE COACHING		
CHAPTER 5 SUB-TOTAL		
PACKAGING - CHAPTER 7		
GRAPHIC ARTIST		
FILM AND SUPPLIES		
MATCH PRINT, COLOR KEY OR COLOR PROOF		
ISBN AND FILM		
PRINTING (RUN EXTRAS FOR MARKETING)		
CHAPTER 7 SUB-TOTAL		
PROJECTED EXPENSES SUBTOTAL		

	FIRST YEAR	SECOND YEAR
PROJECTED EXPENSES CARRIED OVER		
SHOW TIME (PRODUCTION) - CH. 9		
STUDIO SESSION x HOURLY FEE		
RE-RECORDING, ADDITIONS, CHANGES		
INTERVIEWER OR NARRATOR		
SECOND VOICE TALENT		
EQUIPMENT PURCH. FOR LIVE PRESENTATION		
EQUIPMENT RENTAL		
TAPE/SUPPLIES		
CHAPTER 9 SUB-TOTAL		
EDITING (POST-PRODUCTION) - CH. 10		
DIGITAL / COMPUTER EDITING X HOURLY RATE		
REEL-TO-REEL / RAZOR BLADE EDITING		
MUSIC USE (MUSIC LIBRARY SELECTIONS)		
MUSIC SEARCH		
TEST OR PROOF CASSETTES		
CHAPTER 10 SUB-TOTAL		
DUPLICATION , LABELING & SHIPPING-CHAPTER 11		
START-UP (ONE-TIME) DUPLICATING MASTERS		
START-UP (ONE-TIME) LABEL SET-UP		
START-UP (ONE-TIME) LABEL PLATES		
LABELS OR IMPRINTS		
DUPLICATION		
ALBUM (SEE CHAPTER 7)		
NORELCO BOX (SEE CHAPTER 7)		
SOFT POLY BOX (SEE CHAPTER 7)		
OTHER PACKAGING (SEE CHAPTER 7)		
SHRINKWRAPPING OR CELLOWRAP ASSEMBLY		
ASSEMBLE TAPE INTO PACKAGE OR BOX		
GROUND SHIPPING		
TWO DAY SHIPPING		
OVERNIGHT SHIPPING		
OTHER SHIPPING VENUES		
INSURANCE ON CONTENTS IN TRANSIT		
CHAPTER 11 SUB-TOTAL		
SELLING EXPENSES - CH. 12 & 13		
MARKETING AND SALES COSTS		
PROMOTIONAL COSTS		
ADVERTISING COSTS		
PUBLIC RELATIONS		
DISTRIBUTION		
ORDER FULFILLMENT		
CHAPTERS 12 & 13 SUB-TOTAL		
FIRST YEAR TOTAL EXPENSES		
SECOND YEAR TOTAL EXPENSES		
PROJECTED NET BEFORE TAXES		
FIRST YEAR PRE-TAX REVENUE		
SECOND YEAR PRE-TAX REVENUE		

SEEK ADVICE FROM YOUR ACCOUNTANT OR ADVISORS TO DETERMINE AFTER TAX RETURNS AND PROFITS.

Your Time Value

You go to the movies for the evening with Sally, and you pass up a football game with Jim. Your child opts to quit her job to stay home with small children, and her former co-worker lucks out on a great promotion your daughter knows would have been hers. Every choice we make eliminates others. Something you give up is what economics professors call the "opportunity cost" of your decision. The opportunity cost may be a fork in the road of life, or an option with impact on your business. Your time *is* money. Therefore, there's a cost associated with the choices you make.

What's the best use of *your* time? Try the following self-test to find out. It's adapted with permission from Mark Sanborn, a high-content professional speaker from Denver. He uses a cost/benefit analysis to evaluate business activities, and shares his technique with other presentation professionals.

Time cost	1=low time investment	2=moderate	3=high
Effectiveness/ Payoff	1=highly effective in building business	2=moderate	3=least effective
Who does it?	1= outsource/delegate	2=supervise	3= you

	Time	Payoff	Delegate?	Task Total
Preproduction:				
Telephone calls/info gathering				
Meetings/researching				
Determining market				
Selecting packaging and supplier				
Arranging for cover designer				
Writing cover copy				
Writing/reviewing the script				
Gathering source tapes				
Auditioning voice talent				
Negotiating fees, agreements				
Gathering source tapes				
Confirming all's on track				
Production:				
Recording session				
Reviewing session tape				
Transcribing/marking edits				

Reviewing edited tape				
Notes, changes, mark edits				
Soliciting peer review				
Telephone/ meetings				
Choosing music				
Rerecording/editing/reviewing				
Duplication/Packaging:				
Design labels, proof and sign off				
Design cover, proof and sign off				
Order packaging, verify details				
Verify arrival, assembly details				
Meet duplicator to place order				
Listen/approve test cassettes				
Confirm shipping locations				
Other Tasks Not Included above:				

Many people are surprised to see places they could spend more time than anticipated in low-payoff activities. If you have trouble getting a handle on these tasks, try copying the test and sending it to three or four friends who've already published similar audio products. Average how much time they spent.

A Story About the Cost of "Putting It Off"

I know a successful, well established industry professional who felt confused by the things he didn't understand, so he procrastinated. Being a very bright man, he was uncomfortable admitting he was afraid of the unknown. Opportunity knocked, and he ignored it, for 10 years.

He says his colleagues urged him to make tapes, "But, I'm kinda lazy, and I've made a good living with just my teaching. The last couple of years though, this being on the road isn't as much fun as it used to be, and I decided to investigate further, and maybe give audio tapes a try."

That's how, in 1996, Bruce overcame his habits and created two audio programs. One was a promotional tape. The free tape generated dozens of bookings for his newest presentation. They were easy bookings. The customers came from his database, so he could keep all the fees. He reduced regular marketing expenses in half, since he was now fully booked for most of the year ahead.

His second audio project, a 10-tape album, sold out quickly. He duplicated another 500 within six months of release. Bruce cleared $60 a unit on each album, after costs were deducted from the gross. He sold 850 albums before December 31, 1996. He used a few sets for gifts, so 130 albums remained in inventory at year end. His 1996 profit was $51,000, before taxes.

What was his opportunity cost for the 10 years he procrastinated? We will never know, of course. So let's play "what if." For simplifying the math, and taking some account of inflation, let's assume Bruce could have sold an average of 500 albums per year, for the past 10 years, and profited $50/album. The opportunity cost of Bruce's delaying tactics is $300,000. Colleagues who encouraged Bruce were selling tapes 10 years ago, and these figures are in line with their experience.

What really happened? Once past the initial learning curve, Bruce quickly saw how other materials he'd *already developed* for presentations could be adapted to valuable tape products. He's talking to other leaders in his field about going together on producing a simple newsprint catalog, and cross-selling each other's most popular products. He never had the time for planning and development like this while he was a road warrior. Bruce is able to stay off the road five months a year now, without any reduction of his standard of living.

"I try not to think of how much easier it would have been to put the kids through college, if only I'd had tapes earlier," he comments. "I wasn't really lazy; I was ignorant. I don't like listening to tapes myself, and I couldn't believe anyone else really did either. I'm glad my friend Nancy persuaded me to watch the feeding frenzy at one of their product tables. Seeing was believing, and now I'm banking the benefits."

Sample Audiobook Production Budgets

There's more than one way to do a budget. Chapters 2 and 3 cover planning and variables influencing costs. Here is an example developed in collaboration with Global Arts, an independent production company.

Project Description: *An abridged script developed by the author* from a 250-page book, provided on disk. Read by a non-celebrity professional narrator.

Planning/pre production meetings to determine exact needs	75
Minor script refinements for audio	150
Tape, supplies, misc.	200
Narrator for 3 hours finished tape (union, non-celebrity)	1,300
(if non-union, non-celebrity $600.)	
Studio time recording book, 8-10 hours	600
(includes script monitor, engineer)	
Simple editing, digital	800
Additional editing as required, est.	100
Add music, create DAT and chrome cassette masters, 7 hours	290
Misc. unanticipated expenses assoc. with project	250
	$3,765

Marketing: Determined by publisher. Same distribution channels as author's books.

Will a Formula Tape be Acceptable?

Why dump thousands into production if a simple, clean recording and a $50 piece of music from your high school friend will do the trick? Why indeed?

Many sales generating tapes and early tapes from speakers are entry-level products. If you are smooth in your delivery, or can abide a few stumbles or rough spots, a formula-based product, or "package" may be all you need. Music can be faded down and spliced onto your voice at the beginning and end, eliminating more costly cross fading and mixing. You might or might not have an announcement at the end, with copyright and contact information recorded onto the tape. Some people skip the close and put ©, the year, and their identifying information on their labels.

The risks for publishers of a low-budget or formula tape is it *may* convey a sense that the person behind the tape is an amateur. The person or company behind the tape doesn't respect the listener. Yours sounds like other tapes they've tossed. If you go this route, be sure you're meeting the needs of listeners.

The second caution with formula tapes has more to do with human nature. If you tend to be under-prepared, are mindful of your image, or get caught up in the creative possibilities of recording and editing, you can easily use more hours of studio, consulting and editing time than the package price allows for. You may end up going over budget unless you've added a fudge factor of 20% or more.

Products from Presentations

In general, products derived from presentations are simplest to develop. The payback period is shorter, marketing is simpler, and profits can be greater than with any other type of audio product.

Audio Business Cards and Promotional Tapes

Promotional tapes, such as those used for recruiting more "downline" participants in multi-level marketing, can be very low cost to create using standardized scripts. Many are recorded in quiet offices or back bedrooms, from a script a distributor knows by heart already. I've recorded short scripts for clients in their offices over the weekend (when the elevator music was off), and done interviews for broadcast in closed cars on a quiet street. The last location is one a news producer suggested 20 years ago, pointing out that padded headliners, dashboards and seats mimic some of the sound absorption properties of studios. It worked surprisingly well, creating a sense of comfortable conversation.

Audio business cards and informational tapes for marketing purposes are often combined with the company's other marketing materials, so certain budget items won't apply. The budget example here is similar to what many duplicators charge for recording and duplicating a simple promotional or marketing tape.

Jackson Sound Productions
Professional Audio Demo Tape

Common cost to record, duplicate, and package a 20 minute voice over demo tape.

One Hour Studio Recording	@55.00 per hour	$ 55.00
Music and Sound Effects	@30.00 per needle down	$ 60.00
Recording Material and Supplies	@25.00	$ 25.00
Duplication Master	@25.00 1x charge	$ 25.00
250 C-20 Cassettes Duplicated	@ .69 each	$172.50
Imprinting Set-up	@25.00 1x charge	$ 25.00
Imprinting Plates	@20.00 each 1x charge	$ 40.00
Imprinting	@20.00 minimum charge	$ 20.00
Norelco Boxes	@ .15 each	$ 37.50
Laser printed J-cards from templates		$ 75.00
Assembly and Shrink-wrapped	@ .15 each	$ 37.50
250 Laser printed Business Cards to match J-card		$ 75.00
Total Cost		$647.50
Cost per unit		$ 2.59

Voice over demo tapes are used to promote professional voice talent. They can also be designed for the use of prospective market, or give a product demo. Great for PSA's, how to's, invitations, and specialty advertising

Ask your Customer Service Representative about letterhead, envelopes, postcards, brochures, or a complete presentation set to match your cassette and business card.

Jackson Sound Productions Ltd.
3301 West Hampden Ave. Unit C
Englewood, CO 80110
(303) 761-7940 • 1-800-621-6773 • Fax (303) 789-2161
e-mail jspaudio@aol.com

The Peculiarities of A/V Project Quotes

In the production phase, you are paying for person-hours, equipment use, supplies, and knowledge to turn your material into a product master. You'll need others to help you achieve your goals.

One way of estimating is by the "finished minute." Let's use a 12-tape internal training program for the mythical "Pay No Taxes Company" as an example. In-house staff time, benefits, equipment, and materials costs Pay No Taxes Company (PNT) $34,000 for completely edited, approved master tapes. The finished series has plenty of sound effects, a professional script, and does the job dictated by top management and PNT lawyers. Total running time is 10 hours. $34,000 divided by 10 = $3,400/finished hour divided by 60 = $56.67 a finished minute. PNT was willing to invest this much because it wanted to keep all the information within company walls. Their duplicator was required to sign a confidentiality agreement, and turn the project in 48 hours, returning all masters.

This is unreasonable for most spoken audio product masters. A ball-park figure we use is $2,000 a finished hour. Some projects are much less, some projects require more. At $2,000 a finished hour for the production of master tapes, the quote is equivalent to just under $34 a finished minute.

The second method of calculating costs is by time and materials required to complete your project. Let's say you call three studios. They all quote hourly rates. They're bidding the way a construction contractor does, figuring time and materials. Any changes or additions you make will be on top of that initial bid for the work described.

Your Own Numbers

The range of spoken audio available in North America today is astounding, even to people who work in the industry daily. There are cassettes or CDs at all levels, for all tastes.

Your right numbers will fit your market, your subject, and your overall strategy for success, and yours alone.

You now have a format to forecast your success before you make a major commitment of time and money. If the numbers don't work at first it's a signal to go back over your plan, and make the changes to produce a winner. After you know the right combination, you can project three to five years into the future for the life of each product.

If you prefer using our ready-made spreadsheet to create your budget, it's available in Excel for both Windows and Macintosh platforms on 3.5" disks, for $17.00 a disk, including postage and handling. Please use the order form in the back of the book.

●●●●●●●●●
Resources:

Global Arts, John Lane, writer, audiobook producer/consultant 2572 S. Williams St., Denver, CO 80210, 303-698-9310, Fax: 303-698-9310

Jackson Sound Productions Ltd., duplicator, Linda Cano-Rodriguez, 3301 W. Hampden Ave., Unit C, Englewood, CO 80110, 800-621-6773, 303-761-7940, Fax: 303-789-0557, e-mail: dubs @jacksonsound.com, www.jacksonsound.com

Sanborn and Assoc., Mark Sanborn, 695 S. Colorado Blvd., #415, Denver, CO 80222, 303-698-9656, Fax: 303-777-3045, e-mail:MarkSpeaks@aol.com

Brian Tracy, Brian Tracy International, 462 Stevens Ave., #202, Solana Beach, CA 92075, 619-481-2977, Fax: 619-481-2445

Design and Script a Winner

It is in your own best interests to have a full script. In any recording session, there will be surprises and may be changes. Being well prepared and knowing what you need to accomplish helps you keep things under control.

Many would-be publishers resist writing a script, especially if they do lots of speaking or seminars. Well-known sales and business trainer Brian Tracy tells of the battles he had with Antonia "Tony" Boyle, his producer at Nightingale-Conant, over whether he would use a script. Boyle won, Tracy recorded with a script, and since then he's not only used scripts himself, but he recommends the practice to others.

In this chapter, we'll take a look at the pros and cons of using a script, and then consider script designs, and various options, before any writing begins. Many scripts are read by professional narrators, so there's a brief section about narration. The right voice adds a great deal to the overall enjoyment of a good script or story. This chapter concludes with a long section on components of a good script, including examples, so you'll be able to build your script faster.

Do You Really Need a Script?

What would convince you to take time to develop a script? Consider these points:

• A full script or transcript speeds recording and editing.

• A script keeps you on track and organized. Even people who "wing it" easily on the platform or a radio talk show do a better job with a script. Platform competency alone does not guarantee a smooth performance in the studio. The script may not be word for word. A detailed outline script helps you say what you want, when and how you want to say it.

• Predicting costs and making budget decisions is easiest with a full script — and difficult to impossible without knowing what a project will entail. Publishers who refuse to script audio products should be prepared to pay production staff and recording facilities by the hour *without complaint.*

• Narrators cannot audition without a script. Interviewers, directors, producers and engineers cannot prepare ahead of time. Consequently, you set up and prepare in the studio and on the clock.

• Without a script, the engineer or producer will struggle making adequate notes for editing. Their attention is divided. If your voice fluctuates, the engineer is occupied adjusting knobs and volume controls for the consistent levels. The producer, or a production assistant, will be listening for grammar, pronunciation, and marking the time and places where something should be re-recorded. The director is monitoring your delivery and overall cohesiveness, and coaching you so you communicate with listeners — all without a road map on where the session is headed. (When there's no director involved the producer and engineer split these responsibilities.) This is not the best use of highly trained people.

• Spontaneity is important, and makes more interesting listening. Some people find it very difficult to sound spontaneous if they practice beforehand. If that's the case for you, consider reviewing your detailed outline script repeatedly over two or three days prior to recording. In the two weeks before you record, rehearse just the stories and examples word for word, so you have the timing and delivery honed to a fine point. Work with a drama coach, if necessary. People will remember the stories you use long after they've forgotten your main points.

Think of a script the way you think about a travel itinerary. You accept the importance of knowing your destination and days of travel before making airline, rental car, and lodging reservations. You know if you fly from New York to Cairo first class it will cost more than in coach. You wouldn't dream of calling to book tickets without being able to give the necessary dates and destinations. Why should production people be mind readers, any more than your travel agent or an airline reservationist?

So, do what the "big guys" do. Script your program.

Begin with the Customer in Mind

Writing a script that connects with customers in the first minute is easiest once you know who you're targeting and why they'll buy. Ask yourself: What is most important in the minds of my customers?

With that question in mind, begin sketching:

• A strong opening — what does your listener want to feel?
• An organization or logical progression that makes sense to listeners.
• What action you want people to take when they've finished.

What "sound" will serve you best? Should it be an interview — similar to a radio interview, but with questions chosen ahead of time? Or would a one-voice narration work best? Are music or sound effects important to convey your message to your listener? How will you grab attention in the first few minutes?

Fiction, poetry, historical novels and biographies are usually read verbatim, or with minor changes for listenability. How should the reader sound? Professional narrators are chosen for acting ability and because they can bring pages to life. You've seen thousands of examples on television, on stage, and in the movies. Who, specifically, should your main character sound like?

Non-fiction titles or instructional tapes are typically recorded by one voice, as an interview, or on location at a presentation. The author or expert is the star.

If the author could be difficult for listeners to understand, the script can be written to combine credibility with listenability. The author/ expert does an introduction and perhaps some brief commentaries throughout the program. Using this approach, 80-90% of the content is handled by a professional voice.

The script is based on the expert's book, articles, or speeches. The two voices can be recorded separately for convenience, if necessary. Designing the sound this way works especially well for financial and economics titles, science programs, and similar subjects where the expert may be primarily a researcher or scholar. It's also a good format for situations where the expert has a strong accent, a nasal speaking voice, is uncomfortably shy, or is simply a dull reader in long passages.

What's the Best Sound Design?

You may find it useful to translate your ideas into reality by comparing some of the costs and benefits of different sound designs. The most common ones are listed in the following table.

Think about the background and mood you want to create. Do you envision a full-cast audio with sound effects? Something similar to the style of old-time radio, or the award-winning and magical adventure, *Dynotopia?* Your fantasy could be too ambitious to undertake as a first product, but perhaps not. Experienced spoken word producers can usually suggest ways to substitute or modify an original concept, yet stay within budget. There are voice talents, for example, who can sound like 50 different characters, and musicians who are delighted to have their cuts used, for very reasonable rates. Unleash your ideas. Creative thinking is a fun part of the process, so speak up with your suggestions.

SOUND DESIGN	SCRIPT FORMAT	COMMENTS
Narration of text. Abridged or unabridged. Performed or straight read.	1 or 2 voices.	Interesting, varied. Pro actors can do character voices.
Studio recording + taped inserts.	Good script, planning and organization necessary. May include pre-recorded material. Requires good sound quality speech or other "live" source material.	Blends sounds, settings. Can be lively and compelling. Works well if stories and laughter or emotions in live segments. Journalistic/news format.
Interview.	2 voices. Scripted outline. Pro interviewer and information expert.	Conversational, natural. Familiar format. Like a talk radio or eavesdropping. Editing and retakes allows
Seminar or speech.	Least expensive if good sound quality recording, performance and audience response.	Good choice for back of the room product. Music selection and second voice introduction add polish and value. Transcript or catalog of speech speeds editing and excerpting later.

Who Writes the Script?

In a literal sense, anyone can write a script. A *good* script is another story. Writing for audio is a specialized form of scripting, very different from writing the same material for print, television or a screenplay. Allow three to four days per cassette to write, review and rewrite. Few busy people can devote a full eight to ten hours of uninterrupted time to writing.

Using this formula, you'd block out three weeks to script and polish a six-hour album. Six hours prints out within a range of 270-310 8½" x 11" pages, depending on how you set up the pages. It averages slightly over a minute per page.

If you decide to contract the work out, be sure to review samples of the writer's work, and check references. A staff person in your office may be able to write so it sounds just like you talk. That person can flesh out your outline, then make changes after you review and edit the first draft script. The closer to the final script, the more you'll probably want to be involved.

When you're developing an original script, your mind map, presentation notes or earlier publications are a starting point. With subject matter that's specialized or technical you can't always delegate. In such cases, an author/expert has to write his or her own script. Many people can ghost a self-help or nonfiction title. Few "ghosts" can write about the intricacies of scientific research or finance as well as the true expert. An experienced technical writer might, however, be able to take reports, speeches and taped interviews and create a good basis for you to use for the script, and perhaps a book.

With a subject that is broader — like communications techniques or business management — give some thought to hiring a professional writer or producer with audio scripting experience. Your input will be required, but you'll spend less of your time at a keyboard. This combination approach is similar to taking a book manuscript and seeing it improved by a good editor. Collaboration frequently creates a better product, and you'll have your finished script within the time frame you projected.

Abridgments

If you are adapting a book to audio, there are two choices — abridged or unabridged (read in full as written). An abridgment must preserve the essence of an author's skill and story, but be easy enough to follow that you don't lose the listener. No one wants to rewind or struggle to understand the flow of the material. Most listening will be done in cars or other activity settings, surrounded by competing noises and distractions. If your program doesn't make sense, listeners will discard it and may never give you another chance. Worse yet, the listener may be an avid audiophile or a reviewer, and criticize your work to others.

Abridgments vary by degrees. Most bestsellers are either three hours (referred to as abridged), or between four and six hours (abridged lite).

Unabridged books use as many cassettes or CDs as required. A 12-hour reading can be duplicated on eight 90-minute tapes, or, if it suits packaging and marketing better, on ten or twelve shorter playing tapes. An abridger will want to know how many tapes or CDs are planned.

If an audio is adapted directly from a book, an abridgment is done one of several ways. It's easiest to work with the manuscript on disk and a hard copy that can be marked up.

If you don't have either, here's a quick-and-dirty method to get you started. First, take three copies of the book. Mark the edge of pages with different colors of ink, clip the corner of the pages, or somehow distinguish the copies. Using the first victimized book, begin to cross out sections and make notes right on the pages such as "Jump to page 82" and "eliminate character." If you have the manuscript on disk, you'll then make the appropriate deletions and print the abridged draft. If you don't have a computer copy of the manuscript, tear the pages from the spine and discard the unwanted pages. (I know, it's painful to tear apart a book. If you can, use a damaged or shopworn copy.)

Fasten the pages together, or hole punch them and put them in a notebook. Add any transition sentences, chapter breaks, or other notes the script needs, so the recording will be listenable and easy to follow.

When the first pass is complete, read and time representative pages at random. If you read 10 pages in 10 minutes, you can estimate one minute per page. If the type is small, the pages big, or your reading pace times out at two minutes or more a page, that's fine, too. The purpose is an actual reading time so you can estimate how much recording and editing time you'll have.

Do you have enough material to fill the number of minutes you planned? If not, tear apart another book and be less ruthless this time, leaving in more sections you'd originally taken out. Is there a subplot or background story that enhances the main story line? Have you sacrificed some beautiful, moving passages for the sake of time and the central theme? Is there a story you usually tell that clearly affects audiences? Should it be added? Decide what will serve you and the listener best. Put it back in, create it anew, or write longer transitions. Use the third book if you make further changes.

If you're working on disk, always remember to back up your work, indicate the date and version, and number each page.

If you're a publisher of other authors' work, you'll want your author to approve any abridgment. At the major audio publishing houses, abridgers are hired to develop a script that's faithful to the original intent and message. Abridging any work, especially fiction, requires considerable skill.

Locate freelance abridgers through other publishers, writing groups, directories, online interest groups and newsletters.

How Long Should Tapes Run?

The usual length for a two-tape adult fiction title is three hours, or 180 minutes, on two cassettes. With newer tape stock making 100-minute tapes practical, fiction can run 20 minutes longer per tape.

Nonfiction is 45 minutes and up per cassette. Single cassette products tend to be longer than multiples within a series. You might publish a one-tape product of 70 minutes, and a cassette album totalling 140 minutes.

Consumers are reluctant to spend $10 or more for just a few minutes of listening on a single tape. Promotional tapes are free, and typically 10-20 minutes in total length. Many promotional tapes repeat the side one program on side two.

Your program should be long enough to deliver a good product, without wasting the listener's time. If you have enough good material for one tape, make a one-tape product. Don't insult the listener's intelligence by padding it out to two — or six. Your goal is to develop a line of products and that requires growing demand, recognition, and a loyal customer base. If someone tries your first product and finds it's over before it really gets going, they'll return it, or warn friends. People tend to remember negative experiences more than good ones.

Customer feedback influences major publishers. True, they can spread their losses over more products, and weather bad publicity. They have an incentive to minimize returns because of the greater volume. Consequently, they're discriminating about which products they put out under their imprints. If your program is successful, you may be picked up by a large publisher who sees profit potential without much effort or development cost. This can be a win all the way around, for you, the listeners and the larger publisher.

The Components of a Good Script

A good original script is organized, uses descriptive writing, audio English (spoken style), appropriate language, and is adaptable. If you're taking an existing book to tape, the most you will do is an abridgment. If a script is based on a book, but only loosely, your creative task is greater. Here are some things to keep in mind for original scripts.

First, scripts are **organized** in some fashion. Some do this logically, progressing from a basic level of understanding to a more complex one. For example:

"The study of individuals is called psychology. The study of groups of individuals is called sociology. People behave differently in groups. . . and will do things in a crowd they would never do individually. During the next hour we're going to analyze three famous examples of crowd behavior from Canadian labor union annals . . . politics . . . and response to a disaster . . . blah, blah, blah." The program could wrap up with conclusions that can be drawn about human behavior in groups. The tape will be informative, and may also be entertaining.

Some scripts describe a process, such as making a sale, giving up smoking, or planning for retirement. Chronological order (or its cousin, the flashback to prior events) is more popular for biographies and historical works.

Other writers develop a script based on the most common questions about their specialty. This approach means your script may or may not follow the order of an existing presentation or print title. Mark S.A. Smith, a trade show specialist and author of books on sales, has used this method, and recommends it for simplifying the script-writing process. (He learned this approach from National Speakers Association friends, Dan Kennedy and Bill Brooks.)

As Smith explains, "Imagine someone is paying you $1,000 an hour to pick your brain. What questions had they better ask you to get their money's worth?"

Write down the questions this imaginary person would ask you. Your answers will run about three minutes each, so 9-10 questions will run about half an hour per side, Smith points out. If you are typically succinct or long-winded you'll adjust, adding or subtracting questions.

When you're designing a two-tape package, what are the best 50 questions an intelligent layman should ask? Can you group the questions in modules? Using the "20 questions" technique, a nonfiction script comes together quickly. Even if you plan to record at some future date, it's a way to take action, and move from "some day" to a commitment to create audio products by X date.

As a writer, you probably know about scripts using a circular device. You begin with a story. Launch into your theme. Develop the theme with examples, features and benefits. Summarize and restate your theme and main points. End with a humorous tie-in to your opening story, or complete the story.

A circular script can be satisfyingly concluded with a definite ending. Or it can end with a call to action, or questions to ponder. " . . . And so, as Mike walked slowly down the corridor to the president's office, he thought, 'What is the best way to tell her the news?'" For the next three days your listeners will speculate about how they'd deliver the news, if they were in Mike's shoes.

However you organize your script, make sure a listener can follow the material easily. The time-tested method is to list your major points. Make each point a module. If your material is short, the modules can be connected by spoken "segues." (Transition statements are called segues or bridges in broadcasting and audio recording.)

Music can also be used to mark the end of one thought and the beginning of another. Music written into a script this way is referred to as a bridge. Music, a tone, or a sound effect used this way serves an auditory punctuation purpose. It lets the listener choose whether to go on to the next segment, rewind, or stop the player and think about what you've said.

Second, a good audio script incorporates **descriptions and stories**, allowing listeners to visualize in their own minds. Think about the most stirring speeches and radio programs you've listened to. For example, the radio serials of the 1940's came alive with action in "the theater of the mind." Fibber McGee and Mollie's closet packed with household goods was a little different in each listener's mind. Whole families gathered to listen to *The Shadow* or *Sherlock Holmes*. Many popular early evening series were made into television shows in the 1940's and 50's. *The War of the Worlds* radio production by Orson Welles was so realistic it frightened the whole nation. It was scarier than the modern crop of *X Files* look-alikes because it left more to our imaginations. The popular radio stories of the past are steady sellers on cassette. More recently, Garrison Keillor's *Tales from Lake Wobegon* and *Cape Cod Mystery Theater* are modern-day radio yarns entertaining thousands monthly on tape.

Great orators stimulate mental images and provoke action or changes in thinking or behavior. Effective use of spoken English made Eleanor Roosevelt, John F. Kennedy, Martin Luther King, and Winston Churchill memorable leaders. A talent for creating vivid descriptions makes one sports commentator worth more in the pay envelope than an equally proficient but less lyrical broadcaster.

Third, use **"audio English"** — it's how we speak, not how we were taught to write. Many full-time communications professionals recommend writing like we talk in company memos, advertising copy, articles, and reports. Spoken language includes contractions, incomplete sentences, emphasis on certain words, and the subtleties we communicate when we inflect (go up or down on a word).

Write from your mouth to your listener's mind and heart. "Write for the ear," says Toni Boyle, who explains that print and audio are two distinct media. "They're very different styles. In fact, I took a chapter of a book I'm writing — a book with dialogue — and adapted it for audio, as an exercise. Even I was surprised by how different they were, and I do this full time, for a living."

Betty Cooper, author of *Speak With Power,* calls this "Talk Writing," and advises that "a script should always be the way you'd tell it to someone over a cup of coffee or the back fence. You're not out to impress them. You want to get your point across — to communicate." Cooper developed early drive-time information radio programs for The Canadian Broadcasting Corporation, taught broadcasting, and is now a consultant to corporations. I recommend her book *Speak With Power* for anyone striving to be an effective public speaker.

Why always use "audio English" for an informational, sales, or promo tape? Because it will most likely be listened to by one person, a couple, or at most, a small group. You want to establish a personal connection, even though you can't see your listener.

Sometimes the distinction between how we speak and write remains elusive. If you're having trouble, try something a producer pulled on me once, when I began in radio. Take two pages of your preliminary script. Read them into a tape recorder. Then hand the script to a friend and tell your friend the same thing you just read. (My producer snatched them out of my hand. "No props," he said. "Just look at me and tell me the story!") Record yourself again as you retell the material. Your second explanation will almost certainly be more conversational. With a little practice, you'll be able to hear and write in your own "audio English" style.

The **fourth** component of a good script is **appropriateness** — a quality that comes naturally if you know your audience and keep them in mind. A minister wouldn't use the same vocabulary common in a hard-boiled modern detective story. "F...ing" this and that sounds like a character from late-night police dramas, not a spiritual leader giving comfort and guidance. A Shakespeare play has a distinctive sound. It won't be confused with formulaic romances in the grocery store rental tape racks. Keep this in mind if you hire the script out. Be sure your writer understands *your* audience, and doesn't confuse your listeners with another audience. Once again, think your mouth to their ears. One to one.

Profanity, racial and ethnic slurs, negative comments about religion, detailed descriptions of bodily functions, and unflattering stereotypes can result in listener complaints. If you incorporate these into a script, be sure they are necessary to the story, and will be interpreted as you intend. If you have doubts, consult others for their opinions. The line between good taste and freedom of expression is hard to locate sometimes. What's acceptable in a Robert B. Parker novel featuring private investigator Spencer and his sidekick Hawk provokes the ire of the same listener in another context.

Fifth, an **adaptable** script adds value. Don't think of your script as a huge task to be repeated over and over. Instead, look at how you can adapt several products from one well-written, original script. Use it as the basis for articles. Or, plan a transcription-based book or seminar to piggyback on your research and writing efforts. Make your audio script so good — and so "evergreen" — you'll still be reaping the benefits five years, hence from the time and effort you put into it.

Write Once and Adapt Forever

Last, and a bonus tip, is to make sure your script isn't dated. Watch out for references to current events, names in the news, or pop culture trends that undermine the relevance of your words. Instead pick examples, stories, and terms that are enduring. *Jerry McGuire* won't be the hot movie of the day in a year, but athletes and relationships will still fascinate. Many products endure and sell well for 10 years without revisions because the publishers chose examples from everyday life. Dogs chase cats and people fall in love, are competitive, and are intrigued by the prospect of easy wealth, year in, year out.

Using a Transcription

It's easy to derive a script for studio taping from a live presentation transcript. True, it costs money to create, but I suspect the real reason people object to transcribing a presentation is because it's painful seeing "uhms" and "you knows" in black and white. They pass unnoticed when we talk, and jump out at us from the page. They're conspicuous on tape, too, but easy to remove. A transcript lets you rearrange segments as you write, and mark edits directly on the transcript. You can draw a line or arrow at the places you've opted to have someone else ask you a question.

With the program in front of you, all you might need to write would be the introduction and closing remarks. Should you decide to cut out a section of the live presentation, it's easy to write a bridge from what you were talking about to what comes next. The intro and "outro," bridges, and other "drop-ins" to the script are recorded when convenient, and edited into the live recording.

The Close or "Outro"

The end of a program generally includes closing comments from the author or reader. Close on a strong note — either upbeat and positive, or by leaving the listener with something to think about.

If the title is fiction, suggest other titles in the same genre, and a phone number to order direct from the publisher. With nonfiction, be sure to close with a specific call to action. Tell your listener what you want them to do.

EXPERT: . . . and so, now <u>you too</u> can be a shrewd antique and glassware collector. Take your new knowledge and head for the flea markets, auctions or estate sales in your area THIS WEEK . . . and find out how much easier it is to find the treasures among the fakes . . . And be sure to TAKE GUIDE BOOKS to verify the authenticity of your finds.

                  MANY ANTIQUE DEALERS THINK OUR GUIDES ARE BEST . . . because we include extensive indexes and pictures to help you. You can even **save 10% off the retail price by ordering them from our special tape customer order desk** at **1-800-123-4567 ......** No need to write it down . . . the number's right on the cassette.

                  So . . . until next time . . . this is EXPERT wishing you haaaappy collecting!

Music: Up, back down under copyright, up and out in 3 seconds.

Some titles incorporate music at the end. On others, there's a pause before a different voice gives copyright and sales information. Some publishers preview or promote other products. The publisher is the contact for more information. A tape promoting your business includes all the relevant information on the tape and the label. Wording can be like this, or use a variation recommended by your advisors.

ANNCR: *TITLE* is copyrighted YEAR, PUBLISHER, CITY, STATE. All rights reserved.

Or:

TITLE IS THE <u>1998</u> COPYRIGHTED PROP-ERTY OF <u>PUBLISHER</u> AND <u>AUTHOR</u>. ALL RIGHTS ARE RESERVED. THE CONTENTS AND SOUND OF THIS PROGRAM MAY NOT BE REPRODUCED OR TRANSMITTED IN ANY FORM, OR BY ANY MEANS, ELEC-TRONIC OR MECHANICAL, NOR CAN IT BE STORED AND RETRIEVED FROM AN INFORMATION STORAGE SYSTEM WITH-OUT THE EXPRESS WRITTEN PERMIS-SION OF THE PUBLISHER.

What Does a Finished Script Look Like?

Scripts are written in block style, indented for different voices or sound sources. The abbreviated examples above are in New Century School-book and Helvetica fonts, with wide margins, for easy reading down the page. The margins are so the reader, producer and engineer can make notes during the recording session, and when proofing the edited version.

Over the past few years K.C. Truby has recorded dozens of titles. This sample is from *Knowledge Centered Selling* in the *Business Builder* series. It violates the standard format, and KC isn't hung up about spelling, since he reads his own script. He sells more than 500,000 tapes a year — often by the case. You won't see them in stores, but you'll find a lot of lawyers, CPAs and salesmen who recognize his name. They remember his lessons about business success, his stories and folksy style. Notice how Truby uses an ellipsis . . . as a cue to pause . . . and how he CAPITALIZES words for emphasis. When the recording and editing is complete, KC sounds as easy and natural as any of the good ol' cowboys spinning yarns 'round the pot bellied stove down at the Feed and Tack. (For a free copy of *Knowledge Centered Selling,* fax KC Truby with your contact information and mailing address.) It's interesting to compare the script and delivery.

KC: . . . A lack of ideas can COST you. And the biggest cost is opportunity. In my business a customer is worth $2,700 a year on average, and most stay with us for 5 years. That means that any time I DON'T get a new customer I'm kissing off $13,000. That's called the lifetime value of a customer. You ought to figure out for your own place because it puts what you doing today into perspective. If I lose a customer, that I didn't have I just lost $13,000. No new ideas, no new reasons to buy, no new ways to bring in prospects and I'm losing 13,000 a pop.

Now opportunity cost is a hard concept to grab. Its losing what you don't have. What you can't see. And what you can't borrow on. That's tough to get worried about . . .

I'll give you an idea of what I mean. I have a cow. If-en I don't run her in with a bull at the right time of the month, I can't get her SET, now that's ranch talk for "Being in the motherly way" . . . but if I don't get her SET, I'm not going to have a calf next spring . . . A calf that I can sell or raise up to be another moma cow.

But If I don't calve that cow, I don't lose any thing, right? I still have the cow don't I?

What I lose is the opportunity to sell a calf.

Opportunity loss is the one thing that successful business owners stay on top of....

(Another story about a thief stealing a neighbor's spare tire in the middle of the night. The neighbor will move fast to prevent a loss.)

Fear of loss, is strong. Fear of lost opportunities is a strength.

So ok, KC where is all this leading . . . are you telling me a short story, or should we bring a bed roll? No you won't need a bed roll. Here is the skinny . . .

This is a secret that smart business owners are figuring out . . . . . ."

The last 15 words signal the listener that another important point is coming. It will build on the opportunity cost concept. Just as he did with these two stories, KC will state his opinion or facts, add some humor, or a story to make it stick, and repeat the idea. People learn when they're drawn into the lesson. They'll pay good money to learn new information or behaviors and be entertained at the same time.

Good money. Millions. Just ask Truby. He'll respond passionately about how wonderful audio cassettes are for business communication. He even has a presentation about using audio tapes to grow your business.

Printing Out the Script

Format the script using double or triple spacing, in 12-point or larger type. Choose a font that's easy to read. For example, the font used in this book is Garamond 13-point type. Pick any font that works for you and the reader. Use generous margins. Paper is cheaper than studio time. As the day wears on, you will minimize retakes caused by eye strain by doing it this way. Use a header or footnote to date and identify versions of the script, and number all pages clearly.

Printed copies are for the narrator and all recording session crew members. Some people follow a practice learned in broadcast facilities. Each version of the script is printed on a different color, or alternatively, print each person's script on a separate color — blue for the engineer, light green for the narrator, etc. I prefer the second practice. It takes a little more time in preparation, but it simplifies recording and editing. People always write on their scripts.

After a well-deserved post-mortem on the session, where everyone congratulates each other, and you comment about what you'd do differently next time (if anything), nobody has to sift through five sets of scripts (some now on the floor), to find their own complete set. Scripts aren't keepsakes, but you may want them to refer to later if there are retakes. The production crew will keep their copies because the notes are used in editing.

Should the Author be the Voice on the Tape?

Many experienced audio producers believe authors should stick to creating the content. People who are trained in interpreting and delivering a script usually give a better performance. Performance matters to listeners. A few well-known authors have enough clout to narrate their own books — at least until consumers complain. Other authors are great interpreters of their own work.

Bringing a book alive in a recording booth is different from amateur theater, reading to children and friends, or talking on the telephone. Some skills are transferable, and some aren't. Recording sessions can have many stops and starts, even with highly paid professional narrators. Inexperienced narrators find these interruptions unnerving. Newcomers to the studio are prone to focus on their own performance, rather than concentrate on connecting with a listener. That's natural, but anxiety comes through in anyone's voice. Likewise, fatigue, a cold-induced hoarseness or nasality, coffee nerves, or other stresses will be recorded on tape. Many authors improve quickly with rehearsal and voice coaching. If an author will be performing his or her own material, a voice coach and lessons over several weeks can be a wise investment.

Reading your own book is hard work. Few authors believe this the first time into the studio, but almost all agree afterwards. When she finished recording her eight-hour unabridged bestseller, *Kids Are Worth It!*, Barbara Coloroso closed the cover, looked through the glass, and said "I'm never doing this again, you guys. This is exhausting! I'd rather *write* another book than ever read another one on tape!"

We all laughed, stretched, and congratulated each other on managing the recording sessions in record time. It had been hard work, for everyone. The plan originally called for a more leisurely schedule, but a relative was very ill. The family emergency meant she had to cut short the time available for recording. Because Barbara was so professional and cooperative, she was able to compensate, and we stayed on schedule for the audiobook. The total recording time was about 12 hours for over eight hours of finished material—almost unheard of.

Coloroso's personality and experience were the most important reasons the production worked better than we had a right to expect. Her attention was completely focused on helping parents improve family life, so she accepted direction and questions from the control room, trusting we all had the same purpose. She didn't waste emotional energy reacting defensively. She treated everyone with respect and dignity — just as she advocates in her speeches. Consequently, everyone gave their best and worked as an efficient team.

New publishers should be aware, however, that the phrase "Read by the author" on the box often alerts consumers. A customer may insist on a preview before buying or renting. If the point of purchase is a retail store with headphones and a listening option, the problem is solved — if the customer takes the time to listen.

On the other hand, when the narrator/reader is someone known for fine performances — artists such as Blair Brown, Jay O. Sanders, Michael Prichard, Frank Muller, Lynn Redgrave, Grover Gardner, or Donada Peters — the customer has no qualms. Many audio customers bond to narrators, specifying books read by their favorites when they order from Books On Tape™ and other rental companies. That's why the 1996 B-O-T catalog has an 11-page index listing titles by narrator, plus the usual title/author indexes.

Frank Muller — A Master's Voice

Frank Muller, probably the most celebrated narrator in the United States today, composed an essay called "A Reader Inflects," for Terry's Audiobooks, online. You can read the entire essay there, along with Muller's biography and awards. This edited version is used with permission from Frank Muller.

A READER INFLECTS

I'm heading for the studio.

Once again I am about to engage in what often strikes me as the supreme indulgence. There's a blank reel of tape on the deck and twenty more on the shelf. There's a six hundred-plus page bestseller on a stand under a warm microphone in front of a comfortable chair in what my wife calls the "padded room."

The book is a huge, panoramic story exploring several decades in the lives of at least dozen people on at least two continents. There are many more peripheral characters of all descriptions adding all manner of colors and flavors, humours and hatreds to the texture of this epic, each of whom, despite being peripheral, is a human being with a complete and complex identity. And the book is written in the First Person. I'm an actor, it's my job to narrate this book as a single voice recording, and unlike on the stage or in film or TV, I get to indulge completely — I get to play ALL the parts.

This guy, this first person, has four brothers and three close friends, and everybody gets a voice — that's eight characters right there, all white males from the same background and within a few years of each other in age, each of whom I will have to consistently keep distinct and recognizable as they grow through twenty years of shared history, some changing a great deal and others less, each showing the effects of whatever journey they take over the years — for the twenty-eight finished hours of this unabridged recording, put on tape over the course of six weeks.

Then there are the women (can a six-foot-plus 200-pound baritone do women?) — the wonderfully melodramatic, sometimes overbearing, sometimes seductive matriarch — the eight-year-old daughter, the wife dynamic, passionate, tortured, and ultimately tragic, there are the Holocaust survivor parents-in-law who tell their long stories — in the first person — through our first first person of course (hmmm . . . should that fact color the telling — or not . . . if so, how much?) and all those peripheral hicks, Nazis, cossacks, rabbis, tough guys, etc. etc. . . .

How do you keep all this afloat? . . . Do it with passion . . . Passion at the proper pace, preferably. A reading is too fast when there isn't time for an image to reach full fruition in the mind of the listener. It's too slow if the dramatic tension — no matter how heightened or lightened it may be at any given moment — is allowed to drop even for an instant. And building to crescendos, weaving the arc of a story over so many hours, requires total perspective and sure sense of direction.

And intimacy. An audiobook is a very intimate one-on-one relationship between reader and listener. The microphone is the ear of the listener. I often imagine that I'm sitting on a comfortable couch speaking the narrative text into the listener's ear. When the characters speak, they parade around in front of us, and we watch them together. Even during the grandest, loftiest excursions into epic prose, that relationship is an inescapable dynamic which demands proper attention. In quieter passages, when for example a character has an internal thought, a sudden hushed tone, close on the mike, will draw us in and make us listen — fine, as long as I remember one of the other inescapable dynamics of the medium — the fact that people who drive noisy cars still want to hear every word.

Narrators, then, have a tremendous responsibility to be faithful to the author's intent. The author is limited to the printed word. No matter how well a word is chosen, he or she must rely to some extent on the reader's ability to understand, infer, extrapolate. The narrator can inflect — in fact cannot avoid inflection — using the most versatile instrument ever created — the human voice, and in the course of recording a book, will make literally thousands of choices. Skilled or unskilled, a narrator therefore has tremendous impact. He or she can illuminate or flatten, enhance or destroy . . .

OK, the clock is ticking, all the little lights are flashing — clear the throat, quick sip of tea . . . Roll tape.

— Frank Muller

The bottom line? Most fiction authors do not read their own work, for the listeners' sake, for budget reasons, and ultimately for sales. Large audio publishing houses expect to cast professional voices for fiction titles, and sometimes for nonfiction as well. Some authors read their own books or script with outstanding results. Others are painful to listen to.

Still in a quandary about voicing your product? Try an experiment, suggested by Keith Hatschek, producer/publisher of Passion Press titles.

"Pick 20 pages or so from your script. Record them on a home machine. A top-quality recording isn't important. You just need to be able to hear yourself on playback. A dry run in the privacy of your kitchen is a low-risk way to find out how you'll feel about recording."

Play the tape back and ask yourself:

• How long did it take to successfully read 20 pages to your liking?
• Were you frustrated when you had to stop and re-record a section?
• Was it nerve-racking to listen to your own voice?
• How objective are you about how reviewers will hear you?

After listening to the first trial reading, wait a few days before you listen again. With fresh ears consider the following:

• Are you more or less comfortable with how you sound?
• Do you enjoy bringing your own words off the page?
• Have you criticized yourself inwardly over your performance?

- Who else would listen and give you honest, worthwhile reactions, as a colleague or publishing peer?
- Will you promote the title if someone else reads your work?

In Chapter 3 about planning, readers were encouraged to investigate reviews of audio books in *Publishers Weekly* and *Library Journal*. Once again, it will help to pay particular attention to an issue of *AudioFile* focusing on your type of programs. There are regular issues concentrating on poetry, mystery/suspense, self help, and children's titles. Comments from reviewers about other publishers' work can help you create more enjoyable product.

How to Find and Pick Narrators

Choosing the right professional "voice talent" is an instance where experience can be an asset, so ask for help. Producers have an advantage because they've worked with you in the planning and scripting, and have a sense for the intangible qualities you prefer. Studio managers or engineers sometimes make recommendations. They tend to pick the people they work with often and easily. Their favorites are typically very professional.

When the talent you want is a celebrity, the best course is to contact their agent. Agents can speak for the celebrity, or check with their client and get back to you. It doesn't hurt to inquire. Your ideal reader may want to add audiobook narration to his resume, and is waiting to be asked.

Be prepared for price shock. Remember, a voice talent who delivers a fine performance *saves* you money. Studio and editing time is reduced. The right voice talent with name recognition can boost product sales.

Narrators audition. Listen to their other tapes first. If you'll be interviewed, you should be part of a short audition. A good voice is important, of course. Other factors entering into a casting choice, in random order, are:

1. Availability and compatible schedules.
2. Compensation. Fees per hour, per project, or by royalties?
3. Character voices. The best narrators can sound like a cast of many.

4. Right for the content. Is your material highly technical? Emotionally charged? Should it be a man, or woman, sound old, young, or have a particular accent?
5. What vocal qualities do you have in mind? An authoritative voice, or someone light, warm or folksy?
6. What's the talent's reputation "on the street?" Is he or she every studio's favorite to work with? Or do reports come back as "having a rough time, inconsistent and unreliable lately."
7. (Interviewers especially) Can they think on their feet, or will they need lots of coaching, and framing of questions?

Many broadcasters are as tongue-tied as the rest of us without a script or teleprompter. Others relish the give-and-take of an outline script. They have a sense of humor and are skilled at keeping the conversation lively. A great interviewer makes the microphone disappear. You become the star. The purpose of the conversation is to learn as much as possible from you, not for the interviewer to editorialize. They truly "leave their ego at the door." When the chemistry works best, a good discussion program is almost magical. The listener becomes another member of the conversation.

What About Union Talent?

Screen Actors Guild (SAG) or American Federation of Television and Radio Artists (AFTRA and ACTRA) members may charge higher rates than non-union talent. Union talents frequently do a superior job. In some locales you have no choice — nearly everyone belongs to one or both unions. Check with the local union office. Union members use standard agreements.

Here is some advice from another voice specialist who recommends using a voice coach.

Arlie Kendall

303.670.5077

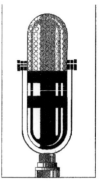

*Having supplied the voice for many interesting projects over the past six years, I feel quite qualified to expound on the downright <u>necessity</u> of procuring a good Voice Acting coach. Voicing is a **craft** and should be learned from a person who has worked in the industry and has, over time, evolved their own skills to a level of mastery.*

A good coach will:

Help you find new deliveries/voices/attitudes Even though many Voice Actors only have "one" voice, it is essential to develop that voice to its' fullest potential. As a professional Voice, you are expected to have the basic deliveries down pretty pat... warm & friendly, bright and bubbly, authoritative, etc. Beyond that, a coach can help you discover voices that live in your body that you didn't even know were there! (Here's a good hint...change your face. Say aloud "I can do anything I put my mind to!" Now, take your right hand and flatten your right cheek and say that phrase again. Hear the difference? You just created a character!) And attitude, this requires an understanding of, even an empathy for, people who look at the world differently than you do.

Teach you to take direction from producers/publishers This is very possibly the most important thing a coach can do for you. The ability to take direction can make or break a voice talent regardless of the quality of his or her voice and/or acting skills. If, after your first read-through of the script, you're asked to raise your pitch or give the read a more sophisticated sound or change a pronunciation... you should be able to, without hesitation, accept that direction and give it back as requested.

Help you overcome or disguise your weaker points A good coach will help you identify and correct any weak areas you may have. For example, in any mundane conversation, I have no apparent speech problems or impediments but in front of a very sensitive microphone, I have a tendency to pop my "p's." I compensate for this by turning my head slightly just before "people" comes out of my mouth or I soften the "p" sound by verbalizing it as a soft "b."

Teach you to interpret a script (How to think like the writer) This is as vital as learning to take direction. You want to get *into* the mind of the person who wrote the script and come from *that* perspective. This is a visualization technique you can learn from your coach.

Teach Breathing/Timing/Projection Learn *where* and *when* and *how* to breathe in the script. Learn the difference between *time* and *timing*. Learn to project (a commonly misunderstood term... it means to *aim* your voice, not increase the volume) effectively.

Teach Studio Protocol and general Do's and Don'ts There are industry-wide do's and don'ts that separate the pros from the rookies. A few examples: *Don't* wear perfume or after-shave to a voice job! A sound booth is generally a small space and some folks are allergic to strong smells. If you are working with other Voice talents, you could affect *their* performance. *Do* take care in choosing the clothing that you wear... some fabrics make a very audible sound when you move, even slightly. *Don't* consume dairy products before a voice job. It will increase the amount of phlegm in your throat which will ultimately alter the timbre of your voice. *Do* learn how to manage multi-page scripts *silently.*

Teach you how to successfully handle cold reads How do you get past the nervous jitters that inevitably occur prior to (and during) recording? Learn to handle a "cold read" (the script has been handed to you *mere moments* before you record!) A good Voice Acting coach can teach you the tricks.

Remember, the essence of communication is intention!

Arlie Kendall

Arlie Kendall
Professional Voice Over

We've covered why it's important to use a script, script designs, and tips on writing. You've read about the how and why of printing scripts. We discussed professional narrators, and ways to prepare if you'll be the voice on your tape. In the next chapter the focus shifts to packaging your products.

•••••••••
Resources:

American Federation of Television & Radio Artists, (AFTRA) 6922 Hollywood Blvd., Hollywood, CA 90028-6128

Antonia Boyle & Company, Toni Boyle, 236 W. Portal Ave., #456, San Francisco, CA 94127, e-mail: ABoyleCo@aol.com

Books on Tape™, Inc., P.O. Box 7900, Newport Beach, CA 92658, Orders: 800-626-333, 714-548-5525, Fax: 714-548-6574, e-mail: botcs@booksontape.com, www.booksontape.com

BookTronics, retailer, 5370 Westheimer, Houston, TX 77056, 713-626-4000

Cape Cod Mystery Theater, Steven Oney, Box 225, West Barnstable, MA 02668. Radio programs on cassette from HighBridge

Barbara Coloroso, Kids are worth it! Inc., P.O. Box 621108, Littleton, CO 80162, 800-729-1588, Fax: 303-972-1204

The Communication Advantage, speaking coach, Dana Gribben, P.O. Box 5038, Larkspur, CA 94977, 510-528-8519

Cooper Communications, Betty K. Cooper, *Speak With Power,* 2209-140th Ave., SW, Calgary, Alberta, T2P 3N3, CANADA, 403-294-1313, Fax: 403-294-1315

Dynotropia, ZBS Foundation, RR #1, Box 1201, Ft. Edward, NY 12828, 800— orders, 518-695-6406, Fax: 518-695-4041

Keith Hatschek, Passion Press, Box 277, Newark, CA 94560, 800-724-3283, www.passionpress. com

Arlie Kendall, voice talent, The Write Stuff, 25 Apache Rd., Evergreen, CO 80439, 303-670-5077

Library Journal, 245 West 17th Street, NY, NY 10011-5300, 212-463-6819

Frank Muller, e-mail: WaveDancer@aol.com

National Speakers Association, 1500 S. Priest Drive, Tempe, AZ 85281, 602-968-2252, Fax: 602-968-0911, www.nsaspeaker.org

Nightingale-Conant Corporation, 7300 Lehigh Ave., Niles, IL 60714, 800-525-9000, 847-647-0306, Fax: 847-647-7145, www.nightingale.com

Publishers Weekly, 249 W. 17th St., N.Y., NY 10011, 800-278-2991

Screen Actors Guild (SAG), 5757 Wilshire Blvd., Los Angeles, CA, 90036-3600, 213-954-1600

Mark S.A. Smith, co-author *Guerrilla Selling* and *Guerrilla Tradeshow Selling,* The Valence Group, 3530 Cranswood Way, Colorado Springs, CO 80918-6338, 719-522-0833, 800-488-0780, Fax: 719-522-079, e-mail: MSASmith@aol.com, www.RXSelling.com

Terry's Audiobooks, Terry Pogue, www.idsonline.com/terraflora/audio

Brian Tracy, Brian Tracy International, 462 Stevens Ave., #202, Solana Beach, CA 92075, 619-481-2977, Fax: 619-481-2445

KC Truby, The Lonesome Cowboy will send you a FREE copy of his latest *Business Builder* cassette tape. Phone 307-472-1941, Fax: 307-472-1950, e-mail: kctruby@aol.com. Specify *Knowledge Centered Selling* for a copy of tape to match script.

Choose the Right Packaging

The best packaging for your program depends on:

- Your target market.
- How and where your tapes will be sold.

Much as you may like one style of packaging, or a particular cover, if it won't sell your audio, you'll be disappointed. Your choice of packaging is part of marketing and should be based on marketplace realities. So if you haven't established your target market and how you will sell, spend a couple of days doing your homework first.

After you've chosen the best packaging for your purpose, give your graphic designer or artist everything they need to do their best work. If you gathered samples of packaging you're going to use, share those. Printers can provide exact templates or dimensions for final art. For early stages of design, use the working templates in the appendix of this book.

Creating an Image with Your Package

Your image matters. Reputation, content, and the look of your products all contribute to your image. Remember, people who use audio describe themselves as time-pressed, busy folks. People in a hurry make quick decisions. Your package must attract and hold their attention long enough for them to decide they want to purchase.

The physical size, feel, choice of words on the covers, your title, whether color or not, the printing, and endorsements combine to give your product an identity. Imagine your tape getting a five-second assessment as a potential buyer for a book chain or catalog sorts through dozens of submissions. Don't let your tape product be cut before it has a chance to be seen, heard and talked about.

Many people who've shown me their products have printed one or two color covers "to save money." They apply their knowledge of printing typical business items at quick print shops to creating product covers. Whenever possible, use color. Four-color printing is inexpensive. Use a specialty printer who does audio packaging all day long, ganging print jobs of like size. Minimum print runs are as low as 1,000 with some printers, however it makes more economic sense to begin with 2-3,000 per run and use extras for promotion.

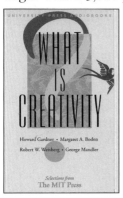

Five thousand four color bookpacks will be less than 40 cents each. Four-color slip-in covers for vinyl are less than 15 cents each. "J" card inserts for hard plastic Norelco-style boxes are about 8 cents. The samples of bookpacks shown here in black and white are all in color, and printed by specialty printers. See resources in the appendix for printers and some supplier names, addresses and other contact information.

Choose Packaging that Works for You

All of the following are popular packaging options. Your product could have multiple markets, so you could package more than one way — one way for catalog orders, one way for back of the room sales, for example. Later on, the same product might be offered in bookpack style, and sold in gift shops.

Bookpacks for Retail

• **Bookpacks.** Booksellers want something that fits existing shelves. That means a standard "bookpack" or what *AudioFile* magazine terms the "retail pack." They're the same thing — approximately 7" tall x 4½" wide, with the look of a paperback book. They can be shelved face or spine out on five-inch deep shelves, or on circular spinner racks. Bookpacks allow booksellers the greatest variety in the smallest space at the least expense. If your goal is bookstore sales, give the booksellers what they want.

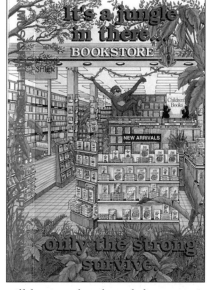

Bookpacks also work for many non-bookstore points of purchase. Truck stops, restaurants, copy shops, gift stores, libraries, catalogs, and mail order customers like the bookpack. For example, the companion audio for this book will be in a bookpack because it is the most universally acceptable, and the most economical choice for packaging when several thousand are printed.

Bookpacks can also be a good option for non-book based products, some premiums and book/tape bundles. Cassette Productions, Inc.

recommends a version of the bookpack that doubles as a mailer.

Many combinations, dies and internal styles exist. All have similar outside dimensions (see template appendix). The paperboard stock varies, depending on which printer you use, and your requirements. Packages hold two to eight cassettes inside, although most contain two or four. Some bookpacks have a rigid plastic mold glued onto the back cover to hold the tapes. Others are ingeniously designed entirely out of paper, using die-cutting and gluing to create either one or two cavities. Random House Audio uses this style.

 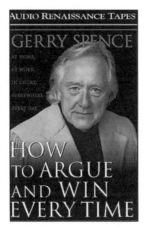 

Packaging artwork is colorful. Bookpacks are printed flat. Because the printing presses have four to six ink fountains, and are computerized, color combinations have little impact on unit cost. If your art is only two-color, chances are it will still run on multi-fountain presses.

Unabridged books and multi-tape programs have too many tapes for bookpacks, so different packaging is better. Solutions that work for both retailer and publisher are "butter boxes," crates, or slip cases for two or more bookpacks, making a set.

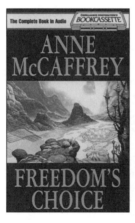 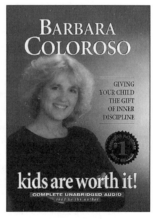

Expect to print 2,500 or more bookpacks per run. Allow six weeks from the time you sign off on all art and supply everything required to the package printer until you receive finished packaging. Turntimes vary with the printer and season. Spring and fall are usually busiest.

Jewel Cases

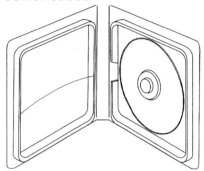

• CDs are normally packaged in jewel cases because they fit on shelves beside bookpacks, are accepted, and are economical.

Blister Packs

• Blister packs are commonly seen in children's book and tape products. Designed for hanger displays and for shelves, blister packs vary and aren't yet standardized for size and shape. Most children's products are one cassette, 5-20 minutes, with a softcover book.

Multimedia Vinyl Cases

• Vinyl albums are plastic cases, also called clear cases, clamshells, library cases or locking cases. This style of packaging is a favorite for seminar multi-tape products, business oriented training, personal development, and continuing education courses. It's the best choice for multi-tape products that will be heavily

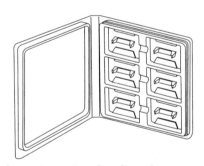

used, such as a review course for job testing. A school or human resources department needs durability and protection for a higher priced learning program.

The larger the album, the greater the perceived value. In the eyes of many who sell products in this packaging. "Bigger is better." The album might cost $3 and six tapes another $6 with assembly, but a larger album frequently fetches a premium price. It's not uncommon to see six tape sets at $99 in catalogs sent to business executives. The same information packaged differently at a bookstore would go for $24.95.

Another reason for vinyl's popularity is customers have received tapes this way for years. They don't question this format, and they resist changing from it.

If your best packaging will be in vinyl albums, spend some time with your duplicator looking at samples, and discussing your product. Albums come in dozens of shapes and sizes, with and without room for workbooks. The extra room inside one of the covers for printed matter is called a literature tray, or well.

An open pocket for a one-piece cover insert (front, spine and back all in one) is called an open trap, or clear overlay without sealed hinges. If you buy albums with hinges sealed you have to struggle to get any spine art down the narrow channel. The best option is to ship untrimmed covers all in one piece to the manufacturer, and by pre-arrangement they will seal the covers into the albums on orders above their minimum, for 10 cents or less an album. Other cover solutions for vinyl packages are silk-screening, embossing or direct printing onto the album covers. The plastic can be formulated differently, and have chipboard inserts or not. There's a lot to know, and how important is it that you master each detail? Or make an expensive mistake? Duplicators can save you a lot of time and get everything right, for the same or very little more than you'd spend buying direct.

Many duplicators keep the most popular sizes of albums in open stock, or can get them within a week, so your orders can be filled without delay. Or, you can keep a modest album inventory, and assemble cassettes and covers as needed.

Libraries will buy regardless of packaging if patrons request or have shown interest in a topic. Distributors catering to libraries offer repackaging and replacement services according to a library's requirements. Many library systems order cases direct from manufacturers and repackage themselves.

Many libraries like vinyl cases, citing durability and protection for cassettes. Using all same-size packaging creates uniformity, so every tape can be labeled with machine-generated call numbers, title and author. Across North America libraries are striving to find the best solution to the challenges of growing audiobook collections. They must protect acquisitions from theft, tape loss or damage, and after-hours book return perils. These are problems faced by commercial audio and video rental stores, so some libraries are following their lead and switching to video clear cases for convenience and durability.

Vinyl is also a good choice for testing covers or experimenting with program titles and price points to determine what sells best.

Norelco Boxes

• Clear plastic boxes, called Norelco boxes, are hinged two-part cases made of hard plastic. Norelcos look professional and finished, like music cassettes. A Norelco-style box has a J card (an insert or liner), so named because when it is removed from the case, it is shaped like a "J". The J-Card goes inside the box, and can be inserted either by hand or machine.

Single Norelco boxes are not popular with booksellers. They get lost among the larger products on shelves. And they are easily slid into a pocket or bag, either intentionally or by a browser who simply wants to have hands free. Double Norelco boxes are available, and the side-by-side tape placement gives a larger surface for printing. Some retailers prefer these over bookpacks.

"O" Cards

• Single or double "O" cards are great for gifts, promotional items, inexpensive components for combo packs, and for low-cost retail items. They work like a wooden match box, with the cassettes snugly held in place inside the O-shaped wrapper. Four-color "O" cards are available for less than 10 cents/each for the single cassette-size (slightly more for double "O" size).

• Soft plastic "poly boxes" come in crystal clear, semi-clear, and colors. You'll recognize this packaging from conferences, or tapes duplicated right there, after the sermon. They are the poorest choice for retail because they're perceived as amateur or low-budget product packaging. Sometimes you'll see a business card slipped inside, or a sticker applied to the outside of the case. For just a few cents more a Norelco box and J-card makes a better impression, and can be priced at least $1 higher.

Soft poly boxes are perfect however for subscriptions, where you send a tape a month. They mail and travel well. The clear or opaque plastic protects the tape, yet doesn't shatter or scratch as easily as Norelco boxes. For safety reasons, if you are making a product children will use, and it isn't being sold in a blister pack, substitute soft poly boxes for Norelcos.

There are two new kinds of packaging just coming on the market. One, a "biobox", and is made of paper. It resembles a flip-top cigarette carton and is designed for a single cassette or multiple cassettes in a package. The other style is a plastic case for two to six cassettes called the "Audio Capsule™." It is similar in size and shape to conventional vinyl packaging. The audio capsule is sturdier, less expensive, and made of 100% recycled material.

The Cover Sells Your Product

Famous or not, if your tape is book-based, and the book is selling well, you have equity in the cover. Stick to the same art, or tweak it to fit.

When you develop cover art from scratch, put yourself in your customer's place. What matters to him or her? What benefits does your program have? How can you communicate your product's value with words and pictures?

Here are some "dos and don'ts" to go over with your graphic designer.

- Do use color.
- Do have an exciting, active, intriguing or descriptive title.
- Do follow tradition, with the title and author on the front and spine.
- Do put the ISBN on the package back, lower right, big enough to scan successfully at check-outs.
- Do list benefits of listening to the tape on the back cover.
- Do say "Read by XXXX," and include a line or two to inspire confidence in the performance. Or say "Read by the author." Let listeners know.
- Do tell how many cassettes, for approximately how much listening time. For example, "4 cassettes, 6 hours".
- Do get clearance from cover photographer to use for audio.
- Do credit any musicians, composer, engineers, or producer
- Don't put your picture on the front cover unless you're a national news figure or celebrity. Put it on the back with biographical information instead.

The last suggestion goes against what some professional presenters believe, says Janita Cooper, president of Master Duplicating in Phoenix, Arizona. "What people want to take home is your information, your inspiration – not you," advises Cooper. "It's hard for some people to believe, because they see a lot of products out there with people's pictures on the front. But I tell 'em anyway."

And what happens when someone overrules Cooper's recommendations? "Well, they're the customer, so we give them what they want," she says, "I always try, though, because we want each and every person who works with us to be a big success."

Don't Forget the Package Spine

Make the spine work for you, too. Use the largest, most readable type you can, short of overlapping the hinge at the edge of the spine. Show the title, author, and publisher's insignia or name, very small, at the top or bottom of the spine. Spines should read from the top down, to be consistent with book practice.

How Important is the Cover?

Very, according to everyone I spoke with.

"The jackets sell the books. A good book jacket makes the difference between whether you'll sell a few or a lot."

–Paul Rush, Earful of Book

"We've done research with customers, and we watch people in the store. Certain colors and covers move, and others sit there. Over the years we've gotten to the point we can tell at a glance whether a product is going to make us any money. Sometimes we get a really nice product, but we can't do anything with it because of the cover."

–Alan Livingston, Booktronics

When new management took control of The Minds Eye, and renamed it Sound Deluxe, the company president repackaged some of the fine recordings that were not selling well. Sales of those titles increased several times over. The product inside was no different. The only change was the packaging.

Is that enough said about the power of a good cover? Do you want some expert guidance?

Test Color and Covers

Take your cue from the big food and soap companies. Test your covers, and your tapes, before making thousands. You'll learn a lot you didn't expect by asking dozens of people for their opinion. Often a small change will make a large difference in customer enthusiasm. And, obvious as it seems, be sure to query mostly those who fit your target customer profile. It's no use talking to dog trainers about your product if the subject is listing real estate in record time.

Once you've arrived at a choice for the cover and package, talk to your duplicator or call specialty printers and suppliers. They'll be able to quote, and probably fax or mail, pricing information for your best packaging choice.

The first audio project always has a learning curve. Allow three months at minimum for the first job, from the beginning of the art development until the packages arrive. Many people take longer because of revisions and changes. If you follow the flow chart, and get your packages underway early in the process, they'll arrive just as your tapes are duplicated.

●●●●●●●●●
Resources:

Alpha Enterprise, Audio Capsule™, packaging, 6370 Wise Avenue, Canton, OH 44720, 330-490-2000, Fax: 330-490-2010

Audio Renaissance Media, Inc., *Tiger Woods* and *How To Argue and Win Every Time,* 5858 Wilshire Boulevard, #200, Los Angeles, CA 90036, 213-939-1840, Fax: 213-939-6436, www.audio-source.com

Audio Scholar, *What Is Creativity* and *Origins of the Human Mind,* Marge Bauman, 10375 Nichols Lane, P.O. Box 1456, Mendocino, CA 95460, 707-937-1225 Fax: 707-937-1869

Bert-Co Graphics, CD packaging, 1855 Glendale Blvd., Los Angeles, CA 90026, 213-660-9323, Fax: 213-669-5700, www.bert-co.com

Biobox™, *TVT,* Steve Gottlieb, 23 East 4th Street, New York, NY 10003, 212-358-0941, Fax: 212-358-0942, e-mail: biobox@TVT.com

Blackbourn Media Packaging, Dawn Dickey, Suite 200, 5270 W 84th Street, Bloomington, MN 55437-1376, 800-842-7550, Fax: 612-835-9060

Blackstone Audio Books, Craig Black, P.O. Box 969, Ashland, OR 97520, 800-729-2665, Fax: 541-482-9294, e-mail: baudiob@mind.net

BookTronics, retailer, 5370 Westheimer, Houston, TX 77056, 713-626-4000

Brilliance Audio Services, *Sanctuary* and *Freedom's Choice,* publisher and duplicator, Lou Dudeck, 1704 Eaton Dr., P.O. Box 887, Grand Haven, MI 49417, 800-222-3225, Fax: 800-648-2312

Barbara Coloroso, Kids are worth it! Inc., P.O. Box 621108, Littleton, CO 80162, 800-729-1588, Fax: 303-972-1204

Disc Graphics, audio packaging/printing, John Rebecchi, 10 Gilpin Ave., Hopptauge, N.Y. 11788, 516-234-1400, Fax: 516-234-1460

Earful Of Books, Audiobook store chain, Paul Rush, P.O. Box 26094, Austin, TX 78755-0094, 512-343-2620, Fax: 512-343-2751, e-mail: earfulau@io.com www.earful.com-audio

David Garfinkel, Overnight Marketing, 2078 21st Avenue, San Francisco, CA 94116, 415-564-4475, Fax 415-564-4599, e-mail: Garfinkel@aol.com

It's a Jungle In There, marketing bookpack for Musicraft, Oregon duplicator, now closed, used with permission

Jack Johnston Seminars, *Male Multiple Orgasms,* 1257 Siskiyou Blvd., #195, Ashland, OR 97520

Knowledge Products, Shirley Cantrell, P.O. Box 305151, Nashville, TN, 37230, orders 800-264-6441, 615-742-3852, Fax: 615-742-3270, crom@edge.net

The Publishing Mills, Jessica Kaye, President, 9220 Sunset Blvd., Suite 302, Los Angeles, CA, 90069, 310-858-5385, Fax: 310-858-5391, e-mail: editor@pubmills.com

Shorewood Packaging, 2220 Midland Avenue, Unit 50, Scarborough, ONT M1P 3E6, 800-387-5137, 416-292-3990, Fax: 416-292-0480

Soundelux Audio Publishing, 37 Commercial Boulevard, Novato, CA 94949

Tangled Web Audio, Forebodings: American Classics, Linda Jones, 1063 King Street West, Suite 133, Hamilton, Ontario, 519-442-5010, Fax: 519-442-2346, tangled@bis.on.ca, www.eidos.ca/tangled/

John Zobrist, duplicator, Musicraft Multimedia, Woodburn, OR, 1-800-637-9493

Before You Step into the Studio

Preproduction is almost complete. You'll soon be in the production phase. Here's a checklist of tasks and mental preparation prior to recording.

In the weeks before recording you'll be busy. You'll:

- Refine your project and marketing based on what's saleable.
- Sign any necessary rights agreements.
- Finalize a budget.
- Meet with the producer about the script, scope, goals, and project timeline.
- Write, review and rewrite the script.
- Collaborate with graphic designer or publisher on a cover/package art.
- Choose or review professional voice(s) if needed.
- Reserve time for a preview studio visit, and recording session(s).
- Schedule time to review rough and final edited tapes.
- Continue marketing efforts.
- Arrange for package printing.
- Find a duplicator to suit your needs.

When you will be the voice on the tape you'll also be:

- Preparing mentally and physically so you're in top shape.
- Rehearsing the script.
- Probably working with a voice coach.
- Visualizing an enjoyable, smooth recording session.
- Visualizing the finished product.

Have a 30-Second Description

Your ongoing marketing begins early. Perhaps you already have a succinct description of your tape. If not, stop and take the time to write what amounts to a draft of the fact sheet or press release. As you call production facilities they'll ask you to describe your audio program. One of the secrets to a smooth recording and accurate cost estimating is knowing "who, what, when, where, why and how" details before the day of taping. A vague description from you, or your producer, makes it harder for others to be clear communicators in return.

People sometimes get stuck telling their story effectively because their thinking is fuzzy. One way to solve this is to adapt a concept from business networking.

Author and consultant Terri Lonier calls it a verbal business card. (Lonier details how useful a "five-minute brag" can be on her marketing skills audio tape, *Working Solo*™, *Volume II, Getting Customers*.) She recommends crafting a brief, easy to under- 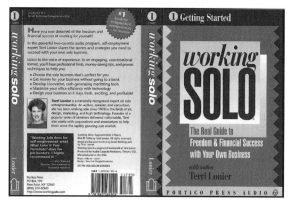 stand description of your service or product. Include the benefits for your customers or clients. Quantify your experience, or results. It might take a full day to write and several more to rework your "five-minute brag" so it holds people's interest. Lonier advises having an "express elevator" 10-second version, for those situations where you only have time for a brief exchange.

With practice, you'll soon be able to say it without hesitation or self-consciousness. At the same time, you'll be making it easier for the person you're communicating with to respond and ask good questions.

Your 30-second description should come easily and directly from your marketing plan and experience with customers. The following exercise gets you started. Fill in the blanks, or adapt to suit your venture.

"Hello . . . My name is_____, and I publish _____, (audiobooks, an album, learning program, seminar, newsletter on tape, etc.) about _____. They're designed for _____ (target customers) who _____ (benefits to listener, or problem solved). In the past (time period) _____ (tape title) has been _____ (sold, mailed, reviewed, adapted for, purchased by) _____ (quantity) and _____ (results.) . . . "

PAUSE. Give the other person a chance to ask a question, or comment.

You'll change the basic script as appropriate when you talk with distributors, reviewers and others who can help make your title a success. When you call people listed in directories and resource guides "cold," remember the KISS principle — Keep It Simple Sweetheart. Assume they're very busy, be courteous, and get to the point. Leave a message or call back at a better time for them. Send a fax or e-mail if they ask you to. Be prepared with a fact sheet or press release of the same information. Be ready to respond with an e-mail response, and a signature file containing contact information. People will appreciate your businesslike approach.

If you are shy by nature, and abhor schmoozing or making phone calls to strangers, this will help get you past the first few sentences without choking. Many people who appear totally at ease and confident as you observe them in action, describe themselves as shy, too. They practiced in front of a mirror, on the job, or on friends and family, when they were getting started.

Now that you can describe your audio project, it's time to make the recording arrangements.

What is a Production Facility?

They go by many different names: recording studio, production house, audio post. Whatever they call themselves, production facilities generally cover the shaded steps in the flow diagram in Chapter 2. They provide *production* and *post-production* services. In terms of your total time and financial investment, creating and selling the production and post-production phases are the shortest, and often the least costly.

Figuring out what makes one facility better than another is more than a matter of hourly rates, or project quotes. A hamburger is a hamburger. It may be expensive and delicious at a five-star resort, or inexpensive and predictable at a fast food chain. If you call six restaurants at random from the phone book, chances are at least five will have hamburgers on the menu. If you call six studios listed in the phone book, most will say they can record and edit spoken word audio tapes. Just because they can, technically, doesn't tell you whether they have the right equipment and experience for your project. In other words, you have narrowed the field, but you need more information.

Most studios sell usage and time to musicians, churches, and local advertisers. They're set up to serve those clients. While this is changing as spoken audio popularity grows, there are still relatively few studio facilities devoted to spoken word. They tend to be clustered in geographical areas near major publishing centers. You'll find good studios devoted to spoken audio in Los Angeles, San Diego, and the San Francisco Bay Area, New York, Denver/Boulder and Chicago, among other areas.

Use a Good Studio

The right studio will have reel-to-reel or digital recording equipment in good working order, a quiet environment for recording, and professional level microphones. The engineer will have appropriate *experience recording speaking voices* for audiobooks, cassette learning albums, advertising or video sound tracks.

A producer managing your project will arrange studio facilities, editing, music, and details. If you won't be working with a producer, try these tips:

- Allow a few days to shop around and compare facilities. The best values may be facilities with nothing more than a line in directory listings. They're booked with referrals and repeat business, and don't advertise for new customers. Ask your circle of friends and business acquaintances for recommendations first. Many times the best source of referrals is an audio publisher in your region. Some studios keep a low profile.

- Book a facility that specializes in spoken word recording whenever possible. A room designed for spoken word recording yields a clean, pure vocal sound. These studios are specially constructed as "dead rooms." The sound is "dead" — meaning it doesn't bounce off surfaces. The doors are heavy and thick, and the walls are well-insulated, which keeps out any extraneous sounds such as plumbing, doors closing elsewhere in the building, airplanes or sirens.

- Find a studio with high quality *voice* microphones costing $1,000-$3,000 each. Many studios use good, but lesser quality, microphones; once you hear how much better you sound on a top-quality studio microphone, you'll be convinced.

- Check with the radio stations in your community. National Public Radio-affiliated stations are in the spoken word broadcasting business. Although many are very small stations, they allocate listener/ member donations and grant money to equipment and maintenance, rather than big salaries. Larger public radio affiliates have more studios, digital equipment, and high-grade phone lines. They feed and receive stories and programs via satellite links, and win awards for news and documentary programming. Contact stations directly to inquire. You may be able to supplement their coffers and schedule studio time, an engineer and (sometimes) talent with one call.

Caveat: Anytime you use a broadcasting facility, your session could be interrupted by reporters or announcers covering a "breaking" story such as a flood, hurricane or spectacular accident. If that happens, you will have to reschedule. It pays to be familiar with a station's news reporting before you call. A small station usually can't afford much staff, and relies on "rip and read" for basic news, weather and sports. Nevertheless, they may prefer to restrict studio use by outsiders.

Understand too, broadcasting facilities are licensed to use the public airwaves, so stations have security issues you might not find in a more casual private business environment. Expect a station employee to work with you, and possibly escort you in and out. There are procedures stations follow to restrict access to transmission equipment, and remain in compliance with federal regulations.

- Still having trouble finding the right studio? Ask a professional audio equipment supplier or local duplicators for suggestions. Many duplicators have in-house studios available for rent. As a last resort contact a wholesale distributor of magnetic tape, listed in the phone book under wholesale recording supplies or manufacturers' representatives. Sales reps travel widely, and know most of the studios. I once found a good studio in Santa Fe, NM this way.

- After you've assured yourself the studio(s) you've chosen have the people capability and the necessary equipment, the next step is to check their references. Then make a studio site visit. Is the lobby lined with platinum records and pictures of bands or music cover art? At a voice studio, like Marc Graue's in Burbank, CA, the halls are lined with signed publicity photos of actors, and others whose voices are familiar from TV and movies, audiobooks and commercials. Sometimes you'll find a more understated look, with awards and plaques honoring the studio's work. It's reassuring to know they've been doing this for awhile.

- Talk with the engineer you'd work with for a few minutes. Ask about the setup he or she prefers, similar recording experience and favorite past projects. You'll hit it off with one engineer, and have a hard time warming up to another of equal skill. To some extent, any creative endeavor succeeds on personal chemistry. If you don't like or feel comfortable with studio personnel, pay attention to your reaction. What's making you uneasy? Personality conflicts could lead to expensive delays and cost overruns. A trusting, goal-oriented team works better together.

Session Set-Ups

Many people do just fine recording seated at a table. Others do better if they can gesticulate and move around, with a high stool to perch on.

Some like their pages flat on a padded table top, others want to prop pages up, or place them side by side on a wide music stand.

The best recording choice is a stationary microphone. If you absolutely believe your performance won't be adequate unless you wear a wireless microphone, say so ahead of time. I've never found an engineer who likes using wireless microphones in the studio, but I've had clients who speak 98 percent of the time in front of audiences, using wireless mics. They've struggled and become frustrated with their own performance at stationary mics. In a couple of instances we switched. They could replicate the energy level of "live" presentations by moving about on a chunk of carpet, even without an audience.

Most people are curious about what goes on in a control room. Which machines and volume controls will the engineer use? What do people talk about behind that soundproof glass? What hand signals does the engineer use? Can the control room and studio "talk" to each other, or will someone have to physically move from room to room for two-way communication?

Do they provide tea, coffee and juices, or should you bring liquids to help lubricate your throat and maintain energy? Do they order food in? How long do they typically record before a break? Can you stop for smokes? Whatever you need to know to help you concentrate solely on your performance should be covered ahead of time. If you have many questions, ask for some time with the studio manager or owner, and limit your time with the engineer to technical matters.

Jot some notes to yourself. A few days before your session call the studio, then fax or mail a confirmation to refresh their memory about details. That helps them be ready on recording day, as expected, when you walk in. You can settle into some practice reading and mic checks without having to wait while the engineer moves furniture, finds the right mic, and asks you lots of questions.

Digital or Analog?

Most studios today record on digital audio tape, or DAT. More and more record straight onto a computer disk. DAT tape comes in a miniature cassette with a mechanism like a tiny VHS tape. Ten DAT masters of up to two hours per tape will fit into a box the size printers use for 500 business cards. Size is an asset, but the primary reasons professional studios use DAT are for superb sound quality and faster editing.

Digital recording equipment converts sound to 0's and 1's many times per second. How often the sound is "sampled" determines the sampling rate. Most DAT recorders sample at 44.1 kHz, which is 44,100 times per second, or 48 kHz, at 48,000 times per second. The higher the sampling rate, the richer the sound. By comparison, many CD-ROMs and internet sound files play back sound at a sampling rate of 22 kHz which is 22,000 times per second, or less, to conserve disk space and transmission times.

Analog recording equipment is acceptable if the studio doesn't have digital capacity. (Analog means sound is recorded in a sound wave pattern on magnetic tape, rather than coded as 1's and 0's. Digital sound is reconverted to sound waves for playback on cassettes.) Until the early 90's, most original recordings were made using analog technology on cassette or reel-to-reel machines. There are plenty of fine recordings still available from reel-to-reel originals. Analog recordings have a "warmer" sound than digital recordings, according to many professionals.

If the studio you're considering uses analog recorders, they probably have high-end professional machines with real-time counters. If they don't, you'll spend extra time later trying to find where specific topics and phrases start and end. It's more cost-effective in the long run to use a production facility where the engineer makes running notes on a recording session, referring to hours, minutes and seconds displayed on the recorder. You'll find a sample log sheet for a recording session in the forms Appendix.

If a studio operator says he'll record you on cassette, and you expect to sell into a competitive marketplace, look further. Cassettes by nature introduce noise onto the tape, canceling out some of the benefits of using a studio to create a clean, easily edited recording. Cassettes are convenient for recording presentations, but have drawbacks as masters. Each generation down (copy) of a cassette adds more hiss. If the original is on cassette and must be edited (one generation down to an edit tape), then mastered for duplication (another generation down) and then recorded onto cassettes for playback and sale (third generation) — the purchaser will be hearing a tape that's noticeably poorer than the original cassette.

While you're at the studio, notice whether reels or DAT tapes are lying around unlabeled, and if the control room looks fairly organized. I mention this because over the years too many engineers have taken a tape off the deck, and handed it to me without taking time to make a label or find and mark a box. I've been a producer for many years, so they can reasonably expect me to put the relevant information on the tapes. As a novice, however, you won't know some information an editor or duplicator will ask for later. It'll take the engineer less than five minutes to make labels, so don't accept session tapes without labels and customary details for the duplicator.

Walking out of a studio with unmarked, unboxed original recording session tapes is like going into unfamiliar woods without water and a few basic survival and first aid supplies. Should you get lost, someone will probably rescue you, but it'll take longer, cost more, and you're likely to be miserable in the interim.

How Many Hours Will You Need to Record?

Low — up to two hours is often enough for a short program with a simple scripted message. When material is familiar and practiced, many people can record, do any retakes, and be gone in one and a half times to twice the length of the finished tape.

If a program was recorded live, you may need an extra hour or more of studio time for additions or re-recording. You'll add an introduction and close. It's usually advisable to bring in a professional voice rather than friends or relatives. Actors from a local theater company or school are one source of trained voices.

Often local radio personalities like to pick up extra money, and can save you time and studio expense. They'll knock it out in less than half an hour and hand you a tape. Don't be surprised, though, if the on-air guy or gal can't adjust their delivery for your needs.

Moderate — two to four hours per finished hour: Audiobooks recorded by experienced professional narrators are typically in this

range. Well prepared, confident authors or experts can complete interviews, discussions or straight script reading within three hours to every
hour of finished tape. Most sessions are scheduled in the morning
because voices are strongest early in the day.

Longer sessions are scheduled over two days for a finished product of
three hours or longer. Even professional voice talents who read all day
for a living reach a point where their voices begin to sound ragged. The
product sounds better and it's easier on everyone's nerves when you
allow more days for recording.

Higher — over four hours per finished hour: Non-professional
voices and anxious, disorganized or perfectionistic voices can require
more recording time. Unanticipated illness, fatigue, and problems
beyond anyone's control can also crop up. See "A Very Bad Studio
Day" in the next chapter for a true story.

New publishers should budget for this level.

Rehearse Your Script

Preparation is the key to sounding confident and natural — on the platform or in the studio. I can't improve upon the advice from the
following professionals:

"One of the biggest mistakes non-professionals make is not being well
prepared . . . 'winging it' is usually a sure-fire prescription for ineffec-
tiveness on the part of the speaker and disappointment on the part of
the audience," is good advice from Tony Allessandra, author of over 50
audio and video programs.

If you are worried about how you sound, give serious consideration to
working with a voice coach. Begin working together at least two weeks
before the recording day, and over two or more sessions. A modest
investment with a qualified acting or narration voice coach can pay
enormous dividends.

Take Care of Your Health

Recording is very draining. If you have a tendency to go short on sleep, exercise or good nutrition, change your ways. Or pretend you're someone with better habits for a few days prior to a recording session. Fatigue, tension, a cold — it's amazing what all comes through in the voice. You might fool a business associate in a ten-minute conversation, but you can't bluff the listener in long recorded programs.

If you need medications, snacks, tea, juices or anything to keep your blood sugar regulated and your throat moistened, take them along. Most professional studios support people who will be working intensely by keeping the cupboard and refrigerator stocked for client use at no charge. Ultimately though, no one knows your body rhythms and needs like you do. On more than a few occasions I've lugged bottles of juice and high-energy granola bars into the studio, rather than rely on the snack machine choices. It is especially important to remain energized through afternoon and evening sessions, when most of us begin to fade. If that means you need to go for a run halfway through the session, do it!

It's a Team Effort

You'll have help in the studio who will become your colleagues for the duration of the production. Good master tapes are a collaborative combination of talents and tasks. The three usual slots in a control room for a serious production are: **producer, director, and engineer.** A producer may also be the director, or may hire someone better qualified for the job.

Some people choose to be their own director and producer. This rarely works well unless you've had previous media and studio experience. Being both performer and director is difficult to impossible for many people because of loss of perspective and objectivity. It's not hard for a five-minute program, but takes its toll and the product suffers if anyone tries to wear both hats for hours of recording. People who've learned to produce audio the hard way agree with producer and writer, Toni Boyle:

"The person who acts as his own producer has a fool at the microphone."

Sometimes people assume an engineer is all they need. Many engineers resist or refuse to act like a producer because they're trained to focus on sound quality, not content or how listeners will perceive something. They feel they must say something to keep you happily recording, rather than sound dumb. Other, much rarer, engineers are wonderful coaches who are willing and qualified to direct. Don't assume too much. When in doubt, ask.

For a humorous look at what can happen in a recording session, borrow or purchase a copy of *You're Good Enough, You're Smart Enough, and Doggone It, People Like You,* with Al Franken as Stuart Smalley from *Saturday Night Live.* It's a satirical recording session. Depending on your sense of humor about self-help gurus, you might find this entertaining, and educational in the process. Experienced producers and engineers laugh out loud, since it's all too close to the reality most of us have suffered through at least once.

Studio Charges

Find out what you'll be charged, and ask for the quote in writing. Is it their policy to charge for studio time you book, even if you cancel that morning? Studios don't like broken appointments any more than dentists and hairdressers. Their bills keep coming whether you are organized, on time or not. Some places are pretty casual about sticking to session times, and some aren't.

Expect to pay as you go. Some studios will discount for cash on the spot. Most will work with you on project costs if you are considerate, and are a candidate for repeat business. They'll appreciate it if you're generally accurate at predicting the time a project will take. They want you to succeed, and come back.

Studio rates differ around the country. The average in Denver was $55/ hour for a spoken word recording session when we called 10 studios in July, 1996.

Ask for an estimate for studio time per hour and tape/supplies charges. An engineer is usually included in the hourly rate.

Then practice, practice, prepare. Prepare, practice, relax. Show Time is just around the corner.

••••••••• Resources:

Tony Alessandra, Ph.D., 7596 Eads Ave., #140, P.O. Box 2767, La Jolla, CA 92037, 619-459-4515, Fax: 619-459-0435, e-mail: Dr Tony A@alessandra.com

Antonia Boyle & Company, Toni Boyle, 236 W. Portal Ave., #456, San Francisco, CA 94127, e-mail: ABoyleCo@aol.com

Keith Hatschek, Passion Press, Box 277, Newark, CA 94560, 800-724-3283, www.passionpress. com

Marc Graue Recording Services, 3421W. Burbank Blvd., Burbank, CA, 91505, 818-953-8991

Terri Lonier, Working Solo®, P.O. Box 190, New Paltz, NY 12561, 800-222-SOLO, Fax: 914-255-2116, e-mail: Lonier@workingsolo.com, www.workingsolo.com

You're Good Enough, You're Smart Enough, and Doggone It, People Like You!, Guided Visualizations by Stuart Smalley, Al Franken, ISBN 0-553-47094-9, ©1992 Al Franken, Performance Copyright Bantam Audio Publishing

Show Time

It's countdown to the big day! The insights in this chapter will help you make it an enjoyable and productive day — one you'll be ready to celebrate afterwards.

Producers are often asked "Should I record in a studio or before an audience?" The answer is "You should record where you'll communicate best."

The first section of this chapter will be helpful for recording in a controlled studio environment. If your product will be read by a professional narrator, you may wish to skip ahead. Recording on location, favored by many platform professionals, is covered later in the chapter. Lastly, there's a true story from one of the country's most confident and experienced speakers, about his very bad studio day.

Be Comfortable

It's natural to have mixed feelings the first time (or few) you record in a studio. That's why I believe people should dress however they will be most comfortable — not how someone else tells them. This is audio, not TV. Studio recording sessions can be long and tiring. You need to be able to breathe easily, without tight clothing undermining your concentration or effectiveness. If in doubt, wear sweats or soft knitted material. Here are some fabrics and items to avoid, or plan to substitute while recording.

- Cuff links (clinks)
- Silk and similar stiff fabrics (rustles)
- Bracelets, necklaces and earrings (noisy, distracting)
- Heavily starched fabrics (sometimes noisy)
- Big metal belt buckles (can hit against table)
- Squeaky or high heeled shoes (if you'll record standing up)

Test the chair or stool you'll use. Listen for swishes and creaks as you move. Switch chairs if necessary before you begin. Tell the engineer if you need a carpet or table covering to muffle a habit of tapping your pen. Speak up if you prefer a music stand or want to stand up. Let him or her know if it's difficult for you to read at certain angles. Experiment during the mic checks, and tell the engineer if you're uncomfortable. Steve Gordon of The Readers Chair publishing house offers these tips:

- A towel over a microphone stand is easy and effective.
- 10-15 minutes experimenting at the microphone, with headphones on, is a fast way for newcomers to learn how to "work a mic."
- Hot water and *fresh* lemon (not bottled juice) greases vocal cords.

Avoid caffeine (jitters), soda pop (belching), and dairy products (coats the throat). Water is a better choice.

Many people dislike the sound of their own voice, or worry needlessly. Can the engineer make your voice sound deeper? Will the engineer or producer tell you if you start talking too fast and running words together? Yes, and yes. What else concerns you? Don't fret about sounding stupid — they've heard similar questions before.

Your first studio recording session is a workplace. If you want friends or relatives to watch, schedule their visit for the end of the session, and ask your producer or engineer for suggestions on how to handle it. Recording sessions are not social, even though they're usually punctuated with laughter and joking. Business partners can contribute important information. Relatives quizzing the control room crew are a distraction and inflate your studio bill. The time to have visitors is after the pressure's off, and the hard part is behind you.

Talk to the Listener

Your job in the studio is to communicate with each listener. Remember, audio is an intimate medium. It's one to one. Form a mental picture of someone, and tell your story or message to that one person. Or, if it works better, imagine your best audience gazing back, and reacting in all the right places.

Tips for a Smooth Performance

Hand signals are the most efficient way to communicate at times, so most engineers and voice talents use them. When you're about to begin a passage the engineer will turn off the control room microphone, so there's no accidental recording. Then the engineer will signal tape is rolling. That's your cue to begin reading or speaking again. As you're reading along you may wish to use a finger across the throat for "cut," or use other mutually agreed upon gestures to signal your intentions. Or you may simply pause, say what you're going to do, then re-read something, pause again, and continue. The pauses are edited out easily later, along with the unwanted first "take." You'll sound smooth.

Learn how close you should be to a **microphone**. It's usually a distance of your balled-up fist between the microphone and your mouth. Mics come in many types, and you "work a mic" depending on its characteristics. Some differences are internal, in how they convey sound to the recording equipment. Other differences are in the sound pattern pick up. Some record voices in all directions (omnidirectional), and others must be right in front of a sound source to pick up well (unidirectional). Some microphones are in between. Some use batteries, others don't. Condenser mics are the best for spoken word, and some cost well over $2,000 apiece.

Follow the engineer's instructions and do the reading or tests they ask for. It takes a few minutes at the beginning of any session for your engineer to be satisfied he or she has "set" the board for optimum sound, and to suit their well-trained ears. Many performers use lots of vocal variety. Now is the time to talk to the engineer about your style. For example, when you shout you will probably move back from the mic. When you're coming to a whispering part you may want to signal, and lean in toward the mic. In general, it's easier to bring someone's voice up than tone down a blast that's off the meter. Bring such things up if you have concerns.

Paper shuffles are a common noise that can be avoided or minimized. Practice turning or moving pages before the recording session. A good microphone and quiet studio are what you want for sound quality, but the trade-off is every little sound will be picked up on the recording tape. The trick voice talents learn is to move pages v-e-r-y quietly, or pause during page turns. The pauses are edited out later.

Retakes happen to everyone. Don't let them fluster you. Focus on communicating, rather than some imaginary scorecard of misspoken words. A professional narrator says something like this:

PRO: Take 2, page 16, middle of the page, third 'graph (paragraph.)
      Pause . . . "The sun <u>slithered</u> around the boulders . . . " etc.

      Take 3, same place.
      Pause . . . (reads again, with different interpretation).

OR   "I can do a better job on her offer of money to the legislator. I'll
      take it again from "You know, Senator, we'd like to support your
      re-election . . . "
      (pauses for engineer to cue tape or nod go-ahead)
      "In 3 . . . 2 . . . 1 . . . You know, Senator, we'd like to
      support . . . "

Mispronunciations and words that aren't clearly enunciated are common reasons for stopping, discussing a correction, and re-recording. You can minimize these with rehearsal, and by checking on any words you aren't sure about. Does the city or person go by Mar-tin-EZ, or Mar-TEEN-ez? Charles, Charlie or Chuck? Nothing undermines your credibility faster than presenting yourself as an expert, then using blatantly bad grammar, or the wrong name. Call the individual's office, a reference librarian, or city in question if necessary, to ascertain how *they* pronounce their name.

Changes on the fly, or "winging it," are fine opportunities to say something you may later regret. On the other hand, another set of eyes or ears as you go through a script can save you grief. Sometimes a producer or other production team member will stop you because you've said something that might be a copyright infringement, libelous, or simply unwise. I once had an upstanding community leader get carried away on the joys of infidelity, all while tape was rolling. The interviewer looked up and rolled her eyes, and I nodded agreement. The engineer muttered "good save," put a "beep" tone on the rolling tape, and relaxed.

Our interviewer heroine swiftly corralled the visiting expert, and redirected the conversation. After the session ended, we found the beep, and three minutes were spooled straight to the trash. The expert had gotten carried away, off on a tangent irrelevant to the product, and of no redeeming value in his personal life. Sometimes smart people say dumb things. The biggest potential problems seem to occur when family members or close friends are part of a story. The stories may be altered substantially for dramatic effect, but when loved ones hear the tape they're unhappy. More than a few edits have transpired later because "so and so, (friend, relative, a client or boss) complained."

The experience that sticks most in my mind was the young man in California whose rise from poverty and gangs was so heroic I cried as I listened to the "live" version he sent for editing. We sent back an edited draft, and a few days after that he called to say "You did a fantastic job! There's only one thing. Momma says Daddy didn't beat her *every night,* like I remembered. She asked us to take it out, and after all — she's my Momma. I don't want to hurt or embarrass her in any way." I suggested a re-edited alternative, to save the powerful story, but my client wisely chose family relationships over dramatic effect.

Pace Yourself

Your first few paragraphs or pages may sound tense. Don't worry. It's common for professional speakers as well as business people and authors to re-record the first part again later, once their voice is relaxed and they've fallen into a comfortable reading rhythm.

Many producers begin with the second tape in a series, or the easiest part of a book — wherever the author/reader is most comfortable. With digital editing it's a simple matter to rearrange later, without destroying any of the original recording.

Recording a long program is similar to running a race. You want to start strong, go along at an even energy level, and finish strong. This is why you need to be in top form, and pamper your vocal apparatus.

Do it in Digital

Whenever possible, record on Digital Audio Tape. DAT is the industry standard in professional studios. Some studios record straight to computer disk, and may back up the session on a DAT. If digital recording isn't available, use the old reliable reel-to-reel method. The worst choice is cassettes. The pros and cons of digital and analog recording were discussed in the previous chapter at greater length and are demonstrated further in the next chapter.

Scout's Rule: Play Safe

Make a simultaneous back-up recording of your session. You'll probably erase and reuse the safety copies later, but every once in a while something gets lost. Maybe you drop the tape into a puddle, or spill coffee on it. You'll look at each other and say, "Thank goodness we have a back-up." Backing up while you're recording is cheap; re-recording won't be.

Room Tone

It's common practice to record a minute or so of the studio with the voice talent sitting quietly inside. Sometimes engineers prefer to do this for each recording session. Later, if a pause is needed somewhere, they'll splice or copy in the sound of the room. It may sound silly, but all quiet spaces have a character. Blank tape stands out when used as a spacer and can subtly, or not so subtly, cause the listener to shift attention away the reader and message. That's why professionals "get room sound." When we need it, it's parked right on the original recording, where it's easy to find.

Keeping Costs Down

The single best thing you can do before recording is to prepare thoroughly. Rehearse and go through the script with a colleague or friend. Make a trial recording or two at home. Other ways you can keep recording time to a minimum are:

- Be organized, with a complete script and copies a few days early.
- Make your tape a priority. Schedule enough uninterrupted time to do a high quality job of recording, to do any re-recording and to evaluate the edited test tapes at least twice.
- Be responsive and available for your production people during the editing, mixing and packaging process.
- Set the tone with your attitude.
- Offer to pay at the time of recording, and as work progresses. This will often prompt a discount.
- Negotiate a project price for multi-day recording. Agree on a fair reduction if you're able to complete your project ahead of schedule.

Recording in Your Own Studio

You may have a background or interest in operating a small recording studio yourself. The cost of high-quality equipment is dropping, along with software and computers. Good second-hand professional gear is available as people trade up. If you're interested in pursuing this option, the best and clearest book I've found for beginners is *Advanced Audio Production Techniques* by Ty Ford. Other resources geared to engineers and musicians are listed in *Mix* magazine, at most large newsstands. *Mix* also publishes a catalog of dozens of technical publications.

The Web has extensive resources. See what you find at www.bookshop.co.uk/fp/ for starters. It's the site for Focal Press, a publisher of professional and academic books for recording, news and entertainment professionals. The Web is good for hours of entertaining research, and, if you're like me, you'll want to try some programs offered as shareware. If so, and if you don't want to live dangerously, practice safe downloading; make sure essential files are backed up first, and you have a virus program on hand. (Some anti-virus programs are freeware or shareware.)

On-Site "Live" Recording

Do you shine before an audience? Is the spontaneous, as-it-happens sound and feel what works best for your listeners, too? Okay. Review your calendar for a likely opportunity. You may want to record more than one session, and pick the best one or two. (Production costs will skyrocket if you try to combine many different sources.) Some presentation professionals record every possible time, and choose the best presentation of each program for clean-up and development into back of the room products.

There are three ways to capture your performance. You do it yourself, you hire someone to record you, or you arrange for a master copy from a company already doing the on-site recording.

Do it yourself — When you've isolated one or two possible dates, I suggest you rent professional level equipment, and familiarize yourself with it before you leave the rental company. Practice the evening before, and color code connectors if necessary. Set up at your presentation with plenty of time to spare, and ask someone in the audience to turn the cassettes over for you. DAT machines switch automatically, and will run for up to two hours per tape. That'll leave you free to concentrate on your performance and audience. Use 90 minute chrome cassettes and plan your presentation so you're not in the middle of a story or main point 45 minutes into the recording. Have a break, group activity, or Q & A instead, so if the cassette is flipped you won't lose anything crucial to your presentation.

If your original master is recorded on cassette punch out the two small plastic "tabs" on the top edge (opposite the open side where you can see the tape). When cassettes are "tab out" no one can accidentally record over the content. Label the cassettes in order, *immediately after your presentation*. Take the tape(s) to your editor, or a transcriber. If you aren't transcribing the performance be prepared to sit with an editor as your tape is polished and mixed on a reel-to-reel machine or the computer. You're the only one who can make decisions on content.

Hire an experienced seminar recording engineer to capture you on tape. Specify DAT or chrome cassettes. Ask the recording specialist to confer beforehand with the people who will edit or prepare your master for duplication, so everyone is working toward the same end. Explain to your recording person how to take useful notes. If necessary, copy the log in the appendix and provide an example of what you want to see. If you have a handout, give two to the recording person. At minimum, you'll get some sort of times or cues on the handout, for you and the editor to use later. Don't expect hotel or contracted A/V set-up workers to do this for you. Their job is troubleshooting for the hotel, and some won't speak or write English well enough to take useful notes.

Many professional presenters invest in recording equipment and carry it with them. In the long run this is the most economical choice. There are a number of high-end consumer or industrial-use machines to choose from. Professional gear runs more smoothly, is quieter,

Marantz MD222

and has recording heads and other parts built for heavy use. The Marantz PMD 221 mono cassette recorder (also comes in stereo) and the SONY series of small DAT recorders fit the bill. Price range: $300–$700.

Professional audio equipment services like EAR in Phoenix, AZ and others all over the country that supply studios can advise you on the pros and cons of their stock. Or you can shop through a catalog. The advantage of buying from a local merchant with a long history in the community is you'll get personal service and trouble-shooting. You can't get that level of service from a telephone order-taker reading features off a screen.

Clip-on and hand-held microphones are used by road warriors and professional services, with several favorites for reliability. Shure®, Telex, NADY and SONY have been around for years. Don't buy any mic based solely on price. Reliability and a good, clear signal are what you want. Older VHF lavaliere mics (wireless) with two antenna receivers will do the job. These are called true diversity systems, which means your voice will be picked up as you move around, even if there's a pillar or other obstacle between you and the receiver. Set antennae at a 40° angle, or roughly like rabbit ears, for the best sound pick-up. Or better yet, go for one of the newer UHF mics with automatic switching between frequencies. The bandwidth for UHF cuts out cabs, cordless phones and other interference that occasionally plays havoc with recording. Price Range: $400 and up.

Get a copy. The third route is to arrange beforehand for a "submaster" of the on-site recording company's master. Ask to have it run in real time. Offer to provide top brand chrome cassette blank tapes for the session recording and for your submaster. Clear it beforehand with the person who hired you to make the presentation. If your contract mentions recording, be sure everything is spelled out. Bring along a copy to show the conference recording company's head honcho if necessary.

From their perspective, the on-site company reports to the people who put on the event, and the individual who hired you. The organization will sell copies of your presentation, as is, with their copyright on the label. I've had wonderful cooperation and assistance from on-site recording companies over the years, as long as speakers arranged for a submaster ahead of time.

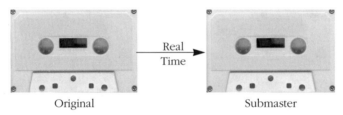

Original   Real Time   Submaster

More References for Platform Presenters

Presenters just starting out can shortcut their learning curve about every phase of the business with several fine publications targeted to professionals. Five I recommend regularly are:

For Professional Speakers Only, Mike Frank
How To Develop and Promote Successful Seminars and Workshops, Howard Shenson
Speak and Grow Rich, Dottie and Lilly Walters
Speaking Secrets of The Masters, Speakers Roundtable
Speak With Power, Betty K. Cooper

The first three on the list are so full of information you'll probably want reference copies by your desk. All five are moderately priced.

The (Very) Bad Studio Day

If anybody should have a smooth recording session, you'd expect it to be Mark Victor Hansen and Jack Canfield, bestselling authors of the *Chicken Soup For The Soul*™ series. They've had over 12 million books in print, and have dominated the bestseller lists for over a year — all after being turned down by one major publisher after another. These two professionals have been platform presenters, media guests, and audio/video product makers for years. Hansen and Canfield together have over 40 years in front of audiences, and dozens of successful audio and video programs. Canfield earned over $100,000 a year in royalties from *Self Esteem and Peak Performance,* an audio program which he recorded for CareerTrack.

I asked Jack Canfield how long he estimated it takes them to record an audiobook, thinking it would make a good example for this book. It did. He began to laugh, and recounted this story to a group of us at a National Speakers Association meeting in 1996.

"You'd guess it would only take a few hours, but we recently went into the studio in the morning, thinking we'd be out before mid-afternoon. It was only a *three hour tape.* We were still there at eight o'clock that night, trying to get through the script. What happened is funny, now, in retrospect. It wasn't quite so funny then."

"Mark was having one of those days. He kept tripping over his tongue. Some words wouldn't come out right. We got too loud, or too into our stories in some places. It was one take after another. But when it really got funny was after dark. A cricket had somehow found its way into the wall in the studio, and began to chirp. We'd already been at the microphones for hours, so we were tired, but we only had three more pages to go. Our schedules were too tight to come back, so we'd say a couple of sentences, the cricket would CHIRP. Mark would run over and pound on the wall. Then run back, we'd do another few sentences. CHIRP. Run to the wall, pound, back, record, CHIRP again. It went on like that until we finished. It seemed like it would never be over," he laughed.

"What a day! That's gotta be the worst either of us have ever done in a studio, on any recording. And no fun for the engineer, either. But, we did finish, and everything came out fine in the end."

The audiobook from that session is *The Aladdin Factor.*

When it's show time for you, remember to keep everything in perspective. Keep your sense of humor, and know you're bound to have an easier time than these two pros did. You can always record another day, or go back later and update your performance. But chances are very good you won't need to, thanks to the magic of editing.

•••••••••
Resources:

Advanced Audio Techniques, Ty Ford, ISBN 0-240-80082-6, ©1993 Focal Press

Antonia Boyle & Company, Toni Boyle, 236 W. Portal Ave., #456, San Francisco, CA 94127, e-mail: ABoyleCo@aol.com

Avid Technologies, Digidesign editing software, Paul Foeckler, 200 East 5th Ave., Suite 341, Naperville, IL 60563

Jack Canfield, Self-Esteem Seminars, *Chicken Soup For The Soul™,* P.O. Box 30880, Santa Barbara, CA 93130, 805-563-2935, Fax: 805-563-2945, soup4soul@aol.com

CareerTrack Publications, Gregg Perry, 3080 Center Green Drive, Boulder, CO 80301, 800-334-1018, Fax: 800-622-6211

Cooper Communications, Betty K. Cooper, *Speak With Power,* 2209-140th Ave., SW, Calgary, Alberta, T2P 3N3, CANADA, 403-294-1313, Fax: 403-294-1315

Harry Fox Agency, music copyright clearance, 711 Third Avenue, New York, NY 10017, 212-370-5330

Mike Frank, *For Professional Speakers Only,* Speakers Unlimited (bureau), P.O. Box 27225, Columbus, OH 43227, 614-864-3703

Marc Graue Recording Services, 3421W. Burbank Blvd., Burbank, CA, 91505, 818-953-8991

Mark Victor Hansen, *Chicken Soup For The Soul™* co-author, P.O. Box 7665, Newport Beach, CA 92658-7665, 800-433-2314, 714-759-9304, Fax: 714-722-6912

Marantz Recording Equipment, Superscope Technologies, Inc., Niko Karvunidis,1000 Corporate Blvd., Suite D, Aurora, IL 60504, 708-820-4800, Fax: 708-820-8103

The Reader's Chair, Delia White and Steve Gordon, P.O. Box 2626, Hollister, CA 95024, 408-636-1296, Fax: 408-636-1296, e-mail: TRC@ReadersChair.com

Howard L. Shenson, deceased, John Wiley & Sons, Inc., 605 Third Avenue, New York, NY 10158-0012

Sonic Solutions, Yuki Miyamoto, 101 Rowland Way, Novato, CA 94945, 415-893-8021, Fax: 415-893-8008, e-mail: yuki@sonic.com

Speaking Secrets of The Masters, Speakers Roundtable, Jim Cathcart, P.O. Box 9075, La Jolla, CA 92038

Time Warner Audiobooks, Maya Thomas, producer, or Samantha Fahnestock, 1271 Avenue of the Americas, 11th Flr., New York, NY 10020, 212-522-7334, Fax: 212-522-7994, www.pathfinder/twa

Lilly & Dottie Walters,*Speak and Grow Rich,* P.O. Box 1120 Glendora CA 91740, PO Box 1120, Glendora, CA 91740, 818-335-8069, Fax: 818-335-6127, e-mail: Call4Sprkr@aol.com

Thomas J. Winninger, Winninger Institute for Market Strategy, 3300 Edinborough Way, #701, Minneapolis, MN 55435-5963, 612-896-1900, Fax: 612-896-9784

Editing "Sweetens" Your Product

You may think your performance was terrible. Perhaps you went on too long, or stopped and started repeatedly, so you assume you'll sound choppy. You mispronounced words, or trailed off where you meant to sound strong.

Welcome to the magic of editing.

In this chapter we'll look at how editing transforms a raw recording into smooth, enjoyable listening. We'll look at different degrees of editing, as well as the "can-dos" and "no-hopers." Lastly, we'll look at how music and sound effects contribute to more powerful results.

How an Editor Makes You Sound Better

Skilled editing enhances any recording. Editing is called "post production" or "posting" in audio and video production. The majority of products offered today have been edited, but the editors hope they've done a good job, so you can't tell. Why edit? Because customers expect clean, clear products. Anything less is likely to work against you.

You've seen print documents on a screen, and know how they're edited. Sections, words, and other sounds are moved, deleted and changed to create the best product. Editing audio is similar. Most audio/video editing today is done on computers, using specially designed software. Beyond the level of word processing though, there's an added dimension to editing spoken word.

When we speak our voices add meanings layered onto words. We use rising and falling intonations called inflections. In American English, for example, the sentence "Did the Giants win?" is said with a rising inflection at the end of a sentence to signal it's a question. The emphasis will be on the words "Giants" and "win." How does it change the meaning if you say it other ways?

DID the Giants win?
Did the GIANTS win?
Did the Giants WIN?
Did the Giants win?

Suppose the recorded voice says the sentence any of the first four ways, and it sounds wrong in context. An editor can modify the loudness of any word or syllable, and change the meaning to sound more natural. There may not be much that can be done with the last sentence though, if there's no "questioning inflection" in the way the sentence is delivered.

Tone, volume, pace, and organization all contribute meaning. We all do this naturally, without thinking about it. And we interpret others' voices over the phone, radio or on tape based on the enormous amount of unconscious sifting and sorting we all do. You've probably said "I didn't mean it the way it sounded" on a few occasions, and acknowledged the mouth doesn't always cooperate with conscious intent.

Editing can save the day when there are such imperfections, especially when the editing is done on computer, using multi-featured software.

Computer vs. Analog Editing

Traditional editing is done on reels of tape, with a razor blade. Editors cut out paragraphs or words, and sometimes set them aside to put them back in elsewhere. Ten years ago you'd walk into an editing room and see tape hanging from a table top or window frame, with notes on scraps of paper or white tape above each "outtake." "Hamburger story," "F. swrs nt glty.," "VO/FF side 3, side 5, side 7." Or you'd see reels stacked beside a producer's desk, each with an interview or segment, waiting to be assembled and shortened.

Some places still edit this way. Thousands of fine recordings created over the past 40 years are a testament to editors' skill and high standards. Manual editing on analog tape is not a strike against a studio, but neither is it the norm any longer.

With modern digital equipment (computerized editing), editing is faster, easier, and we can preview edits. Digital editing allows edits that were impossible before digital workstations became routine studio gear. A few words of a sound file on the screen looks like this:

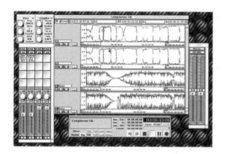

Screen from Sonic Solutions editing software, courtesy of Sonic Solutions

Most editing done on products for sale now is digital editing. The software ranges from high end, such as that used by special effects superstars like Industrial Light and Magic in northern California and major record companies to the inexpensive software designed for experimentation and small home-based projects. These popular programs are in use all across the country and are favorites of hobbyists.

The advantages of using an established working studio to edit are:

- Their computers have enough storage capacity to edit and store programs of several hours length, and still work on other projects. You'll need this flexibility, so you can listen to the rough (draft) edited version, then come back in, make changes, and listen again. (Especially if you have several people who'll listen and sign off.)

- They should have operators/engineers with plenty of relevant experience. Their choices will be better, and their fingers are faster over the keys. When I have two editors who can put a project together, I'll always pay more for the one with Pro-Tools software and several years experience editing audiobooks. Just like I'll take my car to the mechanic who loves Hondas and works on them day in and day out. A helpful friend might offer to do the repair for less, but he's worked at a desk for the last eight years, and all his tools are for American made cars. I need the right mechanic, with the right tools, and appropriate experience.

Good editors are proud of the "art" of their work. Their editing is so smooth that when an author hears himself and beams "I did pretty well, didn't I?," only the editor and producer will know Mr. Expert required 320 edits in an hour-long program to make him sound fluid and natural.

Three Levels of Editing

The clearest non-technical description of editing I've seen was in a booklet written by William R. Guthy, founder of Cassette Productions Unlimited and co-founder of the infomercial giant, Guthy-Renker Corporation. (The 1987 publication is no longer in print.) Guthy described three levels of editing, according to their complexity, studio time and costs. I've modified his guidelines here.

Level one is basic cleanup of a live presentation or studio recording. "Housekeeping" details are deleted. These are extraneous announcements or conversations, like where the bathrooms are, what will happen at lunch, and other information of no relevance to listeners. Long pauses and the 10 minutes of audience buzz during an exercise are cut to a few seconds so the listener won't be bored. This is simple, straightforward editing. Someone with a few full days, experience and a little training can accomplish level one editing unsupervised as long as a full back-up copy exists. A technician may work from notes on a copy of the script, or a transcript. This level is basically following orders.

Level two takes longer, and involves more discretion on the editor's part. Besides all the "housekeeping" deletions the editor listens throughout the tape for "uhms," stammers, off-color remarks, any swearing or objectionable extra sounds. She removes audience coughs, table thumps and long sections of copyrighted music that would put a presenter in violation of copyright laws.

Some of the "tricks" used at this level are changing the "room sound" from cave-like to a lecture hall ambience, or big room to a small intimate sound. The editor might bring down your pitch if you sound tense at the beginning of the script, and suggest some re-arrangement for better clarity. Simple cross fading of music underneath your introduction, the end of sides and under closing comments adds polish to the program. Many publishers opt for this level editing.

Tom Winninger, past president of the National Speakers Association, has published audio learning programs and customized tapes for corporate and association clients for many years. "It's really nice to do a gorgeous edit. It feels good and sure you're proud of it, but it doesn't necessarily mean you'll sell more. If a good presentation with a little clean up, music and nice cover sells and your clients like it, why do more? The content's solid. That's what they really want from you," he observes. "Don't get carried away with the creative potential in editing unless it'll make your product more valuable."

Level three is editing employed by most major publishing houses, some professional training companies and national radio advertisers. Level three and beyond is what the public is used to from television, award winning training programs, documentaries, and Hollywood. Level three gives both the editor and producer freedom to use their full array of skills and equipment.

More creativity is introduced into the process, so a product may have an identifiable sound style or design. A good editor at this level not only tries seemingly impossible edits; he frequently makes them, and they're undetectable. He or she hears and interprets nuances in the vocal delivery, working quickly and easily, and adds power when the voice trails off at the end of a sentence, equalizing it if necessary in other places. The entire session performance is carefully optimized.

Major audio publishers value experienced editors and producers for the "art" and "style" they bring to a production. Their "golden" ears and experience let them hear when part of one sentence or word fits with another, and will be smooth and natural sounding. "Art" means finding the right piece of music to reflect the mood the author and producer want. They use music as punctuation and enhancement for the voice track so the feelings are deeper, the suspense more suspenseful.

A more expensive music library, multiple selections, or specially composed music are used. Sound effects are often added. The resulting final edited masters may have taken thousands of keystrokes, yet the end result sounds seamless.

Maya Thomas, director of production at Time Warner AudioBooks, explains how they work. "I've worked with the same editor for six years so we think alike and can sometimes communicate without words — just a nod or look. He knows my style and preferences in editing and mixing. He does the 'rough cut' on his own.

"I listen and make decisions for the final edit. Then we mix the music and do the tweaking together using Pro Tools (digital editing software from Digidesign). I want something that 'sounds right' to me before it goes to duplication. The mix is creative and fun.

"Again, decisions are a matter of personal taste. The more music background a producer has, the better. I've found carefully watching and listening to films has been useful too. It's helped me develop my 'ear' for editing."

How Many Drafts?

Some producers working full time for audio publishers have authority to make all editing decisions through the finished master tape. Knowing when to delegate (as Maya Thomas talked about earlier) is part of a producer's job. The producer typically sits in after the first "clean-up," making decisions with the editor. This is one way experienced spoken word producers and the editors save publishers time and money. The "work tape" (first edit version) the publisher hears is often very close to what the finished product will be.

First-time publishers often join us in the editing room if we need a third editing session. Changes that may be hard to explain can be easy to achieve collaboratively, when everyone is hearing and seeing the same thing, and can preview changes together.

Tip: Ask your editor to store the music selection used on a tape about two minutes past the end of the program. Make sure the label and package include proper timing notations, so the duplicator will know what to expect. We found it made sense to have easy access to each piece of music later, for the next product, without wasting time and effort searching. We sometimes store the introduction and copyright reading too. Later, if there's a remix or revision, the components are all together. You may be charged again for use of the music cut on another program, but at least you know where to find it.

A Story Illustrates How Modern Editing Pays Off

Once upon a time, somewhere in the 90's, a medical association manager, named Leonard, got some bad news. Imagine the scene as he picks up the phone, and hears the keynote speaker for their yearly convention say she might not make it. "Oh, no!" he thinks, "the press will be there, and both Dr. Jones and her team's cancer research are the big draw." Instead, he says, "We'll do whatever it takes, Mary. Just show up, and give your presentation. Leave everything else to me. We'll make it work. Your tickets will be waiting at the airport. Take the last flight on United, and we'll have a car waiting at this end. Give us your slides, any materials to copy — whatever you need. Harry can take your afternoon session so you'll have a chance to rest. Please . . . we've got a lot of specialists who want to be the first to implement your findings."

Dr. Jones boards the red eye flight, feeling like a zombie. She'd rushed to the airport from surgery, and bought a fresh blouse at a terminal shop. She'd been 18 hours on her feet, including an unexpected six hour emergency operation, and she was just back from three days in bed at home with the flu. She knows the meeting organizers promoted her appearance tomorrow for the audience, and they will be taping. Leonard said he's presold hundreds of copies. She isn't worried about her subject and presentation, but her energy level is so depleted, she doubts adrenaline will be enough to compensate for the debilitating effects of the past week. "Oh, well," she thinks, "I'll rally somehow, then I'll sleep the afternoon away."

The next morning, at 7:10 a.m. Leonard briefs Jerry, the on-site recording engineer, asking that he do everything possible during the live session to make Dr. Jones sound less exhausted than she looked half an hour ago when she arrived from the airport. Jones gets through the presentation, and can't remember a thing later, except the nagging headache. By noon Jerry has a DAT recording, with two cassettes he ran simultaneously. He hands the DAT and one cassette to a cabbie, and scrawls "This'll be fun! Good luck!" across the top of his notes.

The taxi driver heads across town for the 30 minute trip to an editing studio, prearranged at the last minute through Leonard's business contacts in the conference city. The editing room has been on standby for the past hour, "just in case" Dr. Jones sounded as bad as she feared she would.

Fifteen minutes after Dr. Jones' presentation ends, the city's top spoken word editor, Danny, has conferred with Leonard, and is brewing coffee as he flips on the computer. "Good thing we have the edit room for 10 hours," he thinks, as he assures himself most of the set-up is similar to his own equipment configuration. He spends a few minutes with the owner, familiarizing himself with the room's idiosyncrasies. Danny wonders whether this "salvage operation" will take three hours, or 10, so as soon as the DAT arrives he begins loading it into the computer. After five minutes of program are in memory he begins cleaning up the audience coughs, extraneous noises and "uh, uh, uh's." Meanwhile the presentation keeps feeding into the computer in the background.

Ten minutes into Dr. Jones' presentation he decides to call in Allie, a producer, to assist. Ninety minutes later the producer is in the next room, listening to the presentation at double speed on cassette, marking trouble spots on a log. At 47 minutes into the program the sound level drops as two audience members ask barely intelligible questions, so she rewinds, goes to normal speed and relistens. She paraphrases, rewinds, makes notes, rewinds again, and assures herself the questions she'll substitute are essentially the same, but shorter. Allie takes the list of trouble spots back into the edit room. They agree on a game plan.

Using Allie's notes Danny finds and marks corresponding locations in the sound file. He temporarily inserts more space, to make them visually easier to find later on the screen. (He could search by real time, but the track he's changing as he works will be shorter than the original timing.) Soon he resumes making small adjustments to brighten up Dr. Jones where needed.

The producer, meanwhile, scripts an introduction, identifying information about the conference, end of side notification for listeners, closing and copyright information. She reads through the script three more times, marking possible changes. Then she calls Leonard at the conference hotel, giving him a progress report. He gives his okay on the script.

The pair record the "drop-ins" using a voice-over booth at the studio, with Danny at the mic and Allie "on the board." Danny goes back to his computer. She reviews the recorded "drop-ins" and her other edit notes, and returns to the editing room just as Danny is nearing the end of the recording. They put the "drop-ins" into the computer on a different track, and do some minor editing, pulling Danny's takes together and eliminating most of the recorded 10 minutes. The introduction, copyright and association information, and a brief tag at the end of the first side add about one minute, thirty seconds to the total length of the program. The first edit is complete.

Next they match the now-cleaned-up Dr. Jones to her normal vocal speed and delivery, using a lecture tape she happened to bring along for a colleague. Version 1 of the speech is run from the computer onto a reel to reel recorder with a variable speed function. The recording is speeded up slowly on the reel to reel, having the effect of making Dr. Jones sound more energetic. After a bit of experimentation the pair agree on how much to adjust Dr. Jones. Danny rewinds the tape, resets the computer to play, and begins the reel to reel recording. A little more than an hour later Dr. Jones's speech on version 2 sounds natural and energetic. It's ready to go back into the computer.

Now the cut and paste begins, with Danny using elements from all three tracks. The original presentation, edited and in real time is on track one. The studio "drop-ins" are ready on track two, and the speeded up version of Dr. Jones "live" on track three. Elements from track two are copied and laid up against the beginning of version 2 of

Dr. Jones on track three. Other voices from the session are copied from track one, and pasted into version 2 of the speech, in exactly the same spots. After another 90 minutes the three tracks are merged into a coherent program. Finally, satisfied with the improvements, the pair order a pizza. Danny puts two new DATs and four chrome cassettes into the recorders, double checks everything, makes some minor signal processing adjustments, and starts all six recorders. He clicks the mouse to play track three, then listens on headphones to each recorder. An hour later the pizza is demolished, washed down with beer and soda from the studio fridge. The computer/recording machines are showing 68:00 into the full 70 minute program. It only took six and a half hours. Not bad. Interesting news in the program, too.

Back at the hotel it's eight hours after Dr. Jones left the platform.

Leonard greets Danny in the lobby, and receives the two DAT master tapes and four cassette copies, in exchange for a check for $1,200. An area duplicator Danny spoke with earlier that afternoon is poised to crank out 5,000 copies of the edited version, and deliver them to the hotel by the next morning.

Leonard calls his executive assistant at her home and gives the go-ahead to do a mass fax and mailing to 40,000 physicians who didn't attend the conference. Most will receive order forms for tapes and monographs by e-mail within 24 hours. A postal mailing will go to those who don't respond or don't use electronic communication. Verification of the recorded sessions, along with summaries, will be posted online overnight, and the site has a secure order form. Profits to the association coffers from Dr. Jones' presentation on tape, Leonard estimates, will be at least $70,000. Not a bad two days work, he admits to himself.

Forty minutes later Dr. Jones is waking up in her room, and feeling much better. Hesitantly she plays the cassette Leonard slid under her door. At first she's confused, then relieved. In spite of her exhaustion she gave an organized, enthusiastic presentation, sharing the exciting new work her team has pioneered . . . yet she was so sure she transposed words and lost her place several times. Later, in the shower, Dr. Jones realizes what must have happened.

That evening Leonard picks up his messages at the front desk. He finds a card containing theater tickets from Dr. Jones for a sold out Saturday performance of a play she happened to know he'd starred in as a college drama major. *"I don't know how you made me sound this good. You're a genius! Please enjoy the play with a guest. Gratefully, Mary."* He tucks the card and tickets into his inside pocket, and smiling, heads for the reception, where he spots a much refreshed Dr. Jones surrounded by other physicians, vying for a chance to ask questions about her research.

- The editing challenge in this fictitious example used both digital and analog equipment. Most of the work took place in the computer so it was digital editing. The program, however, could not speed Dr. Jones up enough to overcome her tired sound so the edited version was re-recorded onto a reel of tape (analog). that version was again imported into the computer (digital). Finally, it was output to DAT (digital) and cassettes (analog).

What Editors Can't or Won't Do

Delivery: In the example above the problems are fixable. Even the best editor can be stumped, though, when he or she comes up against a "no hoper." Editing can't make dry, boring material exciting or compelling. It can't eliminate voices talking over or under the main speaker. It can't make an accent disappear, or create distinctive character voices if the narrator was stuck in a monotone rut. Or, to quote an engineer with over 20 years experience, "no one's invented the 'excitement' filter yet. If they had I'd have used it on the financial planner who was in here last Tuesday. Good stuff, dull read!"

Interpretation: When a voice talent says something at odds with the content it's usually better to re-record the words, because inflections can't be changed. Imagine a passionate romance novel, for example, "I love you, John" says the smitten debutante, with a sneer in her voice. It's uneditable. It has to be re-recorded so her delivery conveys the appropriate enthusiastic gush of appreciation for John's charms.

Asides, tangents, goofs: Speaking styles can present a challenge, particularly in live presentations and interview style recordings, because the expert may diverge from the script. Perhaps it's an example or joke that works in a live presentation. The audience applauds, and everyone involved in the recording thinks it's pretty funny too. Later on the author listens to the edited first draft and realizes the story could offend a client, or be misconstrued. He gets carried away with himself, for laughs. It was a mistake to use the example on tape. It has to come out.

Slurring and running words together: Suppose, further, that because of the flow before and after the story the only solution the editor can offer is re-recording that segment or deleting a full five minutes from the program, or making an edit that isn't "clean." Listeners will probably wonder what's missing and stop concentrating on the message. A transcript illustrates:

" . . . Point #5, Always Be Prepared whichremindsmeofa story . . . and Pat *never* made that error again! . . . So . . . the important thing to remember is . . . " Take the story out and it doesn't make sense.

The words that run together (whichremindsmeofa) are followed by the story itself, and to the story (and Pat *never* made that error again!). The section from Point #5 on will have to be re-recorded, or the list deleted. The storytelling skills that make Ms. A so good on the platform, such an audience pleaser, worked against her for the tape.

Signal processing is used to enhance recordings. If you have a strong "s" sound some of that can be reduced. Air conditioning noise can be minimized, and we can eliminate some tape hiss from a cassette. Not always enough to make a cassette master good enough for development into a product, though.

Copyright infringement: An ethical editor will advise against incorporating copyrighted music or recorded segments of someone else's material into your program. It is your responsibility to secure permission and pay whatever fees to use other people's copyrighted work.

New goodies: Some leading-edge software can change both the sound and context of words. A deep, resonant "voice of God" male can be manipulated to sound like an old woman, or a child. It's even possible to create voice "fonts." The software, some of it by Voxware™, is being used to create games and educational CD-ROMs, and advance Web capabilities. I grumbled recently to my editor, wishing we already had this software, so we could construct a few replacement words on a long recording. The reader on the project had left the country, and the edit had to be finished before he returned. Having a voice font to work with would have freed us to be outside on a beautiful Colorado afternoon. Instead we toiled under fluorescent lights, staring at a screen for hours.

As with other technological advances, there are frightening implications if used irresponsibly, but voice fonts and being able to manipulate accents and inflections can make editing even faster and easier in the near future.

The Thing About Side Lengths

Spoken audio cassettes are loaded with pre-recorded programs. When the program is going one direction you hear the signal from half the tape width (usually tracks 1 & 3). When the tape reverses, or you flip it, you'll hear tracks 2 and 4. It's a loop of tape, as shown below.

⊗→Intro→→→Body of program→→→→→→→Over
blank←←←←←←←program continues←←←←←⊗

Think of a car on the road between two points. The car travels to the end of the road going one direction, and then turns around and drives back. Tape winds through the A side, and then back on side B. Both sides have the same number of minutes of tape. The most desirable arrangement is to have the recorded material on side A be at least a few seconds longer than side B. That way listeners don't have to fast forward. They don't lose their place, or wonder if they've missed something, and when they hear five seconds or more of blank tape they know the program is continued on the next cassette. Video cassettes, by contrast, play in only one direction.

Test tapes, or proof cassettes for internal use may differ. During the editing phase samples of work tapes are recorded on standard length cassettes for ease of review. The edited example is recorded onto side A, but the technician may fast forward to the end and record the second side from the top of B. Why? It saves time, and money. Sometimes hearing a gap of blank tape scares publishers the first time around, for fear their program was erased. Everything is probably fine. Simply verify that the gap of blank tape will be gone when your product is duplicated for sale.

Adding Sound Effects

General fiction, classics, historical, language and children's titles frequently incorporate sound effects. Self-development tapes rely on
role plays or vignettes, then show a better way to solve a problem. If
your budget allows, and the production will be more valuable to listeners with sound effects, post-production is where you add them.

Street sounds, cocktail parties, telephones, nature sounds, doors, laughter, children at play, animals and business machinery are all examples
of sound effects. Picking effects is fun, and feels like play when you
have the time to enjoy the search. It's less fun when you're looking for
just the right sound, on a deadline. Catalog descriptions are often a
joke. Sometimes you must listen to each sound in a section to find the
one you want. You might listen to 15 "small crowd, indoors" cuts, and
none is right. Yet each sound evokes a different mental picture or
emotional response.

"SFX," the abbreviation for sound effects are from SFX libraries. (Radio
and TV news more often have "live sound," gathered at the scene.) My
favorite library is from the British Broadcasting Corporation library, but
each producer or studio has a preference. Most studios have access to
at least one SFX library on CD. Selections are mixed the same way
music is. The effect may be abrupt, or faded in and out for a different
"feel."

Incorporating Music

Music sets up an expectation in listeners' minds. Music evokes a mood.
One piece of music may work well at the front and end of a recording, but has nothing within the piece for bridging between segments.
You may need two or more pieces of music to create the mood
accompaniment for the text.

Music library selections are copyright free, and inexpensive. There are
many good libraries to choose from. Publishers use either music
library selections or commission exclusive music from composers.
Copyrighted music can be used with written permission and payment
of license fees. There are organizations that handle permissions all day
long. See the end of this chapter and the Resource Appendix.

Locating Music and SFX Libraries on Your Own

Music libraries began on a large scale in the 1970's. Over the years they've come down in cost. Many music libraries offer free demo CDs. They advertise in the back of A/V production magazines. A large book-store rack usually has magazines catering to musicians and video makers. Or you can check with local production facilities. Most have copies of their favorite trade publications in the waiting area, and will part with an out of date copy if you ask nicely.

Estimating Editing Time and Charges

Few products are edited and out the door in a day, like the Dr. Jones example. Therefore you want the editing facility to have enough capacity to assure your program can be stored for up to several weeks, in case you must wait for approvals and feedback from others. Digital files are loaded and unloaded into computer memory in real time — an hour program will take at least an hour going in, and later being laid back to cassettes, DAT or whatever format is chosen. During those times the equipment is tied up, so studios charge for these ser-vices.

It's common for non-book based, unscripted tapes to go through several edits. As long as the original master is left intact it's always on hand to go back to. Editing time is reduced if the people who "proof" the project listen to drafts in a timely manner. Making numerous changes can add up fast.

Allow 10 hours of billable editing for every hour of finished tape on your first project. You and your editor will become used to working together and the amount of editing and mixing time required will go down. As a rule of thumb I usually figure six and a half hours for all editing, mixing and mastering of a 60 minute master, plus the two hours for loading into and back out of the computer.

Some programs are fast, some take a little longer. These figures repre-sent a moderate amount of editing. Your situation may be entirely different.

At the conclusion of the editing, or post production, phase you'll have a finished, fully edited and approved master tape. It's properly timed, and needs no further changes. Now you need someone who can make copies, either on cassettes (analog) or on CDs (digital). The next chapter is about duplicators and replicators, and how they make your one edited master tape into the hundreds or thousands of copies for distribution and sale.

●●●●●●●●●
Resources:

Antonia Boyle & Company, Toni Boyle, 236 W. Portal Ave., #456, San Francisco, CA 94127, e-mail: ABoyleCo@aol.com

CareerTrack Publications, Gregg Perry, 3080 Center Green Drive, Boulder, CO 80301, 800-334-1018, Fax: 800-622-6211

Deyan Audio Services, digital editing, producing/directing, Robert and Debra Deyan, 6617 Rubio Ave., Van Nuys, CA 91406-5634, 818-902-1777, Fax: 818-902-1777

Digital Masters, Audiobook recording, editing, Rick Dasher, 138484 Ventura Blvd., D4, Sherman Oaks, CA 91423, 818-386-9646, 818-386-9172, e-mail: digitalm@earthlink.net

FTM Studios, 1111 S. Pierce, Lakewood, CO 80232, 303-922-3330

Marc Graue Recording Services, 3421W. Burbank Blvd., Burbank, CA, 91505, 818-953-8991

Jackson Sound Productions Ltd., duplicator, Linda Cano-Rodriguez, 3301 W. Hampden Ave., Unit C, Englewood, CO 80110, 800-621-6773, 303-761-7940, Fax: 303-789-0557, e-mail: dubs@jacksonsound.com, www.jacksonsound.com

Sonic Solutions, Yuki Miyamoto, 101 Rowland Way, Novato, CA 94945, 415-893-8021, Fax: 415-893-8008, e-mail: yuki@sonic.com

Spoken Word Audios, John Runette, studio, director, editor, Los Angeles, CA, 310-398-9858

Duplication and Labeling

You have the edited master. You're excited. It's time to make copies to share and sell. You'll need copies of your master. You need an audio duplicator. The first objective of this chapter is to give you enough information to be an informed consumer, and be able to work smoothly with your supplier. The second is to provide assistance as you design distinctive labels that are mini billboards.

If you've decided on CDs, the same process is called replicating because every CD is a clone of the CD master. Most duplicators either do CD replicating on site, or send your master to a colleague specializing in quality CD replication.

Whether CD's or cassettes, there's one essential first step *everyone* should take.

Back Up Your Master!

ALWAYS, always, always have a back-up set of your edit masters in a safe place.

A "back-up" or "submaster" is insurance. This can save you thousands of dollars. There are at least four reasons.

The first reason is peace of mind. Businesses close, new owners take over, buildings are damaged in natural disasters and fires. Federal Express, UPS or the postal service loses your package in an accident or through human error. More likely, someone mismarks your master or puts it in the wrong box while distracted. Though such things are rare, that's no consolation if your program is lost.

I finished a 30-minute *extensively edited and mixed* radio documentary a few days before it was to air on the Canadian Broadcasting Corporation in Calgary. My production partner and I were weary after 10 hours of mixing and hunching over editing blocks. We left the finished documentary behind in the control room. It would have been simple to label it clearly and take it with us, but we were inexperienced. Because I goofed, the next day another studio user inadvertently recorded over the reel. If we had left the source tapes behind, too, we would have been out of luck.

Ever since then, we back up recording session tapes even if clients say "never mind." We do the same with edited masters sent for duplication. We insist the publisher acknowledge in writing when they decline back-up masters.

The second reason is to protect your investment. Electronic masters are like original manuscripts. You'll generate income from those assets. The IRS sees it that way, and so should you.

Third, many duplicators ask to keep edit masters on file so they can respond quickly when you reorder. If a "running master" the duplicator has been using to make your cassettes wears out or breaks, they will make another "running master" from your edited master program. You won't be charged for subsequent "running" masters, because it's a normal part of doing business for duplicators.

This is an efficient and convenient system, but you'll need to retrieve your edit master if you decide to make any changes later. It's more convenient to have a copy yourself.

Fourth, you can respond quickly when:

• You're asked to customize your product for a client or industry.

- Material or terms you used are dated. A quick fix is all you need. If you can take your masters back to the same studio you used before, you'll save time, especially if your duplicator is out of town.

- You've evolved into a much better presenter, and want your audio product to reflect your improved delivery.

Whenever you work with a studio or producer, expect to get at least two copies of any finished product master, clearly labeled and timed. Most professionals figure this into the cost of a job and will do it automatically. Ask. If they can't or didn't make a second back-up master, ask the duplicator to make the "submaster" of your only edited master before they go any further. You'll pay extra and up front for recording time and supplies. Do it.

Get a back up even if your turnaround time is tight, or even if you have to pay an "up charge" for a rush job if necessary. Protecting your investment and sanity is your responsibility.

ID everything clearly with the title, date, version and timing. This sounds obvious, but many studio professionals hand over an unmarked tape. Even a piece of tape, a grease (editing) pencil marking or ball-point on the liner card or reel is better than no label at all.

Here's a (Composite) Story to Reinforce This Point

Tom is hot! He trains management professionals in the hospitality business. Give him six months of hands-on consulting in almost any hotel property; he'll reduce costs and staff turnover and increase revenue. His clients send him referrals and talk him up to others in the industry.

As the organization grew and moved to larger offices, nobody thought to keep track of where the backup tapes of his four-cassette program were stored. The recording studio he'd used was strapped for space. As a policy, they gave clients two masters, then dumped the computer sound files for the next job. No problem. Tom's duplicator had a set of edit masters, and cranked out reorders as needed.

Soon his seminar on tape was selling 50-100 units a week. A respected industry journal featured Tom's work, and gave the training tapes high marks. Tom's assistant took dozens of phone orders, and rang their duplicator for another 1,000 sets. Tom bought champagne dinners for the whole staff. Everyone rejoiced.

Two weeks later, on a Wednesday, Tom had a message slip about a call from someone he didn't recognize — "Ms. Martin, ABC Duplication. Please call."

"Martin?? Martin???" he thought. Assuming it was a sales call, he put the slip aside. On Thursday a second message said, "Urgent! Need to talk with you by Friday!" Ms. Martin's number was underlined. The co-worker who spoke with Martin reminded him. "Don't forget, it sounded important!" she called over her shoulder as she dashed out the door to pick up her child from day care.

"OK," Tom called after her. "I'll do it. Promise." He vowed to himself to return Ms. Martin's call from the airport. He went on filling his brief-case, double-checking the flight time and hotel reservation.

Early the next morning at the airport, he ran into his old college room-mate, so they passed a pleasant 45 minutes catching up on the past nineteen years. As he settled into to airline seat and pulled out some paperwork Tom reflected on how he was a workaholic. His old buddy, it seemed, had a life. He vowed to take a break that week-end, spend it with his family, and put work on hold.

On Monday morning Tom felt great — until he returned Ms. Martin's call. He listened in dismay as she told him his seminar masters had been thrown in a dumpster, crushed by the refuse truck, and gone to the landfill. The duplicator he used fled town leaving suppliers and employees in the lurch. Everything that wasn't retrieved by the pre-vious Saturday morning had been destroyed or sold. Ms. Martin had been on the phone for two days, alerting the customer list.

(This really happened. If it had not been for Martin's efforts, dozens of companies would have been in Tom's predicament. Sure, she told me later, she picked up a little new business. Mainly though, she could sleep at night knowing she'd done all she could. The publishers she was able to reach picked up their masters and project files under the watchful eyes of state officials. By Saturday afternoon all the equip-ment had been auctioned off, and everything left over was dumped.)

What did it mean for Tom? He spent over $5,500 recreating his masters from the duplicated cassettes. His staff spent two days tracking down the package printer, an out-of-state company known only in the trade. The printer, once located, refused to give Tom credit terms. "Whaddaya think I am, a bank? Your guy owed me big time. The only way I'll print the job is prepaid." Tom's advice — "Back those babies up — and know where you put them!"

Picking a Duplicator

Most major metro areas have more than one duplication company. Your best supplier might even be halfway across the country. Location is not as important today as the right service, price and quality for your needs. Fortunately there are many reputable companies offering good pricing, service and quality at each level.

Small companies tend to excel at personal service. When launching a tape with an initial order *under* 500, you will probably find a better match, but slightly higher per tape costs, from a duplication or replication company serving customers in your area.

The big large companies have a wider array of state-of-the-art equipment. Automation means they can complete runs faster, which in turn means the lowest per-cassette duplicating prices. The largest duplicators are geared for high-volume major publishers, corporations and multilevel/promotional tapes.

Ideally, your duplicator can deal with fluctuations in week-to-week volume, and longer-term business cycles. If it's slow when your order comes in, it could go right through, and be ready for pick up/ shipping before Friday, ahead of schedule. If they're swamped, you need to be confident that they'll still have your job done on time.

Can Everyone Work from DAT?

Most companies can handle your edited master in any format. They will be able to play or convert a master on DAT, cassette, reel to reel, or a CD. Most can also copy the audio track from a video tape.

One-Stop Convenience

More and more duplicators sell convenient extra services in addition to copying tapes. Some companies write scripts, record, edit, mix, duplicate, package and ship for you— all under one roof. Priced individually, these services could end up costing you more money, and you'd spend much more of your time. Besides convenience, you'll have experienced people working for you, with greater buying power. The minuses are that duplicators may offer services based on their favorite packaging or employee experience. A duplicator who likes vinyl packaging, for example, and is unfamiliar with fiction titles sold in bookpacks, could steer you toward what he knows rather than what the marketplace demands for a title like yours.

Duplicators offer extra services for a simple business reason: they make money on the mark-up. Even so, your duplicator's price will often be better than what you would get buying services separately.

Show You're in the Know

When you are gathering information, here are some tips.

- Pricing is per master, not the total number of duplicated tapes or CDs you order. Three thousand total will be priced as 1,000 x 3 within a three-tape set.

- Half down and the balance on completion of the first order are standard payment terms. Your tapes ship or are released when you have paid in full. Request a credit application or provide your standard application for reorders and long-term business with a duplicator.

- Ask for references, and call them. You especially want to talk with people whose projects and needs were similar to yours. If you need 100,000 tapes in two weeks, can they do it? Do account executives over-promise to get the jobs, then under-deliver? Or do they exceed expectations? You want a vendor who can help your company grow.

- Does the company you're considering have a toll-free number and after-hours messaging? A fax machine and customer accessible e-mail? Do they check messages, fax and e-mail regularly? Or do they have the equipment off in a corner, and check when the day is slow? Accessibility is important, especially for road warriors.

Businesses are rapidly moving to electronic communication. It's faster and more economical. E-mail often eliminates the need for snail mail, overnight delivery and faxing. Attaching art or graphic files to an e-mail message is convenient. People send and retrieve messages on their schedule, 24 hours a day, worldwide.

- Ask for the per tape unit cost *and total job cost.* You can't make a true comparison otherwise.

You may be able to negotiate a lower price later. The larger your volume of business, the more room the duplicator has to come down. They have economies of scale, but profit margins in audio duplication have eroded the last few years, so most quotes are already competitive.

- If they don't volunteer, ask about their quality checking. A duplicator I talked with recently has installed equipment that quality checks *every single duplicated cassette.* Companies are more and more quality conscious. If the company you talk with doesn't "QC," move on.

- Ask for and listen to their demo tape or a representative sample of their work on a program similar to yours. If they hedge, find out why.

- Understand the difference between high-speed duplication methods and options for labeling your tapes. Both are discussed later in this chapter.

What Duplicators Will Ask

When you request a quote from a duplicator/replicator, they'll need the following information. You can help set the tone for a professional relationship by having everything organized before you call. In order to make this simpler, you might want to copy the duplicator information in the appendix. File it and make copies for faxing. The duplicator will want to know:

- Your company name, address, phone, fax, online and sales tax identification number.

- How many minutes your master tape(s) run. An evenly divided 70
  minute program fits on a C-70. Your program will be priced at twice
  the longest side. Have your cassette times in front of you. If your
  recording is on cassette, the label will be marked with the maximum length.

- How many cassettes or CDs you want from each edit master.

- What grade of tape you require. Normal tape, a/k/a "voice," ferric,
  or Type I tape stock is the norm. "Music" grade is between "voice"
  and "chrome" and recommended for some jobs. Chrome (Type II)
  is for music duplication and live voice recordings. "Metal" is most
  expensive and overkill for spoken word.

- Which shells (plastic cassette cases) do you like? Clear, white, black,
  or a color? Two colors? Clear, white or black are most common.

- Do you prefer paper labels, or would you like the information
  stamped onto the cassettes? Imprinted (stamped) is the most popular
  choice.

- Will you provide approved camera-ready label copy, or will the
  duplicator handle the typesetting? If you're providing finished art,
  when will it be ready?

  You will be responsible for proofing and signing off on *all* art. Your
  duplicating job cannot be put on the production schedule until
  you've approved labels.

- What color ink do you want on the labels?

  One color ink is the norm. Black is most common. Blue is popular
  too. Expect an extra charge and possibly delays for additional or
  special mix colors.

- Have some idea what packaging and assembly services you'll need.

Where and how you expect to sell your products influences your choice of packaging, as covered earlier in the packaging and planning chapters.

- Know the date you'll need the completely assembled cassettes or CDs. If it's critical to have them by a certain time, specify morning, afternoon or 5:00 p.m. Otherwise your order will be loaded according to smoothest work flow for the duplicator's crew. It's a good policy to order far enough ahead to leave a few days leeway before your true "drop dead" date. If there's a power outage, or some other interruption in work flow at the duplicator's, you'll still be okay.

- Do you have specific boxing and shipping requirements? If you need smaller, lighter boxes to take with you on the road, say so. If you need a consistent size box or labels to unusual specifications, make sure the duplicator has the specifics in writing. Their shipping department needs to know so they can order cartons accordingly. If you know you'll be sending case lots repeatedly to wholesalers, catalogs or other locations, you may prefer to run your own shipping labels and ask the duplicator to keep them on file for your products.

- Will you need other services? Product storage, fulfillment and inventory records are services many duplicators now offer in response to customer requests. Using your duplicator's staff and warehouse to fill orders you fax or e-mail daily can be a bargain or a disaster.

- Last, the duplicator will probably make an estimate of your experience in the business. One of the ways newcomers can get into a bind is expecting everything to happen faster than it does.

Doug Brand, chief engineer of Jackson Sound Productions in Englewood, CO, decorates his control room with cartoons and sayings. My favorite, placed where clients are sure to see it, sums up the attitude of many of us who've toiled for years on too many last-minute "I need it yesterday!" projects. Brand's sign says,

"Lack of planning on your part does not constitute a crisis on my part."

It humorously points to a common problem. Rush jobs may mean a sacrifice of sound quality. Given adequate time the engineer can assess, massage the sound, and give you the best sounding product.

To reiterate, when you call duplicators they will want to know the:

- length
- quantity per master
- tape type
- shells
- labeling
- ink colors
- packaging
- turnaround time
- shipping
- and any special instructions

With all these variables it's clear why many companies steer you toward a package, or, ask for a few minutes to work up your quote.

Minimum Orders

You'll find some duplicator/replicators have a minimum order of 100, 250, 500, 1,000 or higher units per master. This is a business decision. There's nothing personal about it if they decline your business. It's no reflection on your program or its market potential. The duplicator has chosen a market niche where they can compete and be most profitable. When your title is selling briskly and your runs are larger you'll have quantities that fit their customer profile. You may go back to them later and be able to work together.

Problems with Orders

When an audio cassette fails because of something the duplicator is responsible for, you will get a replacement free. Components, equipment and the people behind the scenes turn out so many tapes that something may slip through quality control. The duplicator might have received a small amount of bad bulk tape from their supplier, a cassette may have been imprinted or loaded backwards, with side A on the side labeled B, or it's the wrong program. Errors are uncommon, but we're talking people and machines here. Stuff happens. Murphy's Law lurks everywhere, as you've undoubtedly discovered.

Often duplicators ask for defective tapes back in order to verify what went wrong. Some returned tapes turn out to play fine, indicating it was a wrong setting, or a problem in your customer's tape player. Dirty players can sound dull or muffled when they do play, and "eat" tapes. Customers need to be reminded to clean their players, just like they clean VCR's to keep the heads free of tape particles, grit and grime. People procrastinate — even when they know better.

Getting the tape back and diagnosing the problem is a way to prevent similar problems in future jobs. They may have just upgraded to new equipment, for example, and something didn't operate just right. It's their problem, and you'll get free replacement tapes, and a big thank you for bringing it to their attention.

Some publishers do such large volume they find it's helpful to have a sheet to fax or give to customers. CareerTrack developed a sheet of tape problems and solutions they'll send on request.

"High Speed" Duplicating Defined

Tapes are duplicated in real time, or by one of two high-speed methods.

How fast copies are made is a function of the equipment used. It might take 30 minutes to copy a 60-minute program on a home boom box, and less than a minute to copy the program at a professional duplicator's. The more copies a duplicator can make per hour, given equal quality and sound, the lower the unit cost is going to be to you.

To illustrate, when you use real-time dubbing on a two-cassette boom box or "dubbing deck" to copy 30 minutes of a language program onto one side of a 60 minute cassette, you're doing it in real time. Many musicians prefer real-time dubbing, contending their sound is reproduced more faithfully than using high-speed dubbing.

One popular method of speed duplicating for sale and promotional tapes is called "in-cassette," where programs are copied at high speed, cassette to cassette. You've seen these machines at work at conferences, churches and in smaller offices. If a duplicator says they use standard length tapes, like 45, 60 and 90 minutes, they are most likely duplicating by the "in-cassette" system. Your cassette master goes into one slot, and multiple blank tapes are recorded with your program, simultaneously. Many more copies can be made in an hour using in-cassette duplicating than you could do in a day using a home or office dubbing deck.

The second popular system for "high speed" duplicating is called bin-loop (or loop bin), It's least expensive per unit, and accomplished on highly automated, computerized machines.

There are thousands of duplicating companies around the U.S. Linda Caño Rodriguez, of Jackson Sound Productions, Denver, CO, has been in business over 30 years. She's seen spoken audio grow from almost nothing to today's dimensions. She explains the duplication process.

Photo courtesy of Gauss

"The first step in audio duplication, and one of the most critical, is the creation of the duplicating master. This master is developed from your finished recording and is either transferred to 1/2" analog tape on a Studer Master Recorder, or recorded onto Digital Audio Tape for loading into a Digital Bin. From either of these two master formats, the program is then recorded onto pancakes of high quality cassette tape. After these pancakes of tape are recorded, they will be loaded into cassette shells using high speed loaders. Next a test cassette, which is an exact duplicate of the final product, will be forwarded to you for your approval."

After you've approved the test cassette, your program is loaded into cassette shells. On the fastest equipment the ratio is (128:1) for voice and (96:1) for music, or, to put it another way, an hour-long program is loaded in 30 seconds.

Tapes then go from loaders to automatic labeling machines for either on-shell or roll labels. Once the labels are applied and quality checking has been done, tapes are seg-

Photo courtesy of Gauss

regated in trays, by title, and moved to the assembly area. Either machines or hand labor may be used to assemble tapes into your boxes or albums.

Virtually all commercial tapes you buy in chain stores are high-speed duplicated using bin-loop, or digital bin systems. It's the way the best-seller audiobooks, all top-selling seminar and self-help programs, and promotional tapes are duplicated.

Which Method is for You?

Both methods have advantages, so evaluate based on your situation.

Bin-loop duplicated tapes are custom-loaded to the exact length of your program, based on twice the longest side length. If your program is 26 minutes long and 13 minutes on the longest side, your copies will be 26 minutes. If it runs 16 minutes on the longest side your copies will be 2 x 16, or Cassette-32's, called C-32s. Every cassette will sound the same. When you duplicate 150 or more per master, bin-loop is more economical.

"In-cassette" is a good method for testing and customizing programs in smaller quantities. The primary reason it is more expensive than "bin-loop" or DAT bin methods is labor. Someone must monitor machines almost constantly, removing duplicated tapes and inserting more blanks. Each tape is checked by someone. Labels are typically laser printed and hand applied. All assembly into packaging is by hand.

A tape that costs you $1.50 in a Norelco box using the bin-loop method @ 250 units/run will be another $.50 to $1.25 duplicated the in-cassette way. If all you need is 25-100 tapes for review and feedback, in-cassette is the ideal method. It's fast and easy.

While it doesn't make sense to tie up lots of dollars in inventory, there's more motivation to sell product if you have more on hand. Sometimes this is a chicken-or-egg dilemma for new publishers. Over time they can spend far more on the cost of the goods by cautiously sticking with in-cassette duplication over the alternative bin duplicating method.

Cassette Shells

Black, white and clear shells are readily available, so many duplicators offer all three at the same price. Colored shells, Side A one color and Side B another, and high tech or high performance shells may be a special order with additional lead times and charges. Cassette shells are preloaded with leader tape. In the beginning, they're called C-0's because there's no magnetic tape inside the shell.

"Test" or "Proof" Cassettes

This is a sample of exactly what your program will sound like when duplicated. Some people call them reference or proof cassettes, rather than test cassettes, but the purpose is the same. A test cassette is your final chance to check your program, and the duplicator's work at mastering and duplicating your program before it's loaded into shells. Test cassettes are an important step to protect both you and the duplicator from an unsatisfactory product. Test tapes are the sound equivalent of a printer's "blue line."

Don't give in to the temptation of believing that because the duplicator's own marketing cassette sounded great, yours will too. Take the time to listen through.

If there are any sound problems (unlikely), be sure to take notes. Tell the duplicator approximate times on the tape, or some sort of content cues, to find the problem. Experienced duplicators can usually troubleshoot any problem and suggest solutions. Engineering is part art and part science. The duplicator will remaster your program and run a second test cassette.

The cost of creating another bin-loop or cassette master will be borne by you when a problem on the test cassette is due to a content, delivery or editing problem you missed earlier in the process. If the duplicator somehow goofed, the duplicator will absorb the remastering expense.

Guarantees on Duplicated Tapes

Reputable duplicators guarantee their work, They can do this with confidence because they use good components, quality check their duplicated tapes, and are in business for the long term. They have many loyal repeat customers, and grow through referral.

If you choose to go with the lowest bid, be sure you're comparing equivalent quality, service, and guarantees. A few companies cut corners with low wages and poor maintenance of machines, or low-ball a job to get you in the door. After a few months, they must either increase prices to where they make a profit, or go out of business. If the duplicator closes without notice, you're stuck, no matter what you were promised or guaranteed.

CD or Not CD?

Yes, if you have a fiction bestseller. Otherwise, cassettes are a safer choice. The major drawback to audio CDs is the relatively small installed base of CD players vs. cassette players. Since spoken word reproduces fine on cassettes, the large publishers have not felt enough customer pressure yet to produce more than the best-selling titles on CDs. They produce what they can sell.

Other considerations to factor into your decision are:

- Cassettes offer longer playing time than audio CDs. (Up to 100 minutes per cassette, vs. 74 for CDs.) It takes three CDs to make a three hour book, vs. two cassettes.

- Cassettes have a "bookmarking" feature — a user can see at a glance where she left off. The tape can be played immediately from that point, without searching. Cassette "bookmarks" are portable, whereas a CD moved from player to player will lose your place.

- CD players don't slip as easily into a pocket, fanny pack, or onto an arm band. They aren't as convenient while walking or jogging.

- Cassettes don't skip on rough or pothole-riddled roads.

- CDs are higher tech, new. Cassettes are low-tech, old technology.

- CD players are gaining in popularity. Portable players work in cars with simple plug-in adapters.

- Inexpensive boom box-style CD/cassette decks make home dubbing to tape simple and practical.

- Initial start-up costs for CDs are higher than for cassettes.

Incorporating audio programs makes excellent sense for CD-ROMs where several media can be combined to create a valuable learning or entertainment product. Publishers enjoy a substantial savings by putting everything on a single CD-ROM vs. producing the same material on a video, audio tape or CD, and print materials.

CD Manufacturing and Costs

CDs are created by automated pressing machines. Clear plastic disks are each laser-etched as an exact copy of a glass master disk. Aluminum and a protective coating are applied next. The operation takes place inside a unit that's monitored through glass windows. Completed CDs are stacked like rings on a post. You'll find several good examples of CD production featured on duplicators' Web pages.

CD clones are imprinted with labels in one to four colors. Most are packaged in sleeves or jewel-style cases. CD-ROMs are included in magazines, glued to book covers, or included with software bundles.

An audio CD costs $1.00, or less, replicated at 1,000 units. Duplication costs are dropping. Packages used in retail are small and easier to ship than audio albums or bookpacks. Inserts and sleeves for CDs are printed by the same companies that make audio and video packaging.

Labels

Cassette labels come in three basic flavors. They're either stamped or silk-screened straight onto shells, applied paper labels or sheet labels run through your laser printer.

Taking these in reverse order, the lowest tech and easiest start-up is using sheet labels. Check first with your favorite copy shop if you expect them to copy your labels. Some won't. Avery, Ace Labels and others make sheet labels for laser, standard printers,

and copying. Hand labeling from sheets isn't cost effective for published products, but it's a good alternative for experimenting, and test runs.

Pressure sensitive paper labels used to be the standard. They're paper, usually on rolls. Roll labels can be printed in colors on a variety of stocks, so you can have neon colors, or a metallic background. Labels are printed on sheets, then die-cut to fit the various types of automatic labeling equipment. A duplicator fits the roll onto a machine and quickly labels several hundred tapes automatically. It's efficient and fast.

On-shell printing is the lowest cost method, at five cents per cassette or less. The method is called "imprinting" or "Apex" style, and has become the industry standard. Some duplicators include on-shell printing in cassette duplication prices and some add it as a separate charge. The benefits to you are:

- Low cost, especially over time and reorders.
- No stock of labels to keep track of or reprint.
- Many colored inks available at no extra cost.
- Works on clear and opaque, and all color shells.
- Start-up costs for imprinting plates are inexpensive.
- Imprinting removable with solvent, and easier to remove than labels.
- Won't catch in car players and peel off with age, like paper labels.
- Four color on-shell printing possible, though not generally used.

Label Art as Advertising

After looking at hundreds of tape cassette labels for years, only a few are memorable. Savvy publishers can take advantage of labels to reinforce their logo recognition and identification. Labels can carry through elements from a cover with type fonts and a design. The After awhile listeners begin to associate good listening with certain publishers.

Labels can work for you twice because cassettes are passed along. A potential customer for more of your titles may only have the label information. It's up to you to help them identify and find you with an ISBN number, phone, fax and online options. (Some  publishers use a post office box to avoid having to remake label plates if they move or their area code changes.) This voice demonstration tape has a cable car label in four colors to reinforce the fact that Toni Boyle is in San Francisco.

What Goes on the Label?

At a minimum, your label should include:

- Your product title and any subtitle
- Author
- © for the content, the year the first tape is produced, the publisher, all rights reserved
- ISBN, so people can locate you
- Cassette number and A or B, or side numbers in a series

Your copyright information, publisher contact information and the program title or module subtitle should be on *every label*.

In addition, ℗ for the performance copyright, logos, the Dolby insignia if Dolby noise reduction is used, and the running times for each side appear on many labels. (Dolby is a signal processing technique with some licensing restrictions. Ask your duplicator about including it.)

Some publishers put different information on the B side labels. For example, their address on Side A, the phone number on B.

Type Fonts and Sizes

The easiest to read fonts work best.

Imagine someone trying to read your label while behind the wheel. I like large print for the tape numbers and sides, possibly because I grew up navigating Los Angeles freeways.

Duplicators can set up your labels. If you find their work is unappealing, you may prefer to do it yourself, or have your graphic artist create the label art and films, using the duplicator's template or specs.

Use point sizes as large as are practical. We begin with the title in 36-point and work up or down until it fits within a form that's 200% of actual size. If the publisher has a preferred font, we use it, or something similar. The labels are proofed at 200%, then printed at 48-50% to leave a little white space. Use the templates in the appendix.

Set-Up Fees and Art Costs

Duplicators have expenses to start a new order. Those are charged as one-time set-up fees for a bin-loop or "running" master made to fit their equipment. Running masters are not transferable, as a rule, because they're formatted to different equipment. (You own your edit masters. Duplicators keep the running masters if you move your account.)

Imprinting plate costs for your labels are usually passed through. If typesetting or artwork needs to be done, those charges may be extra. Cover design and printing are always extra. Any packaging, assembly, fulfillment and shipping charges are priced in addition to duplicating.

It works best if you provide finished cover art and okay a color proof before the duplicator or manufacturer creates printing plates. You will be responsible for the job cost, just as with other printing, once you have signed off on cover or package art. Errors are often missed when rushing to meet a deadline. Proof carefully!

Thoughts About Shipping

Think about establishing policies and procedures that minimize costs. That means procedures that save you dollars, time and loss in transit. If you've already faced these challenges, you might want to skip to the next chapter.

Cost. Ask your duplicator for shipping estimates. Lately, several vendors I use and trust have discovered their supposedly lowest cost shipper was no longer the best. The difference on a recent quote was $2,000 from the highest to lowest shipping bid.

After a recent price hike by shippers, I kept records to compare per-pound costs for a shipment we do frequently. The postal service was close to UPS ground — sometimes better.

Cartons. Standard mailers for single products work if you're fulfilling individual orders. Mailers can be modified and printed in quantities as low as 50 at a time with your company name and sales message. Check with box manufacturers close to home.

There is no standard carton size for audio because packaging and quantities are so varied. Specify double walled, or 200 lb. burst strength and ample taping to protect your products in transit. Whenever quantities warrant, have cartons shrink-wrapped on a skid for shipping. The best carton size for your needs may be something the duplicator doesn't keep in stock. If you need all your products in the same size cartons, offer to pay extra if necessary. Unless you specify, duplicators may recycle incoming boxes as they see fit. While this is environmentally sound, the dimensions can change with each order. You could end up reboxing to suit your needs or to maximize storage room.

Be sure also to communicate how you need the cartons marked. Cartons are usually labeled with your product title, the quantity in the carton, and may have the date, your address or ISBN. If you have several titles with the same or similar names, you'll want to identify each version on the outside too. We use a marker on three sides for quick recognition in the storage area. Colored stickers work better for some people.

If you use recycled cartons, be sure there is nothing visible on the carton to confuse shippers or people at the receiving end. Either mark the other shipping information out thoroughly, or mask over it with carton masking spray paint or tape. Racing to meet a UPS pick-up cost me several hundred dollars once when a shipment was returned to a supplier and shelved as new materials. I had to absorb the cost of an extra run and overnight delivery. We didn't find the first shipment until the carton was opened weeks later, and we figured out what had happened. Automatic scanners probably read the wrong address, because a part-timer in our office hadn't eradicated earlier markings on the box.

If your duplicator is local, consider picking up your orders or using a courier if your duplicator doesn't deliver.

Freight carriers. In 1996 our company experimented with a small color catalog. Because orders came from all over the country, we evaluated three popular carriers. The consensus was that too many shipments arrive damaged because of rough handling. Some formerly adequate boxes and tape had to be replaced with heavier duty supplies. When all costs were factored in, we decided to ship most orders via the carrier with the best record for handling and tracking orders smoothly, not the service with the lowest per pound shipping charge. (The chosen carrier provides free shipping boxes.) The delivery service can tell us who signed and received the package . . . and forgot to tell our customer. If an order isn't delivered, it's a few clicks of the mouse or a phone call. The shipper finds the package and takes care of the problem promptly. Time savings and customer service won out for us. We could invoice immediately and payments came back faster.

Responsibility in Transit

Once cartons of your audios leave the duplicator's premises, it's the carrier's responsibility to deliver your product safely. If there's damage, your duplicator must file a claim, as the shipper. The same thing applies if you ship it directly from your location. Loss and damage in transit are a nuisance and you can lose sales. We insure everything to total value and pay extra if necessary for scannable tracking. You want your products to arrive at the point of sale in good condition.

The happy result of all your effort is making money. Sales are the subject of the next two chapters.

●●●●●●●●●●
Resources:

Antonia Boyle & Company, Toni Boyle, 236 W. Portal Ave., #456, San Francisco, CA 94127, e-mail: ABoyleCo@aol.com

Brilliance Audio Services, *Sanctuary* and *Freedom's Choice,* publisher and duplicator, Lou Dudeck, 1704 Eaton Dr., P.O. Box 887, Grand Haven, MI 49417, 800-222-3225, Fax: 800-648-2312

Cinram, duplicator/replicator, Peter J. Jensen, One Tower Lane, Suite 1700, Oakbrook Terrace, Illinois 60181-4631, 630-573-5209, Fax: 630-954-0812

Eva-tone, duplicator/replicator, 4801 Ulmerton Rd., Clearwater, FL 34622, 1-800-EVATONE. www.eva-tone.com

Gauss, a division of EVI Audio, Joseph O'Connor, 9130 Glenoaks Boulevard, Sun Valley, CA 91352, 213-875-1900, Fax: 818-767-4479

Jackson Sound Productions Ltd., duplicator, Linda Cano-Rodriguez, 3301 W. Hampden Ave., Unit C, Englewood, CO 80110, 800-621-6773, 303-761-7940, Fax: 303-789-0557, e-mail:dubs @jacksonsound.com, www.jacksonsound.com

Media International Inc., duplicator, 4-color imprinted labels, Duane Lundeen, 6312 Roosevelt Road, Oak Park, IL 60304, 800-200-8701

Mellex International Corp., cassette shells & packaging, John Cristiano, 150 St. James Ave., Saint James, NY 11780, 516-862-6829, Fax: 516-862-1903

Precise Media, duplicator, Layne Scharton, Pomona, CA 91768

Sonopress, Inc., duplicator, 1540 Broadway, 28th Floor, New York, NY 10036, 212-782-7668, Fax: 212-782-7650

Sony Disc Manufacturing, Thomas E. Farrington, 3181 N. Fruitridge Ave., Terre Haute, IN 47804

World Media Group, duplicator/replicator, Brad Cates, 6737 East 30th Street, Indianapolis, IN 46219, 317-549-8484, Fax: 317-549-8480, e-mail: wmg@indy.net, www.al.com/wmg/

Profiting From Your Investment

"There are nearly as many ways to market audio products as there are audios," says Jay Zwicky, marketing director of Sounds True Audio.

In chapters 12 and 13 we'll look at some of the most popular ways to market and sell tapes and CDs. Chapter 12 is about selling at presentations (back of room, or BOR), sales from newsletters, direct mail, and using promotional tapes. This chapter also contains additional tips on working with the media, online sales, and stimulating more orders from existing customers.

The next chapter, Selling to Stores and Libraries, addresses three areas people frequently inquire about — libraries, bookstores and catalogs. You'll find a brief introduction to how wholesalers and distributors fit into the picture. These markets are the strongest for top-selling authors and subjects — in other words, popular mass market audiobooks, children's titles and self-help. Audiobooks are currently enjoying another dynamic growth spurt. Sales increased over 30% in the last quarter of 1996.

That's great news for start-up and growing publishers. There's not so good news, too. The sustained effort required to be successful discourages many. This won't be a surprise, if you read Chapter 3, and worked out a marketing plan. Let's look further now at how you'd implement your plan.

Success = A Plan, Focus, and Persistence

The plan you developed in Chapter 3 is your blueprint. If you've done your homework, chances are good any changes you make in your active marketing will be refinements, not major changes. Your energy, time and money will be funneled toward reaching and selling to your target market.

When you rely on back-of-the-room sales, you must learn to tell the audience about your products in a non-irritating way. If you believe in your learning resources and the value your tapes can bring to people, it is much easier to be impassioned about your products. Excitement and confidence sell products.

This requirement to be focused and persistent is one of the hardest things for new publishers to accept. Yet it's the "being out there" marketing of themselves and their products that keep sales going. Unless your products are in enough hands, word-of-mouth advertising won't be sufficient to carry your sales upward. Don't be discouraged, though. There's a bright side.

Smaller publishers have an advantage over large ones. You know your customers better. This is particularly true in niche marketing. If you were an English literature professor in an earlier life, you'd know the classics. You'd belong to the professional organizations and know who supplies course materials for college students. Textbook reps might buy enough to cover all the costs of launching a tape series the major publishers wouldn't touch because they don't know how to sell it.

As a former professor, you'd also know there's a Shakespearean festival in Ashland, OR, every year. Booksellers, gift shops and even the theatre might buy cases of your Shakespeare tapes. And you'd be in a position to go straight to the most interested buyers.

Or perhaps your marketing plan includes finding an industry supplier to front the money to sponsor your tape series so you can focus on creating more tapes. You can find a sponsor, but it'll be an enormous stroke of luck if your first call, or first 10 calls, hit pay dirt. Your connection to a corporate sponsor might turn out to be another parent on your kid's soccer team — or someone you meet in an airport van. You wouldn't have found that connection unless you were willing and able to let people know about your product and dreams.

No matter how you market, you need what Terri Lonier, television commentator, consultant, and author of the *Working Solo*® series of books and audios, calls a "marketing mindset." You're always marketing, always on the lookout for opportunities. You don't have to be obnoxious; you do have to be focused, persistent, and work your plan.

Back-of-the-Room Sales Tips

Speakers and trainers are missing an opportunity when they don't have good quality products. Audio is often the first step, because tapes are relatively easy and inexpensive to create. Videos, books and other learning aides for audience members may be more attractive, but unrealistic, given the demands of running a business and being on the platform.

Mike Frank, C.S.P., C.P.A.E., is a past president of the National Speakers Association, and author of *For Professional Speakers Only*. Frank is well qualified, because he's successfully worn three hats since 1967: Professional speaker with over 3,000 presentations to business and association groups, owner of a major speakers bureau (has booked over 10,000 engagements for clients), and producer of over 100 public seminars featuring dozens of the world's top speakers. He knows!

On page 28 of his book, Frank says, "Books and cassettes — well packaged and professional in topic and development — are powerful tools in demonstrating one's grasp of and position in their field."

"They are also money-makers. A few top speakers earn in excess of a million dollars a year from tape or book sales. Many more can match or top their speaking fees through product sales, made either to the attendees (usually at public seminars) or directly for distribution in several different ways."

When tapes are offered alongside books and videos on a sales table in the back of a room, at least 10 to 15 percent of customers will opt for audio. Audiences are motivated to purchase when the subject hits close to home for them. A "how to" on the alleviation of family stress is just one example. It's not unusual to sell upwards of $25 a head in audio products at these presentations. In an audience of 100 people if 20 attendees spend $25 each a presenter can take in $500 and have a unit cost of only $50. When the products for sale are in the $75-250 range the unit costs go up a few dollars, and profits soar.

Are dollars the only motivation for selling products at presentations? No. There's another reason. Jim Cathcart, a long-time sales trainer for Fortune 500 companies, asks a room full of sales trainers "Do sales trainers need products?" There's a brief silence. "NO!" he answers. "Sales trainers don't need products. Sales *learners* need products! Without products to use for review, reinforcement and follow up, how will the people at a training or speech possibly be able to make full use of the shared knowledge? The answer is they can't. That's why you need products. You cannot possibly help people change unless you give them the tools to put new behaviors into practice."

Back-of-the-room sales work for many presenters. *Always* make sure you've cleared it with the people who hired you. One of the quickest ways to destroy your reputation, and bookings, is to pitch products when you agreed you wouldn't.

Here are some tips for better back-of-the-room sales:

- Have a draped display table of learning materials and products in the room. Position your display and sales tables for maximum visibility without blocking people who need to enter or leave.

- Be set up 30 minutes before your presentation begins so people can browse and talk about your products among themselves.

- Give away one or a few products as "door prizes" or "gifts" before the first break or before lunch, to stimulate interest and sales. Make the awareness activity something fun and lighthearted.

- Refer to what's on your tapes before the first break at a half or all day presentation. Tell one of your signature stories, or give some solid information, then say something like this: "By the way, that story, and three others about X are on the Y album." Say it as a throwaway line, transitioning to another point, or to the break.

- Tell your audience your audios go far beyond what can be covered in the limited time the speaker has with the audience. (Don't lie.)

- When your tape is essentially the same as the presentation, emphasize the value from listening over and over. Stress the better results the attendee, by having your message on tape. Mention the pass-along value, so one purchase can be shared back at the office.

- Tell the audience you created the tapes in response to requests from people just like themselves. (Don't say so if it's untrue. You'll risk looking foolish if audience members don't agree.)

- Offer to autograph all purchases, including tapes. Some people who do this do not shrink wrap, or they autograph extra covers or J-cards for the customer to insert after the product is opened. This is smart because the customer then has an extra cover to give away.

- Offer discounts, especially for multi-product "jumbo packs."

- Use a free tape or booklet as an incentive for orders over $100.

- Promise, and adhere to, an unconditional guarantee of satisfaction. You'll reduce resistance to buying. Although a small percentage of customers may take advantage by purchasing, duplicating and returning your tapes, a guarantee substantially increases sales.

- Accept checks and credit cards for purchases.

- Offer free priority shipping when you run out of tapes on site.

- Charge sales tax, or include it in the price. Remit taxes to proper agencies. Be especially mindful when selling BOR frequently in a jurisdiction. Taxing agencies know about seminar sales.

- Include an order form or catalog in materials packets, or with each purchase.

- Offer a limited-time discount for orders placed within X days. Impulse drives many BOR sales, so add some urgency to the purchasing decision by picking a short time frame — a week or less.

- Decide whether you will accept purchase orders, and under what circumstances. When someone wants to purchase three units via purchase order for a library system or corporation, you'll be prepared.

- Pre-sell products so all attendees get your tape. Many companies and associations are opposed to sales pitches from the platform. They're open, however, to learning materials and added-value products. Any method to increase their payoff using employee "windshield time" during the workday gives them more bang for their training bucks. They'll find money somewhere in the budget for learning materials.

- Build in follow-up tapes for seminar attendees, as short refreshers, and ways to stimulate their thinking and productivity. The tapes can be bulk shipped directly to the training department, sales managers, or others, who dispense them to attendees. Hand-to-hand transfer of tapes on your customer's end stimulates further discussion and positive results. The people who hired you can build on your ideas, develop more dialog, and track results. Your value is enhanced far beyond the cost of the audio cassettes.

What if sales are disappointing?

- Try different covers and prices to see how either influences sales.

- If you know you have good products, and are having trouble selling, ask colleagues to sit in while you pitch. Review your performance together afterwards. Your body language or wording may need fine tuning. Their comments may sting, but you'll get valuable feedback.

- Tailor your pitch so it's appropriate to your audience. Many people object to product sales, and say so on feedback forms. A 10-minute spiel drives people away from the sales table, and can tarnish your company's reputation. Are you being sensitive to your audiences?

Lilly Walters and Dottie Walters, co-authors of *Speak and Grow Rich,* encourage their readers and seminar audiences to create bundles of products. Thousands of presenters have learned about the business of speaking from this dynamic mother-daughter team.

"Back-of-room sales occur because the presenter has inspired in the attendees a desire to invest in the products for themselves. Subtly sell all the way through your talk. If the audience feels you 'selling from the platform,' you are not doing a good job. When your program material is good, people will want more." *Speak and Grow Rich,* offers much in the line of practical ideas, backed by years of experience.

If you're entering the speaking and training field, I highly recommend you also read *"How to Develop and Promote Successful Seminars and Workshops"* by Howard L. Shenson. Unfortunately Shenson passed away, so his book has some dated information, but his proven and research-based strategies can help anyone learn how to succeed with adult audiences. Shenson's chapter 12 is devoted to back of the room sales. Shenson also authored other valuable books on consulting.

Newsletters/Newstapes

Newsletters: The best marketing strategy for many businesses is to get in front of clients and customers on a regular basis. Newsletters are the best way to gain and hold a "front of mind" position, so when your customer is ready to make another purchase or seeks advice, they'll think of you and look no further.

Newsletters can be print, audio, or over the Internet. Many newsletters are a combination of formats, available to suit the customer. Some are free, others for fee. You can include product references and an order form along with easy alternative options to buy by phone, fax or online when you publish your own newsletters.

The single best "how-to" book on the subject is Elaine Floyd's *Marketing with Newsletters*. The fat trade paperback is jam-packed with smart advice on marketing any business. It contains hundreds of photos and illustrations of what works and what doesn't.

How to boost sales, add members & raise funds with a printed, faxed or Web-site newsletter.

Elaine Floyd
author of Advertising From the Desktop

Order your own copy direct from the publisher. They'll include a copy of Newsletter News, Floyd's own newsletter and a resource list. Libraries and bookstores also have the book, or can get it for you.

Being featured in other organization's newsletters is a good strategy. Articles from you, or featuring you or your products, build a business. Research the newsletters in your target market, then approach them with an offer of free feature articles. Any regular publication comes up against deadlines and keeps a few articles in reserve for the edition with a hole in it somewhere. If your information dovetails with the editor's needs, you'll get exposure.

Find the right newsletters for your target market in the *Oxbridge Directory of Newsletters,* available at many public libraries. While you're at it, look for the professional associations and trade organizations, nonprofit organizations and magazines serving your target market. You'll probably find a few you didn't know existed. Gale Research Company publishes a number of these directories. If you need help getting started, ask the research librarian. Popular directories may not be on the shelves for self-service.

Ongoing education is essential in most professions. Physicians have been purchasing subscription audio cassettes for over 25 years. Your pediatrician, cardiologist, internist or other specialist probably subscribes to at least one such series to help stay abreast of work by others in their field. Attorneys, CPAs, and other professionals have similar programs. Some professions allow members to learn via cassettes to maintain their certification in their specialty.

Newstapes as member benefits are another popular use of cassettes. The National Speakers Association sends a tape-a-month, called *Voices of Experience,* and a magazine, *Professional Speaking,* to all members. The tapes teach, increase member retention, and facilitate more communication between members. NSA's practice is to offer different information in each format, making them complementary. Some associations use a tape version of the printed newsletter as an alternative. Many such tapes follow a magazine format, with regular departments and columns each month.

Subscription series are a close cousin to newstapes. There can be big profits and powerful business-building opportunities using instructional tape series. Cassettes are mailed, or information is downloaded at regular intervals. The series are sold up front, and after two or three years there are enough recorded editions on the shelf to recycle some for new subscribers. These appeal to people who prefer ongoing learning at regular intervals. The costs, compared to attending a seminar out of town, is attractive. Products such as these may be condensations of industry-relevant books, or part study, part tips, part motivation. Howard Brinton Seminars is a company specializing in the Real Estate industry. Their tape series include print and tape material every month. All subscriptions start with the calendar year, and are pro-rated, to simplify recordkeeping.

Catalogs

Grady Hesters and Linda Olsen have been publishers in the audiobook and catalog business for years. Putting out a sales piece like their four-color, 100-page Audio Editions catalog isn't for the faint of heart, or for those with a skinny wallet. Hesters makes an observation for someone coming into the business today: "It takes $3 million to make $6 million. You have to buy good lists, pay for all the design and printing, postage and overhead. Then you send it out, and hope the return is better than two percent," he says.

Olsen concurs. "It's a tough business. There's an art to successful catalogs. With Audio Editions we always strive to have the hottest bestsellers and an extensive selection of titles. We can't justify keeping an audio in successive catalogs unless it generates enough revenue. The explosion of audiobook titles, and more customers, makes the management challenge all the more interesting. Our customer service and fulfillment side have to be able to get the orders entered correctly, and then shipped right out. The ideal is to ship the same day we take the order."

Audio Editions, The Publishing Mills, Sounds True, and Knowledge Products are just a few examples of many companies using catalogs as an effective component of their marketing strategy.

Most newcomers and small companies aren't ready to do a four-color catalog. They want their products in existing catalogs instead. There are two types; printed catalogs (like you receive in your mailbox) and online catalogs. Many audio publishers use both.

When you pick the catalogs you think would be right for your products, use common sense. If you were looking for antiques, you'd gravitate to a street with a cluster of stores close together, wouldn't you? Using the same logic, if you have a tape series on business Spanish, your first calls should be to catalogs targeting international business travelers. Don't waste your time on catalogs featuring products for young families. Pass those catalog names along to a friend with a set of children's tapes instead. (You never know. He might be married to the sister of a language-school executive.) While this will be obvious to some of you, I've learned many otherwise intelligent people don't have a marketing (or shopping) mindset.

Reference volumes list thousands of catalogs, by category. Some catalogs include audio products, but don't specialize in them. For example, *Wireless* (print) features tapes by Garrison Keillor, a popular humorist and creator of the fictional town of Lake Wobegone,

MN. Keillor's show is a hit on National Public Radio, which also sells tapes via the Internet. Click and Clack, aka Tom and Ray Magliozzi, weekly tell listeners to call an 800 number, *or* visit the "shameless commerce division of CarTalk.com" for tapes and CDs of "The Best of Car Talk." The Web site is a true example of their irreverent opinions, fun-loving attitude to life, and good automotive advice.

Wireless probably doesn't have enough interested customers who would buy audios on Zen Buddhism. Such a product would be a better fit in catalogs featuring spiritual and religious products.

Publishers who belong to the New Age Publishing and Retailing Alliance (NAPRA) would be a good starting point for the Buddhism audio. The *NAPRA Review* is published every other month, and is chock full of publisher ads. Many of the publishers are probably open to adding religious and spiritually-oriented titles to their own catalogs. After reviewing your product and marketing strategy, a few may want to try your audio.

Catalogs offer different splits on the sale. If your tape sells for $24.95, you might get half of the sales price, or even more. Some catalogs order product, pay for it at a discount, and fill orders from their location. Others take their percentage of the sale price, then forward the rest by check, along with mailing labels. You fill the orders. This second method is called drop shipping.

Smart Practice™ is a company of over 250 employees today. They ship products around the world to health care professionals, including veterinarians, eye-care specialists, chiropractors and physicians. The company began with a simple subscription audio series, recorded by co-founder Naomi Rhode, 25 years ago.

Jim Rhode, president, wrote their catalog copy himself, and kept a close eye on all the details. "One of the best business decisions we ever made wasn't mine. In fact, our staff came up with it on their own. They'd been after me for several years to go four-color, but I thought it was too expensive, and I put it off. Finally, as a new catalog was coming up, they took the initiative. I was presented with a color catalog — ready to go. You can imagine I had mixed emotions, but we went with their version. Sales shot up! I learned two important lessons from that. To trust and delegate more to our wonderful staff, and to print every catalog in color."

Many companies start with modest one-page order forms and a description of products. As sales grow, and their customer lists expand, they invest in more pages, and through agreements with other vendors they add products.

Vermont Audiobooks is an audiobook store on such a growth path.

"When I retired from IBM, I said I wanted to work from home, sell something through mail order, and be computer based. Selling audiobooks on the Internet fit the bill exactly. My wife manages the inventory, and I do the Web site development and marketing.

"So far our Web site has been reasonably successful."

Mail Order and Direct Response

Mail orders can result from advertisements in card decks, co-op mailings, newsletters and mailings to your own customers. You can buy mailing lists through list brokers and mailing houses that are listed in the phone book. Companies that specialize in mailing services will sort, stamp, bag and mail your pieces for you for less than you can do it yourself. As with catalogs, you will need to send out thousands of pieces to get a small percentage return in orders. The more targeted and up to date your list, the better. Lists must be "cleaned" often to stay current, because people change positions, addresses and other information. A good list will not have many "bad addresses" or duplicates.

The best list for you is the one that "pulls" in the orders. Then you can create your own list of customers. They will be the most likely candidates to buy another audio or service later.

Many good books exist as guides to mail-order success. Two of the best resources are *The Complete Direct Marketing Sourcebook* by John Kremer and *More Than You Ever Wanted to Know About Mail Order Advertising* by Herschell Gordon Lewis. Many more are on bookstore and library shelves.

Anyone using tapes to promote their services, or for recruiting people in multi-level marketing, should hold off spending any money on marketing (including tape production) until they have read at least one of Dr. Jeffrey Lant's books. Why? Because Lant writes audio scripts and advertising copy that sells. His talent has made him a very rich man. He's become even richer writing and speaking about how others can imitate his success. He understands what motivates people to buy. Dr. Lant's personality rubs some people the wrong way, but according to everyone I surveyed, his ideas and recommendations do work.

How to Make a Whole Lot More Than $1,000,000, and *The Unabashed Self Promoters Guide*, are two of Lant's popular "how-to" books. See for yourself how a master marketer does direct marketing online, too. Lant and company have an extensive print catalogs and a mall on the Internet.

Direct response sales are made where people pick up the phone and order in response to what they get in the mail, see on TV or hear on the air. The well-known and very successful Anthony Robbins' 12-volume audio program, *Personal Power*, sold via infomercial. The product sells, sells, sells for approximately $180, direct to consumers.

Infomercials are expensive to make — figure $150,000 and up. Very few make real profits. The majority don't last long. This marketing method is a poor choice for low-priced products bought one or two at a time by consumers. If you watch a few infomercials, you'll see the product prices are often over $100. Health and beauty products seem hottest at present. The customers for direct response sales are different than the typical audiobook buyer.

If you believe you have a set of tapes, products or a message with the potential for big profits, you can approach an established infomercial company. If they agree, they'll bring their hard-earned experience and money to the deal. Guthy Renker Corporation is a pioneer and leader in this area. Contact their headquarters in Palm Desert, CA for a copy of their guidelines on submitting your products for infomercial consideration. Or, contact the companies who make the programs you see on TV.

Online Orders

The Net is not going away.

The opening words of the book *Online Marketing* by Jay Conrad Levinson and Carl Rubin make the case: "Success in business means selling – nothing we've seen so far comes close to the potential of the online marketplace."

Their book is a good place to start if you've shied away from going online, or if you're using a commercial online service such as America Online or Compuserve for e-mail, but not much else.

Many publishers have one or more Websites. There are three top general Websites for books and tapes. BookZone is one of them.

Mary Westheimer, of BookZone, explains "We don't consider ourselves a bookstore as much as a catalog. We work for publishers, who hire us to create their presence, then get out of the way when it comes to the transaction. We "capture" the order but do not charge a percentage on sales. People can order directly from the publishers or through us. That's great for publishers, as it helps them to build their mailing lists, but it means that it's harder for us to track sales. As always, though, I must emphasize that sales is not the only value of a Web site. In this, the Gutenberg Age of the Net, we always urge publishers to see it at least equally as an exposure avenue."

Investment in an online presence is a bargain compared to other methods of marketing. I expect by 2005 the Net will have become as much a part of our daily life as copy machines and ATMs.

Surf the pages listed below (and any others recommended by friends) for a crash course in the Web. The following sites are among many informative locations to learn how to navigate, in language we laymen can understand. All begin with the suffix http:// and will work with upper or lower-case names.

www.bookfair.com.	Read the Info pages.
www.ParaPublishing.com	Free stuff, updated lists, links.
www.Bockinfo.com	Clear explanations, online help.
www.AudioPublishers.org	Links to dozens of publishers.
www.wgts.org/audiobooks/	Terry's Audiobooks — don't miss.
www.AudioFile.com	Reviews, updated industry info.
www.BookWire.com	Bestsellers, *Publishers Weekly*.

To look at how publishers show and sell a variety of information and entertainment products online, here are a few sites to get you started.

www.BookZone
www.ReadersNdex
www.Amazon.com
www.Audiobooks.com
www.TatteredCover.com
www.Barnesandnoble.com

Radio, TV, and Print Coverage

Media coverage as part of an overall promotion plan can be effective when you have a newsworthy or controversial subject. Commercial broadcasting needs advertisers, so they look for program ideas and guests to interest a large audience. The producers of talk and interview shows want lively, knowledgeable guests. In other words — you need a "hook" to hang your story on (as in a "hook" to catch channel surfers, and keep them listening).

If you are shy by nature, you will have to assume another persona, or at least put on another hat for marketing. Think of yourself as a coach or neighbor, sharing information. When your plan includes media exposure, you must train yourself to tell listeners how to buy your products.

Hundreds of broadcast producers peruse *Radio-TV Interview Report (RTVIR)* from Bradley Communications for guest ideas. The number of talk shows has increased from 1,000 a few years ago to more than 3,000 in 1996. Consider placing an ad every four to six weeks in RTVIR.

If you aren't getting response and invitations from your efforts, try rewriting your advertising copy. Hire professional public relations or promotion specialists with good references to help you, if necessary. The same applies to the specialized training you may need to handle whatever someone asks on live TV or radio.

I've seen media coaches in action. I think they're worth every cent when they teach you how to deflect unwanted questions, and how to return to your main points. In essence, you learn how to remain in control, rather than giving it up. You're able to make your on-air stint accomplish your goals, and assure the program producers and host are also pleased.

Imagine you've listed yourself on GuestFinder.com, or run an ad in an industry publication. What will you say when a producer from the show of your dreams calls? From a producer's point of view, the potential guestlist calls are "pre-screening." You're on a short list. How you handle the phone interview will determine whether you're invited to be on-air, or the producer moves on down the list.

I have worked inside TV and radio, and produced interview shows. Working with an experienced media coach can help you turn interviews into tens of thousands of dollars in sales. I've pulled the plug on guests who were so nervous, or boring, that we would lose our audience. If you want to make the most of media appearances, use professionals for coaching. If you are nervous, work up to the big markets, gaining experience and confidence first.

Even when you are comfortable with interviews, you cannot control the unexpected. Anyone who can salvage some sales from the following tale, vented in frustration on the Publishers Marketing Association listerve, is a marketing hero. The following is used with permission, and, unfortunately, John McCabe says, it's all true.

"Today I was interviewed for a LIVE BROADCAST on a radio show in New York City. As I was waiting to be interviewed, I heard them introduce the guest before me. Then all of a sudden that guest was connected to my phone line, and not to the radio interviewer, and we were wondering what was going on. We started to converse with each other and were having a good laugh. Then the radio techs figured out their problem and connected him to the show and left me hanging. Then, after the

first interview was over, the host came to me and called me "Rodger" (my name is John), and asked me a question that had nothing to do with me or my book. In a calm way, I told him he must have his interview sheets mixed up. I told him my name. So, I had no formal introduction, and listeners had no idea who I was, or that I wrote a book, or what the name of the book is.

Then the host asks me a question and I am answering it the best I can. And he is silent. So I keep talking. And he is silent (obviously he was trying to figure out what was going on). So I try to keep talking. And he is silent. Finally I didn't know if I was even on the air, so I ask "Gary?" And, after a bit of silence, he says "Yes, I'm here." Then he asks me about how I clear my nasal sinuses. Obviously not a question meant for me. So I tell him that the question must be a question for the next guest. And this is being broadcast LIVE in NEW YORK. Then someone is knocking on my door. Loudly. So I shut the door of the room I am in and the door SLAMS shut. Loudly. Then there is someone making noise next to the wall outside of the room I am in. It is the fix-it man, Mr. Buttcrack. He is here to rebuild the water heater closet that is outside next to the room I am in. Why didn't I know about this? Of course I can't do anything about it now. I am on the radio LIVE in NEW YORK. So he starts pounding apart the water heater closet. Loudly. Meanwhile the neighbor, Miss Iwannaseducesomebody, has decided that Mr. Buttcrack is going to be her target for the day and she is out there trying to strike up a conversation with him and is, with her Australian accent, talking above the noise of his hammer — loudly. And I am hoping the radio listeners in New York can't hear this. Meanwhile the other neighbors' two pit bulls are on my roof — Yes, on the roof — and they are barking at the other neighbors' cats who make a lot of noise scampering across the roof to get away from the pit bulls. And the postal carrier shows up to try to calm the cats down from where they are up in the tree, while the dogs are barking, while the gardner shows up and starts cutting the lawn with the loud lawnmower, while the cable company guys show up and are underneath the house — right under the floor of the room I am in — talking loudly in Spanish to their supervisor who speaks Korean, while the guy on the radio keeps calling me "Rodger" and keeps flubbing his questions, while Mr. Buttcrack is pounding apart the water heater closet as Miss Iwannaseducesomebody with her Australian accent is trying to lure Mr. Buttcrack over for lunch while the pit bulls on the roof are barking and the postal carrier is calling for the cats to come down out of the tree, while I am trying to do this live interview on the radio as my voice is *being broadcast LIVE in NEW YORK, and I forgot I had connected the fax machine to the line I was on and the fax machine turns on all by itself for no reason and makes the SQUEALING FAX NOISE loudly broadcast LIVE to radio listeners in NEW YORK as I scramble to hold the phone and run across the room to turn the fax machine off, as the interviewer finally gets my name right, as the interview ends, and he forgets to mention the name of my book, or my 800 number. As the dogs are barking on the roof and the Korean lady is yelling orders to the Spanish guys under the house as I hear Mr. Buttcrack with his pot belly and tool belt holding his pants at the appropriate slant telling Miss Iwannaseducesomebody that he has electric charm as the postal carrier tries to talk above the sound of the lawnmower as she is calling the cats to come down out of the tree as the pit bulls bark as I am hoping this didn't really happen. *#$@!*

So I try to go to sleep after the interview from hell, but Mr. Buttcrack is making too much noise. And I don't know why, but I swear I am hearing what sounds to be a dozen helicopters hovering in the air and I'm wondering if I really am dreaming. And I turn on the TV but all I get is static because the cable is messed up. So I go outside and am walking on Main Street and I see some friends and we stand and watch the media circus and the large crowds of people gathered outside the Santa Monica Courthouse as they wait for the O.J. verdict to be read as a dozen helicopters hover not too high above our heads.

Then, after the verdict is read, and most of the people are cheering, this brisk TV newsguy, Mr. Hairspray, comes up to me and grabs my arm and asks me if I want to be interviewed by Miss Boufanthairdo LIVE on the air to tell my feelings about the O.J. verdict. And I look at him and say, "No." Then, remembering my day, I turn back to him and say, "Not only NO, but HELL NO!"

If he only knew.

John McCabe (NOT Rodger)
Author of *Surgery Electives: What to Know Before the Doctor Operates*
(thejmccabe@aol.com)"

If that discourages you from ever being on the air, what about print media? Directories, updated yearly, are expensive to purchase. Before you buy, see what your local library has to offer. They're likely to have a copy of *Editors and Publishers Yearbook* and *Standard Rates and Data.*

When you approach newspapers, heed this insider's advice:

Getting free publicity for your product in the form of a news story is as much a matter of patience and polite persistence as it is luck. The first rule for approaching a newspaper for a story is to know the paper. Read it. Make a note of bylines, sections, and get an idea of who covers what before you make your pitch. Nothing turns an editor or reporter off more than a person who calls pitching a story who freely admits he or she doesn't read the paper or know the difference between the lifestyles and the sports sections. Sound stupid? It is, but such gaffes happen frequently.

Don't limit yourself to one idea for pitching your story. Read the business section, note whether stories are covered that might include an angle for your business. Locally made products — whether toys, tapes or transportation are often featured. Don't expect an instant, large, front-page feature. Judgements made by reporters and editors often have to do as much with how they are feeling that day as they do with other news competing for space.

Watch for national trends that might dovetail your tapes into a lifestyles or arts and entertainment story. The subjects featured on your tapes might make a lifestyles or religion page story on say, America's search for spirituality. Your recording process might be part of a story on local studios. While you may not be always featured prominently and may be included as part of a larger package, it's one way of getting your name out to the public and it costs you nothing but time and some effort.

Study local columns in different sections of the paper. Often a business or name will be included in a column about changes (promotions, relocations, expansions, contracts) in the business community. Getting a mention typically involves nothing more than a phone call or writing a short press release and sending it to the person responsible for the column.

The best way to approach a reporter or editor once you think you have a story idea regarding your audio cassette is to write a straightforward, one-page press release and send it to them. Minimize the hype. No balloons, baskets or gimmicks, although a small sample of what you're promoting can be appropriate. Make sure all the details, including your name and a phone number (numbers) where you can be reached during the day are included. Basic facts such as a phone number seem obvious, but they often are overlooked. Follow the press release with a polite phone call a week or so after you've sent the release. Try to drop a personal reference into your conversation regarding a previous story the reporter has written. Mild flattery never hurts — journalists enjoy ego strokes as much as the next person, perhaps more — and it shows you've done your homework. If you're turned down keep persisting politely — perhaps a phone call once a month — if only to remind them that you're still available if they change their mind or if a new angle occurs to them or you.

Justin Mitchell, newspaper editor

Give-Aways

Tapes marketing other aspects of your business can also pay off. Whether paid for or free, it's in your best interests to keep a record of all tapes shipped so you can:

- Follow-up for future business opportunities.
- Track your domestic and foreign sales.
- Know when to reorder from duplicators and package vendors.
- Check your units shipped against units paid for.

Although millions of tapes a year are duplicated for multi-level marketing and motivation purposes, tapes are used by hundreds of other businesses for a wide array of promotional uses.

Insurance sales specialists send audio business cards to introduce themselves before they phone. Barrett, an employee staffing and leasing company with 40 offices in eight states, gives away a free tape called *Outsourcing*. They want to help potential customers understand the value and benefits of using Barrett employees. *Investors Business Daily* sends an audio cassette free with every two-week trial subscription to the newspaper. A non-profit agency made a tape they hand to prospective foster parents, so people will make informed choices about opening their home to children who may only stay a short time.

The Human Factor

Why do some publishers sell $1,000,000 worth of audio tapes a year, and apparently equivalent publishers barely cover their costs?

A new employee in our company asked that question in 1994, after she observed four speakers selling vastly different quantities of audio products.

All were knowledgeable, and skilled on the platform. We concluded each had valuable audio product content, with equal production and sound quality. (I knew that to be true.) In addition, they had very low return or failure rates on their audio products.

Other commonalties were: the same audiences, similar fee ranges, product prices at roughly $10-$12 for a single tape to $40 for a four-pack. Gender, background, age and topics were also ruled out as determinants.

Now, years later, I am still fascinated by the continuing disparity in sales for these four speaker/publishers. I believe the single most important factor in distinguishing who sells and who doesn't is the attitude of the publisher — the personality and values behind the imprint. Let's take a look at what distinguishes these four independent audio publishers in the metal health field. (The individuals described below are all based on real people. Names were changed to protect their privacy and confidentiality.)

Publisher A, Alan, sells $250,000 yearly in audio products through back-of-the-room sales and mail/phone order from catalogs. Lately he has added bookstores and libraries, and started courting broadcast interviews. I expect he'll continue to grow his audio division by 20 percent a year for the foreseeable future.

"The pass-along and word-of-mouth factor has generated the best profits at a lower cost per sale for us. We are mindful about shipping products to speaking locations or selling through bookstores," Alan observes. "Back-of-the-room sales require staffing the table. You have to hire a temp, pay transportation and lodging for a staff member, or split the profit with the organization sponsoring the presentation. After the speech, our office must ship any leftover products to another speaking location or back home. By the time products are returned to inventory, some units have been lost or damaged."

"I look at everything we do with our information as part of our publishing business. The decision not to take a lot of product on the road and sell BOR is new. We analyzed our cost per sale for a typical quarter, and adjusted it upward for the new, higher shipping costs. Turns out what used to make sense doesn't anymore. So, we sell fewer on site, and more by phone and fax orders these days.

"Our first couple of tapes were just to help people who really needed to go back over the information a number of times, depending on where they were at. I made them with a home recorder and microphone because people kept asking me for tapes.

"Today we have a full-time marketing person who does a great job on the phone with reviewers, distributors, and broadcast producers. We've use four-color printing in our catalogs, and always subcontract out the design work. Our overhead is higher, but our sales have gone up substantially. We've repackaged and given new titles to quality products we believed in, but were slow movers."

Publisher B, Susan, sells close to $12,000 a year, almost entirely through catalogs, and will probably double that in 1998 because one of her three products was picked up in two more catalogs.

She believes it is not nice to sell, and considers it unprofessional. She doesn't tell audiences she has products. She has chosen not to add staff to create handouts, handle orders for products, or take care of shipping. Susan is fully aware her decisions are costing her sales. She doesn't want to talk about it, and is happy with her choices. Her income is sufficient for her needs; therefore money and greater exposure are not important enough motivators for her to reconsider.

Publisher C's values also influenced his sales. Todd sold about $4,000 in 1995. I predict he will sell $45,000 worth of audios in 1997. Audiences want to buy because of his clever titles and dramatic platform presentations. He has a gift for teaching adults, and he's worked to make his presentations connect powerfully with individuals. Todd does *no marketing*. His presentations are so strong they sell both him and his products, on the spot. He is a master at selling from the platform without being offensive.

Although Todd's first product has been out for four years, he was sidetracked with health problems. By cutting the "C-level" priorities in his life to a minimum, he was able to meet existing bookings, recover his health, and spend more time with his family. "Now I'm in a better place to tap the income potential from back-of-the-room sales. I believe I can substantially shift my income stream over the next five years from one mode of delivery — speaking — to offering access to what I teach through products. I'll make more audio tapes, a video, do another book, and may do some consulting. I've had offers, and it beats traveling in bad weather. My goal is keeping my health and making the transition to a less hectic lifestyle."

Publisher D, Janet, has the greatest potential for sales increase. In 1994 her company averaged about $200,000 in audio sales from half a dozen products. I anticipate during 1998 she will more than double that figure. Why will Janet probably see the biggest gain?

She enjoys all phases of information delivery and marketing: the platform, promotional tours for books, TV and radio call-ins, and interviews. Her enthusiasm and convictions are infectious. She has a passion people respond to.

She is flexible, working with established publishers and self publishing, depending on the products and what fits company goals. As a policy, based on advice from Dan Poynter, author of *The Self Publishing Manual*, she's kept all electronic rights. This has proven a profitable decision already.

While she likes to bank checks as much as the next person, Janet sees profits as the means to expand the business and have more to share with others. She runs the numbers and knows where her income is generated. New products are designed to meet what customers tell her they want — not what she thinks they should have.

She tells everyone who may be interested about her business and products. A commitment to serving the customer makes it possible for her to self-promote, confidently and comfortably. Janet's basic attitude to life is upbeat and open. Financial gain, health, family, and work are balanced in her day-to-day life. I expect her company to enjoy a steady sales increase from continuing word-of-mouth advertising.

Many of the publishers mentioned in this chapter also sell through booksellers, and to libraries. That's the focus of the next chapter.

●●●●●●●●●
Resources:

Amazon.com, www.Amazon.com

Audio Editions, Grady Hesters,1133 High Street, Auburn, CA 95603, and Audio Partners Publishing Corporation, Linda Olsen, 1133 High Street, P.O. Box 6930, Auburn, CA 95604, 916-888-7803, Fax: 916-888-7805, e-mail: BOOKAUDIO@aol.com

Books on Tape™, Inc., P.O. Box 7900, Newport Beach, CA 92658, Orders: 800-626-333, 714-548-5525, Fax: 714-548-6574, e-mail: botcs@booksontape.com, www.booksontape.com

Cathcart Institute, Jim Cathcart, P.O. Box 9075, La Jolla, CA 92038, 619-456-3813, 800-222-4883, Fax: 619-456-7218, e-mail: JECathcart@aol.com, www.cathcart.com

Columbia House AudioBook Club, 1221 Avenue of The Americas, 17th Floor, New York, NY 10020

The Complete Guide to Direct Marketing, *(Open Horizons Publishing) and 1001 Ways To Market Your Books* (5th edition, pub date 9/97), John Kremer, Open Horizons Publishing, P.O. Box 205, Fairfield, IA 52556, 515-472-6130, Fax: 515-472-1560, e-mail: johnkremer@bookmarket.com, www.bookmarket.com

Direct Marketing Association, 6 East 43rd St., New York, NY 10017

Editor & Publisher Publications, 11 West 19th Street, New York, NY

Mike Frank, *For Professional Speakers Only,* Speakers Unlimited (bureau), P.O. Box 27225, Columbus, OH 43227, 614-864-3703

Guerrilla Marketing Online, Jay Conrad Levinson and Charles Rubin, Guerrilla Marketing International, P.O. Box 1336, Mill Valley, CA 94942, 800-748-6444; Guerrilla Marketing Online Strategies

Guestfinder, online media guest service, www.guestfinder.com

Guthy-Renker Corporation, informercials, 41-550 Eclectic, Palm Desert, CA 92260

Jimmy B's Audiobooks, 5225 W. Rosecrans Ave., Hawthorne, CA 90250-6621, 310-643-7640, jimmyb@audiobooks.com

Knowledge Products, Shirley Cantrell, P.O. Box 305151, Nashville, TN, 37230, orders 800-264-6441, 615-742-3852, Fax: 615-742-3270, crom@edge.net

Jeffrey Lant Associates, Dr. Jeffrey Lant, P.O. Box 38-2767 Cambridge, MA 02238, www.worldprofit

Terri Lonier, *Working Solo®,* P.O. Box 190, New Paltz, NY 12561, 800-222-SOLO, Fax: 914-255-2116, e-mail: Lonier@workingsolo.com, www.workingsolo.com

Midwest Book Review, James A. Cox, Editor-in-Chief, Diane C. Donovan, Editor, 278 Orchard Drive, Oregon, WI 53575, www.execpc.com/~mbr/bookwatch

Justin Mitchell, journalist/editor, c/o AudioCP Publishing, 1660 S. Albion, #309, Denver, CO 80222

More Than You Ever Wanted To Know About Mail Order Advertising, Herschell Gordon Lewis, Prentice-Hall, Inc., ISBN 0-13-601039-3

NAPRA (New Age Publishing & Retailing Alliance), P.O. Box 9, Eastsound, WA 98245-0009, 360-376-2702, Fax: 360-376-2704, e-mail: napra@bookwire.com, www.napra.com

National Speakers Association, 1500 S. Priest Drive, Tempe, AZ 85281, 602-968-2252, Fax: 602-968-0911, www.nsaspeaker.org

Para Publishing, *The Self Publishing Manual,* ISBN 1-56860-018-6, Daniel F. Poynter, ninth edition, P.O. Box 8206, Santa Barbara, CA 93118-8206, Order line: 1-800-PARAPUB, Free info kit: 805-968-7277, Fax: 805-968-1379, Fax-on-demand: 805-968-8947 (some free documents), www.parapublishing.com

Personal Power, Anthony Robbins, c/o Audio Renaissance, Los Angeles, CA

The Publishing Mills, Jessica Kaye, President, 9220 Sunset Blvd., Suite 302, Los Angeles, CA, 90069, 310-858-5385, Fax: 310-858-5391, e-mail: editor@pubmills.com

Radio/TV Interview Report, Bradley Communications, Landsowne, PA

ReadersIndex.com, www.ReadersIndex.com

SmartPractice™, Jim and Naomi Rhode, 3400 E. McDowell, Phoenix, AZ 85008-7899, 602-225-9090, Fax: 602-225-0245, www.smartpractice.com

Sounds True Audio, Jay Zwicky, Mkg. Mgr., 4135 Aurthur Ave., Louisville, CO 80027, 303-665-3151, Fax: 303-665-5292, e-mail: soundstrue@aol.com, www.puzzlergulch.com/ Sounds_True

Vermont AudioBooks, RR1, Box 60, Richmond, VT 05477, 800-639-1862, e-mail: vtaudio@together.net

Lilly & Dottie Walters,*Speak and Grow Rich,* P.O. Box 1120 Glendora CA 91740, PO Box 1120, Glendora, CA 91740, 818-335-8069, Fax: 818-335-6127, e-mail: Call4Sprkr@aol.com

Wireless catalog, P.O. Box 64422, St. Paul, MN 55164 -0422

Selling to Bookstores and Libraries

Do you dream of seeing your books and tapes on bookstore shelves? Or in libraries all around the world? I hope so. The first step to making a dream come true is being able to define what that dream will feel, look, and be like.

Many publishers have bookstore sales as their goal, and for some this will be a profitable route. Library sales are a better route, because of differences in the way these two large marketplaces buy products. Libraries rarely return books and audiobooks. They do not require such substantial discounts before they'll buy.

Whatever is written today may be outdated in three months, so this chapter is brief and general. I urge you to read journals, articles and several of the most recent editions of the good books available about book promotion and sales. These people are the real experts.

If you are just beginning your publishing venture, you will find hundreds of publishers of all sizes contributing to online discussions.

Reaching Booksellers

Audiobooks are marketed similarly to print books. We covered this briefly in Chapter 2. The distribution chain and review system are the same, although on a smaller scale.

Reaching booksellers is a non-issue for authors who've contracted with other publishers to develop the audio. In such cases, the author's job is to do appearances and cooperate with their publisher's marketing efforts. The comments that follow are for those of you who will market your own products.

Titles for a mass audience should go to national reviewers four to six months before the "pub date." When you are publishing in print, and simultaneously in audio, make sure your press releases highlight an audio option. Headphone clip art is available over the Net and in commercial collections of "click art" on CDs. Use the symbol for easy recognition on fliers and announcements for your title.

A good review will spur booksellers' and librarians' interest. Because of the backlog of tapes to review, most audiobooks that make it to the "A" pile will lag several months before reviews appear in print. In addition to *Publishers Weekly, Library Journal, Booklist, Kliatt, Billboard,* and *AudioFile,* there are dozens of other publications that may review audiobooks. Think of specialty publications in your subject area. Read recent issues. Mail to the appropriate columnist or reviewer, using the address in the publication. Follow up in two weeks by phone, fax or e-mail to be sure your tape arrived. Many publishers include a stamped post card or fax back form, asking the addressee to indicate whether the tape will or won't be reviewed.

If you're looking for insight into what titles the major houses have in production, visit www.audiobooks.com. Upcoming titles from major audiobook publishers are listed in the section called "In the Studio." I made the mistake of printing the list once, and went through more than 20 legal-sized pages for three months' forthcoming titles.

When you sell to booksellers, they expect to purchase at 20 percent to 50 percent off the retail price. There's little incentive for retailers unless they have enough mark-up to stay in business and make a profit.

Distributors Specialize

A distributor is essential for maximum nationwide marketing to retail stores. Buyers for chain stores, discount membership warehouses, and major library systems are inundated with requests to review and purchase titles. The scope of a buyer's job forces her or him to limit the number of products they can listen to. Distributors who've established relationships with buyers, and who have provided strong-selling titles in the past, will have an easier time reaching decision makers.

Distributors are independent businesses with different policies. Many publishers work with one retail distributor, and a second distributor for libraries. If you go this route, booksellers and libraries can order from your distributor, and you can refer all inquiries.

Some distributors specialize in audio products. Penton Overseas has evolved from a publisher of language tapes to much more. They now represent dozens of small publishers to the book trade. Professional Media Services, ReZound, and others offer similar services.

Once again, I strongly suggest buying a copy of *AudioFile's* annual *Audiobook Reference Guide*. Use the order form in the back of this book. Complete distributor and wholesaler information is in the *Reference Guide*. Contact the distributors who seem most suited to your title. Follow their submission procedures. Read their terms carefully.

When a distributor responds positively, don't sign whatever they send just because you're excited they said "yes". Many distributors have floundered in recent months. Distributors' performance and financial stability has been a regular topic on listservs. Some have gone bankrupt, and publishers were left unpaid. Investigate before you sign. If the company is sound, they'll still be there next week, willing to handle your products because they believe your titles will sell. And remember — everything is negotiable.

Wholesalers

Wholesalers and distributors cover many of the same functions. You may want to work with a wholesaler, or more than one, in addition to your distributor. Or, you may decide to use only one "master distributor" who will be your exclusive representative to the book trade. Ingram Audio and Baker & Taylor are the largest wholesalers of books and audiobooks. There are a number of small companies. If you have a regional title, look for a regional wholesaler.

The Problem of Returns

One of the quickest ways to go out of business, is to fill a big order and then see the product come back. Many booksellers currently order on terms that are similar to consignment. They want the product on their shelves — as many as one or two copies per superstore or location. They just don't want to pay for them until they're sold. Since audio products sell best when the staff is enthused and can comment or recommend titles, the huge store approach to merchandising works against new audio publishers.

You must know how much loss and risk you are comfortable with. Remember, your cassettes and CDs will compete with hundreds of other titles on the shelves. Don't mortgage the house for the brief thrill of seeing your tapes shelved beside your favorite best-selling authors.

Years ago, booksellers bought books at a discount and resold them at retail. Today they can stock their stores with primarily free merchandise, and pay after they ring up a sale. Your wholesaler or distributor accepts returns, and sends the damaged goods back to you, or takes a credit against your account. Wholesalers and distributors add in some delay before they pass on your percentage. When you have a fast-selling title, this may be acceptable. If your product doesn't fly out the door, you can be thousands of dollars out of pocket.

Organizations like the Audio Publishers Association were formed because marketing and promotion are more cost-effective when publishers pool their resources. Co-operative mailing campaigns are low risk, low cost, and sometimes the most realistic way to reach booksellers. Publishers who participate in co-op mailings should always include their distributors and wholesalers on fliers so booksellers have the option to order through easy, familiar channels.

When you sell directly to booksellers, libraries and organizations offer them set discounts. Decide what is acceptable by reviewing what other publishers do. Then establish your terms and conditions, *and stick to them.* You can require all or part payment from wholesalers and distributors when they order your products. Your volume will be compromised, but the peace of mind may be worth it. Books on self publishing explain discounts and "T & C's" in detail.

How the Publishing World is Changing

Major publishing houses are corporate entities, being bought and sold like many other corporations today. At present they are willing to go along with the consignment approach to book selling. Until they change their policies, the rest of the industry — especially the much lower dollar volume small publishers — will be stuck with the present practice.

Audio Bookstores

A number of entrepreneurial audiobook lovers have wondered about opening their own audio bookstores. There are many already operating around the country. Some are small single owner stores. A few are larger, with multiple locations. Most rent as well as sell titles.

"We've been at this for nine years," says Jimmy Belsen, owner of Jimmy B's Audiobooks in Hawthorne, CA. "Everything moves. We don't have it in the store unless it moves. It's taken us a few years to get everything working smoothly, but now we have a very good business with lots of customers who come in regularly. We get to know them, and notify them when a new book comes in that we think they'll like. There's a lot of personal selling. We always recommend audiobooks based on what each customer likes, not our own personal preferences."

When I visited his store at the foot of Pacific Palisades, in the south coastal Los Angeles area, Belsen was involved in a massive update of his online catalog pages, at www.audiobooks.com.

Paul Rush, owner of the Earful Of Books chain or audiobook stores says "Audiobook merchandising is entirely different from book merchandising. An audio store is more like a video store. We merchandise with a heavy emphasis on new releases. Visuals are very important. Most of our titles are face out, for example."

"Bread and butter customers are regular users and they come in at least once a week, sometimes more. Our customers are tremendous readers. They don't have time to read all they'd like. That's why they're listening," Rush adds.

Belsen agrees. He displays *Publishers Weekly* bestseller lists prominently in their store windows. Customers want to know what's "hot." He pointed out how many titles are now available in audio. Most of the 15 showed headphones, and four came on CDs or cassettes.

"CDs are coming. They show up now about as often as audiobooks did a few years back, when we began posting this list every week." Belsen thinks CDs could be dominant nationwide within five years.

Frank Johnson, Jr., of Audio Diversions, located in McLean, VA, also sees strong interest in CDs. "Customers ask for discs, and more titles are being produced in both formats." The biggest negative, all three agree, is so many users can't "bookmark" a CD. Listeners can't rewind and replay easily. This is a real handicap for language courses, Rush points out.

If your subject is of regional interest, contact local stores directly. Be sure you have prepared a telephone pitch that clearly describes your title and how it can benefit the store before you call. Be courteous, businesslike, and respectful of their time. Sometimes what sounds like a brush-off or the run-around is not. Expect to continue contacting someone, courteously and professionally, if necessary. If you make it easy for the buyer to give you a straight answer, he may decide to give your products a try.

Rush's criteria for a regional title is based on how the title is merchandised, and the story. "We have to really believe in a regional title. *Texas Bound* is a collection of Texas stories read by Texas readers. It's won awards, and does well in our Lonestar state (TX) stores."

The Library Market

"Sometimes I wish a few of our audios would wear out sooner so we could buy more. They circulate 300-400 times before they wear out." says Carol King, audio acquisitions specialist for the Denver Public Library system. Yes, you read right. Up to 400 times. That's why you won't find much left on the shelves by the time you get to the local library at four PM on Saturday. While some librarians would disagree, saying the "circs" per audiobook are under 100 x, all agree audiobook budgets cannot keep up with demand.

Sally Gilson of the Winnefox Library System in Oshkosh, WI has worked with other area librarians to form an "Audio Books Circuit . . . as a way for very small libraries to offer a greater variety of audiobooks than they could afford to purchase on their own. More, more, more say the audiobooks listeners."

Growth in the library market has also meant growth in distributors and leasing companies who serve the libraries. Companies like Taped Editions make it easy for librarians by offering quick tape replacements, repackaging to suit, and all the preparation so an audience can go straight onto shelves.

The libraries order a regular quantity of audio titles, say 25 new books a quarter, and the leasing company ships an assortment to fit their requests. The library returns all the tapes that are no longer circulating, in exchange for the new titles.

Audio usage is accelerating. Continued growth will depend on word of mouth advertising for media coverage, and quality products developed with an understanding of what the marketplace will buy.

In chapter 14 we'll see how the delivery systems for those audios may change in the future.

●●●●●●●●●
Resources:

AlBert's AudioBooks, 5015 Cornell Road, Unit F, Agoura Hills, CA 91301, 818-889-7492, Fax: 818-889-5983, e-mail: AMY516@aol.com, www.audiobooks.com/retailers/alberts/home

Audio Diversions, audiobook retailer & online catalog, Frank Johnson, Jr., 6639 Madison-McLean Drive, McLean, VA 22101, www.idsonline.com/audiodiversions

AudioFile magazine, the annual *AudioFile Reference Guide,* and *AudioBooks On the Go,* Robin Whitten, editor and publisher, P.O. Box 109, Portland, ME, 04112, 207-775-3744, Fax: 207-775-3744, orders 1-800-506-1212

Baker & Taylor Books, 2709 Water Ridge Parkway, Charlotte, NC 28217, 800-775-1800, Fax: 704-329-8989, www.baker-taylor.com, e-mail: btinfo@baker-taylor.e-mail.com

Ingram Book Co., Ingram Audio, 1 Ingram Boulevard, La Vergne, TN 37086, www.ingrambook.com, 800-937-8200

Jimmy B's Audiobooks, 5225 W. Rosecrans Ave., Hawthorne, CA 90250-6621, 310-643-7640, jimmyb@audiobooks.com

Media Books, publisher, 560 Sylvan Ave., Englewood Cliffs, NJ 07632, 201-894-8550, Fax: 201-894-1831. Carmen LaRosa, VP and general manager at sales and marketing office, 536 Lawrence St., Port Townsend, WA 98368, 360-379-3009, 3013. E-mail: CarmenLa@localnet.com

Penton Overseas, Inc. long established publishers of language tapes, distributor, Hugh Penton or Jean Gonzales, 2470 Impala Drive, Carlsbad, CA 92008-7226

Professional Media Service Corporation, distributor, 19122 South Vermont Ave., Gardena, CA 90248, 800-223-7672, Fax: 800-253-8853, e-mail: Promedia@class.org

Publishers Weekly, 249 W. 17th St., N.Y., NY 10011, 800-278-2991

Quality Books, Inc., library distributor, 1003 W. Pines Road, Oregon, IL 61061-9680, 800-323-4241

Fast Forward to the Future

Profitable audio publishing is nearly always based on more than one title. As you gain experience, you'll naturally evaluate what went well, and what didn't happen as you originally planned. Who bought your tapes? How did they buy? Where were your marketing assumptions correct, and where were you off base?

Are there supplier problems to solve before you start another audio project? Do you have questions to go over now, before you come up against new deadlines and larger orders? Will the production people you want on the project be available when you need them?

If you opted for a simple production on your first project, is the same script style and format appropriate for your next audio? Will part of planning for the future include using your master tapes on a CD-ROM format, or marketing online? What will you have to do differently?

Most of these are questions only you can answer. However, there are other questions you can't answer, because they involve new technology. This chapter indulges in a bit of crystal-ball gazing, with comments from people who work with cutting-edge digital audio.

Will CDs Take Over?

The stance taken by duplicators and marketers of spoken audio, for now, is to stick with cassettes, while keeping very close track of sales and trends reported in the trade. When popular tastes for music switched to CDs a few years ago, the change came swiftly.

A minority of customers currently request spoken word CDs. At the time this is being written, their choices are limited. Major publishers are providing more titles on CDs as demand increases. The time frame for CDs to overtake the audio cassette is at least three years, or until after the turn of the century. I suspect different technology will replace audio CDs long before consumers will give up low-cost, easily accessible and convenient cassettes.

Ellie Remar Bouchard, a manufacturer's representative, has worked within the audio and video duplication business for many years. She hears both sides. Bouchard knows all the suppliers. She knows how excited many friends are about new technology. And, as an expert in sales, she also understands and watches consumers.

"It doesn't matter how much media coverage there is, or how great CDs and Digital Versatile Discs (DVDs) are. If the customer can't see enough reason to switch from cassettes, there won't be a big move to CDs. Cassettes are inexpensive, convenient — and everyone has the means to play them already. From the consumers' point of view, cassettes are a good product, so why would they change?"

And, Remar Bouchard notes, cassettes are an international format.

CDs indisputably sound better when played under quiet conditions. Road noise, radial tires, other conversation, and attention to driving reduce the advantages of CDs. While many cars priced over $30,000 have CD players in them, the percentage of vans and sport utility vehicles being manufactured with CD players dropped in 1996. (Adapters can hook up portable CD players to cassette decks.)

The Buzz About DVD

Digital video disks (DVDs), also known as digital versatile disks, are heralded as a great new technology that will supplant other delivery systems for video, movies, and software.

The major advantage of DVD is its storage capacity. One DVD disk has enough capacity to playback a full-length movie, so 90 percent of Hollywood's output could be sold on DVD. Retailers like the format, because it attracts consumers into their stores. Picture and sound quality are excellent. Software manufacturers can create even larger programs when they're delivered on DVD.

DVDs look like just CD-ROMs, with a gold instead of silver colored aluminum coating. The disks are made with two to four ultra-thin layers for greater capacity. The tiny pits pressed into blank plastic discs are even smaller than on a conventional CD, further increasing the capacity for 1's and 0's that can be read by lasers. Pits on a DVD disk are about 1/38th of a micron. By comparison, a human hair is 40 microns in diameter, on average, according to Terry O'Kelly of Kodak.

The drawbacks for spoken word on DVD are:

• DVD is so new that there are few players in homes yet.

• Reading DVD requires a new machine, at hundreds of dollars for a cumbersome, *non-portable* player the size of a VCR.

• Some, but not all, computers that read CDs are able to read DVDs.

• You can't record onto DVD (at this time).

• It appears DVD will be confined to software and movies for the foreseeable future, or until the music industry switches from Audio CDs.

• DVD production costs, at about $100 thousand in production, and $6 a disc to replicate per thousand mean it's priced out of consideration for publishers unless it becomes a mass audio format.

If, or when, either CDs or DVDs sweeps the spoken word market, existing programs can be converted from analog or digital masters with relative ease. Publishers who wait for CDs or DVD, and disparage the lowly cassette, risk losing years of potential sales in the interim.

In-House Digital Production

Creating and editing your own audio products is becoming a more realistic option every year. Software prices are dropping and computers are increasingly more powerful. Inexpensive storage devices that hold a gigabyte or more of information make it possible to work with memory-hogging audio files, without having to break them into smaller pieces. Many programs exist for Windows-based and Macintosh computers. Most were created for musicians or video editing.

I debated bringing our editing in-house and decided against it. There's an intangible value from collaborating with highly skilled computer editors. We create better products working together.

The two software product lines I see in professional studios are from Digidesign (part of Avid technologies) and Sonic Solutions. Both companies sell a range of products priced according to features. The investment can make sense. You won't find much of a selection in most computer stores or consumer catalogs. Too often, I've found, undertrained salespeople in computer stores want to steer you to off-the-shelf programs, without comprehension of the challenges spoken word editors face. Buy a tool designed specifically for the job.

You'll find more knowledgeable assistance, as well as competitive prices, from EAR Audio in Phoenix, AZ, or similar studio outfitters. EAR is one of a number of *professional* equipment suppliers. To find one in your area call or e-mail Digidesign or Sonic Solutions. They know the local vendors. Basic software starts at about $800. (Digidesign's *Pro-tools* for the Mac is called *Session* for Windows.)

The software's selling price is less of a consideration than the learning curve involved. Do you have the time to learn an audio editing program thoroughly? Is this the best use of your time? Is there someone in your organization with the aptitude and passion necessary for long, tedious sessions at the computer monitor? If so, will that individual stay on your payroll once they've reached a high level of proficiency? Do you have those "golden ears" studio people sometimes refer to? Do you have a highly trained ability to hear subtle sound differences, then make exactly the edit for the best possible sound? That's what distinguishes truly well-made products.

The Web is Changing Everything

Sound delivery and processing is already widely used, listened to, and available on the Internet. As modems become faster, and more people use simple internet access through their TVs, the Web will take on more importance.

•Three examples, of the dozens of software manufacturers, are:

> Real Audio: http://www.prognet.com (Progressive Networks)
> Voxware™: http://www.voxware.com (compression, voice
>   processing software)
> Liquid Audio: http://www.liquidaudio.com (primarily for music)

How else will audio be different in the future? Here are some comments from people who work with the Net daily.

• Patrick D'Arcy, an enthusiastic San Diego-area application developer, uses Real Audio software to "stream" programs to listeners over the Internet. The files play continuously. D'Arcy explains, "It's like pulling a chain through a hole one link at a time." This is an advantage, he says, over sound wave files that must be downloaded. Such files require more transmission time and hard drive space. "That's not necessary with Real Audio technology," says D'Arcy.

"There are over 1,500 radio broadcasters already online. Spoken word through the Internet has a potential audience of over five million people by best estimate (as of late 1996). That's one application for the software. The other use is 'corporate radio,' sort of a secure internal computer-based intercom system. Fed Ex, Sun Micro Systems, and Intel, do internal radio broadcasts. The best news is, Internet Explorer and Netscape have Real Audio as a free download (it's imbedded in Explorer)," D'Arcy adds.

"Listen to an audio clip and decide for yourself. Evaluate RealAudio on many audio publisher sites, or at www.netseminar.com."

• John Gibson, of EAR Audio, believes we will see many companies providing audio programs directly to customers with multicasting. They'll bypass the retail distribution chain, printed catalogs and on-site sales, and deliver products directly to clients and customers. The major attractions to Net delivery will be convenience and economy.

Programs will be prepaid, using credit cards or electronic funds transfers. After payment, customers receive a code. They access and use the programs at their convenience. The technology and delivery means are already in place. Gibson says and, "we ain't seen nothin' yet."

- A Cupertino, CA company, Audio Highway, markets a device called "Listen Up." The remote-control sized unit fits into a docking station. Using their software you can program a computer to surf the Net during the wee hours of the morning, pulling down and recording only what you choose to hear. In the morning you pluck the unit from the docking station. As you go about your day you can listen to up to an hour of investment news, magazine summaries, or audiobooks, stored in the digital memory chip. A plug-in adapter for your present car radio/cassette unit lets you use your existing playback system, or use batteries. President Nathan Schulhof says units with three hours of digital memory (enough for most abridged audiobooks) will be on the market by 1998.

Recycling Will Be Big

Ali Lotfi, of Lacerta Group Inc., and Douglas Booth from Intermedia Video Products presented a workshop in June 1997 for duplicating and replicating executives. Publishers in audio publishing could be affcctcd by changes looming for cassette products.

Lacerta, Lofti explained, recycles audio and video cassettes by grinding them up and separating the molecules chemically. The components can be reformulated in other products. He and his brother operate a pilot plant jointly with DuPont in Richmond, VA, processing magnetic media. According to Lotfi less than one percent of video tapes, and fewer audio tapes, are recycled. Most magnetic media goes to landfills. The problem right around the corner is two fold. 1) Approximately 20,000 landfills in 1972 have declined to only 2,100 expected to be operating by the year 2000. We've run out of space. We must recycle more than the current two percent of all the plastics consumed in the US. 2) The cost of raw materials, combined with dropping retail prices for multimedia products, will force manufacturers to look for lower cost components. Recycled plastics and polyester appear to be economically viable using the process now being tested by Lacerta/ DuPont.

"In the future only those industrial organizations which have a workable strategic plan for properly managing their waste can achieve or maintain both long-term commercial viability and a distinct competitive advantage," Lotfi concluded.

Douglas Booth, of Intermedia Video Products, is heavily involved in recycling tape units, without destroying or substantially changing to the cassettes. Intermedia serves Hollywood studios and large corporate clients, primarily for VHS video. (There are tax breaks for recycling unsold products, preview tapes and defective product.)

Intermedia completely erases the magnetic signals on all tapes, strips the labels off, eliminates any identifying markings, cleans the shells, tests, sorts and reboxes the tapes. Most are sold back to duplicators in large lots, at 20-25 percent lower unit cost than virgin cassettes. Completely erased and clean recycled cassettes can be reused with no appreciable difference in the product quality.

Booth cautions there is a big difference between "recycled" and "cheap". Reputable companies like Intermedia are genuine recyclers. Vendors who, with cash in hand, buy up tapes for resale, without erasing and stripping identifying markings, can and do sell at rock bottom prices to duplicators.

"If the price is very low the tapes often have not been degaussed (erased), so you could end up with someone else's program bleeding through onto yours, or worse. You don't want *Debbie Does Dallas*, or similar X-rated content, to show up after your credits on the end of a tape," Booth told the audience. "It's buyer beware when dealing with used tape brokers."

At present audio publishers needn't wonder what program could have "lived" on their tapes in an early incarnation. Bin-loop and digital bin duplications use fresh tape stock and new shells. That could change fairly quickly in the future.

Conservation of our resources is not an "if" question. It's a "when?"

A Last Word

Future editions of this book will be revised based on feedback from readers. Please tell us what you found helpful — or what you didn't find covered, and wish you had — in *Words On Tape: How to Create Profitable Spoken Word Audio on Cassettes and CDs.*

E-mail your comments to HowToAudio@aol.com, or fax us at to 303-751-5655. We want to hear from you.

Best wishes for great success and satisfaction in audio publishing.

●●●●●●●●●
Resources:

Audio Highway, Nathan Schulhof, 20600 Mariani Ave., Cupertino, CA 95014, www.audiohwy.com

Avid Technologies, Digidesign editing software, Paul Foeckler, 200 East 5th Ave., Suite 341, Naperville, IL 60563

Patrick D'Arcy, www.netseminar.com

Digital United, CDs and DVD, Mark Magel, Croton On Hudson, NY 10520

EAR Professional Audio/Video, John Gibson, 2641 E. McDowell Road, Phoenix, AZ 85008, 602-267-0600, Fax: 602-275-3277, e-mail: info@ear.net, www.ear.net

ITA, The International Recording Media Assoc., Charles Van Horn, exec. dir., 152 Nassau St., Suite 204, Princeton, NJ 08542, 609-279-1700, Fax: 609-279-1999

Intermedia Video Products, Douglas Booth, 9200 Deering Ave., Chatsworth, CA 91311, 818-882-3073, Fax: 800-228-2209

Lacerta Group Inc., Ali Lotfi, Richmond, VA

Media Lab, Inc., CD-ROM creation, digital technology for web, Win/Mac, 400 S. McCaslin Blvd., Louisville, CO 80027, 303-665-0374

Replication News, Clive Young, editor, Miller Freeman PSN Inc., 460 Park Avenue South, Ninth Floor, New York, NY 10016, 212-378-0400, Fax: 212-378-2160, e-mail: pro@psn.com

Sonic Solutions, Yuki Miyamoto, 101 Rowland Way, Novato, CA 94945, 415-893-8021, Fax: 415-893-8008, e-mail: yuki@sonic.com

Resources

ABI/Inform, www.library.upenn.edu/index

About Books, Inc., Tom and Marilyn Rosses' *The Complete Guide to Self-Publishing*, 3rd edition, P.O. Box 1306, 425 Cedar St., Buena Vista, CO 81211, 719-395-4790, Fax: 719-395-8374, e-mail: abi@about-books.com, www.SPANnet.org

Scott Adams, Dilbert creator/author e-mail: scottadams@aol.com

Advanced Audio Techniques, Ty Ford, ISBN 0-240-80082-6, ©1993 Focal Press

AlBert's AudioBooks, 5015 Cornell Road, Unit F, Agoura Hills, CA 91301, 818-889-7492, Fax: 818-889-5983, e-mail: AMY516@aol.com, www.audiobooks.com/retailers/alberts/home

Tony Alessandra, Ph.D., 7596 Eads Ave., #140, P.O. Box 2767, La Jolla, CA 92037, 619-459-4515, Fax: 619-459-0435, e-mail: Dr Tony A@alessandra.com

Alpha Enterprise, Audio Capsule™, packaging, 6370 Wise Avenue, Canton, OH 44720, 330-490-2000, Fax: 330-490-2010

Amazon.com, www.Amazon.com

American Booksellers Association, Terrytown, NY, 914-591-2665

American Federation of Television & Radio Artists, **(AFTRA)** 6922 Hollywood Blvd., Hollywood, CA 90028-6128

American Library Association, 312-944-6780

Antonia Boyle & Company, Toni Boyle, 236 W. Portal Ave., #456, San Francisco, CA 94127, e-mail: ABoyleCo@aol.com

Judith Appelbaum, *How to Get Happily Published,* ISBN 0-06-273133-5

Audio Book Club, 2295 Corporate Blvd., NW, Suite 222, Boca Raton, FL 33431-0810

Audio Diversions, audiobook retailer & online catalog, Frank Johnson, Jr., 6639 Madison-McLean Drive, McLean, VA 22101, www.idsonline.com/audiodiversions

Audio Editions, Grady Hesters,1133 High Street, Auburn, CA 95603, and Audio Partners Publishing Corporation, Linda Olsen, 1133 High Street, P.O. Box 6930, Auburn, CA 95604, 916-888-7803, Fax: 916-888-7805, e-mail: BOOKAUDIO@aol.com

***AudioFile* magazine,** the annual *AudioFile Reference Guide,* and *AudioBooks On the Go,* Robin Whitten, editor and publisher, P.O. Box 109, Portland, ME, 04112, 207-775-3744, Fax: 207-775-3744, orders 1-800-506-1212

Audio Highway, Nathan Schulhof, 20600 Mariani Ave., Cupertino, CA 95014, www.audiohwy.com

Audio Literature, Lisa Hunt, 370F West San Bruno, San Bruno, CA 94066

Audio Publishers Association, Jan Nathan, exec. dir., 627 Aviation Way, Manhattan Beach, CA 90266, 310-372-0546, Fax: 310-374-3342, e-mail: apaonline@aol.com, http/www.audiopub.org

Audio Renaissance Media, Inc., *Tiger Woods* and *How To Argue and Win Every Time*, 5858 Wilshire Boulevard, #200, Los Angeles, CA 90036, 213-939-1840, Fax: 213-939-6436, www.audio-source.com

Audio Scholar, *What Is Creativity* and *Origins of the Human Mind,* Marge Bauman, 10375 Nichols Lane, P.O. Box 1456, Mendocino, CA 95460, 707-937-1225 Fax: 707-937-1869

Avid Technologies, Digidesign editing software, Paul Foeckler, 200 East 5th Ave., Suite 341, Naperville, IL 60563

Baker & Taylor Books, 2709 Water Ridge Parkway, Charlotte, NC 28217, 800-775-1800, Fax: 704-329-8989, www.baker-taylor.com, e-mail: btinfo@baker-taylor.e-mail.com

Bantam Doubleday Dell Audio Publishing, Christine McNamara, Director of Marketing, 1540 Broadway, New York, NY, 10036, 212-354-6500, Fax: 212-782-9600, e-mail: McNamara C@BDD.com

BASF Magnetics Corporation, 9 Oak Park Drive, Bedford, MA 01730-1471

Bert-Co Graphics, CD packaging, 1855 Glendale Blvd., Los Angeles, CA 90026, 213-660-9323, Fax: 213-669-5700, www.bert-co.com

Biennix Corporation, *The Money Hunt Guide to Growing Your Business* and *Managing Your Legal Career,* Cliff R. Ennico, 2490 Black Rock Turnpike, #407, Fairfield, CT 06432, 1-888-243-6649, www.moneyhunter.com

Biobox™, *TVT,* Steve Gottlieb, 23 East 4th Street, New York, NY 10003, 212-358-0941, Fax: 212-358-0942, e-mail: biobox@TVT.com

Blackbourn Media Packaging, Dawn Dickey, Suite 200, 5270 W 84th Street, Bloomington, MN 55437-1376, 800-842-7550, Fax: 612-835-9060

Blackstone Audio Books, Craig Black, P.O. Box 969, Ashland, OR 97520, 800-729-2665, Fax: 541-482-9294, e-mail: baudiob@mind.net

Wally Bock,*Cyberpower,* and other publications, e-mail: wbock@bockinfo.com, www.bockinfo.com

Booher Consultants, Inc., Diana Booher, 4001 Gateway Dr., Colleyville, TX 76034, 817-318-6000, Fax: 817-318-6521, e-mail: Booher@Compuserve.com

BookExpo America, 203-840-5476, Fax: 203-840-9476, bookexpo, reedexpo.com

Booklist, 630-892-7465

Books on Tape™, Inc., P.O. Box 7900, Newport Beach, CA 92658, Orders: 800-626-333, 714-548-5525, Fax: 714-548-6574, e-mail: botcs@booksontape.com, www.booksontape.com

BookTronics, retailer, 5370 Westheimer, Houston, TX 77056, 713-626-4000

BookWire, www.bookwire.com

BookZone, Mary Westheimer, P.O. Box 2228, Scottsdale, AZ 85252, 800-536-6162, Fax: 602-481-9712, mary@bookzone.com, www.bookzone.com

Bradshaw Cassettes, Matthew Fox, P.O. Box 720947, Houston, TX 77272, 800-627-2374 (1-800-6bradshaw), Fax: 713-771-1362, www.Bradshawcassettes.com

Jim Brannigan, marketing consultant, 340 Woodhouse Avenue, Wallingford, CT, 06492, 203-269-0065, Fax: 203-269-3818, e-mail: JBrannigan@Worldnet.att.net

Brilliance Audio Services, *Sanctuary* and *Freedom's Choice,* publisher and duplicator, Lou Dudeck, 1704 Eaton Dr., P.O. Box 887, Grand Haven, MI 49417, 800-222-3225, Fax: 800-648-2312

Canadian Broadcasting Corporation, headquarters in Toronto, Canada

Jack Canfield, Self-Esteem Seminars, *Chicken Soup For The Soul™,* P.O. Box 30880, Santa Barbara, CA 93130, 805-563-2935, Fax: 805-563-2945, soup4soul@aol.com

Cape Cod Mystery Theater, Steven Oney, Box 225, West Barnstable, MA 02668. Radio programs on cassette from HighBridge

CareerTrack Publications, Gregg Perry, 3080 Center Green Drive, Boulder, CO 80301, 800-334-1018, Fax: 800-622-6211

Cathcart Institute, Jim Cathcart, P.O. Box 9075, La Jolla, CA 92038, 619-456-3813, 800-222-4883, Fax: 619-456-7218, e-mail: JECathcart@aol.com, www.cathcart.com

Chivers Audio Books, Paul Jobling, Box 1450, Hampton, NH 03842-0015

Cinram, duplicator/replicator, Peter J. Jensen, One Tower Lane, Suite 1700, Oakbrook Terrace, Illinois 60181-4631, 630-573-5209, Fax: 630-954-0812

Cline-Fay Institute & Love and Logic Press, publisher, 2207 Jackson Street, Golden, CO 80040, 800-338-4065

Barbara Coloroso, Kids are worth it! Inc., P.O. Box 621108, Littleton, CO 80162, 800-729-1588, Fax: 303-972-1204

Columbia House AudioBook Club, 1221 Avenue of The Americas, 17th Floor, New York, NY 10020

The Communication Advantage, speaking coach, Dana Gribben, P.O. Box 5038, Larkspur, CA 94977, 510-528-8519

The Complete Guide to Direct Marketing, (Open Horizons Publishing) and 1001 Ways To Market Your Books (5th edition, pub date 9/97), John Kremer, Open Horizans Publishing, P.O. Box 205, Fairfield, IA 52556, 515-472-6130, Fax: 515-472-1560, e-mail: johnkremer@bookmarket.com, www.bookmarket.com

Cooper Communications, Betty K. Cooper, *Speak With Power,* 2209-140th Ave., SW, Calgary, Alberta, T2P 3N3, CANADA, 403-294-1313, Fax: 403-294-1315

CPU, Inc., Jeff Baker, CEO, Commerce Way, Arden, NC 28704, 800-545-3828, Fax: 704-687-3558; western U.S. plant in Irvine, CA

Custom Duplication, Inc., Dirk Flexon, 3404 Century Boulevard, Inglewood, CA 90303, 310-670-5575, Fax: 310-412-2731

Patrick D'Arcy, www.netseminar.com

Deyan Audio Services, digital editing, producing/direcitng,Robert and Debra Deyan, 6617 Rubio Ave., Van Nuys, CA 91406-5634, 818-902-1777, Fax: 818-902-1777

Digital Masters, Audiobook recording, editing, Rick Dasher, 138484 Ventura Blvd., D4, Sherman Oaks, CA 91423, 818-386-9646, 818-386-9172, e-mail: digitalm@earthlink.net

Digital United, CDs and DVD, Mark Magel, Croton On Hudson, NY 10520

Direct Marketing Association, 6 East 43rd St., New York, NY 10017

Disc Graphics, audio packaging/printing, John Rebecchi, 10 Gilpin Ave., Hopptauge, N.Y. 11788, 516-234-1400, Fax: 516-234-1460

Disc Makers, duplicator/replicator, 7905 N. Route 130, Pennsauken, NJ 08110, 800-468-935, Fremont, CA 1-800-869-0715

John Patrick Dolan, attorney, 3 Pointe Dr., Suite 302, Brea, CA 92621, 714-257-3414, Fax: 714-257-3424

Dove Audio, Dove Entertainment, 8955 Beverly Blvd., Los Angeles, CA 90048, 310-786-1600, Fax: 310-247-2924 or www.doveaudio.com/dove/

Dynotropia, ZBS Foundation, RR #1, Box 1201, Ft. Edward, NY 12828, 800— orders, 518-695-6406, Fax: 518-695-4041

Durkin Hayes, 2221 Niagara Falls Blvd., Niagara Falls, NY 14304, 800-962-5200

EAR Professional Audio/Video, John Gibson, 2641 E. McDowell Road, Phoenix, AZ 85008, 602-267-0600, Fax: 602-275-3277, e-mail: info@ear.net, www.ear.net

Earful Of Books, Audiobook store chain, Paul Rush, P.O. Box 26094, Austin, TX 78755-0094, 512-343-2620, Fax: 512-343-2751, e-mail: earfulau@io.com www.earful.com-audio

Editor & Publisher **Publications**, 11 West 19th Street, New York, NY

Eva-tone, duplicator/replicator, 4801 Ulmerton Rd., Clearwater, FL 34622, 1-800-EVATONE. www.eva-tone.com

Executive Insights, Shari Posey, Long Beach, CA

Mike Frank, *For Professional Speakers Only,* Speakers Unlimited (bureau), P.O. Box 27225, Columbus, OH 43227, 614-864-3703

Franklin-Covey, Co., 1958 S. 950 E., M.S. 20, Provo, UT 84606-6200, 801-496-5000, Fax: 801-342-6689

FTM Studios, 1111 S. Pierce, Lakewood, CO 80232, 303-922-3330

David Garfinkel, Overnight Marketing, 2078 21st Avenue, San Francisco, CA 94116, 415-564-4475, Fax 415-564-4599, e-mail: Garfinkel@aol.com

Gauss, a division of EVI Audio, Joseph O'Connor, 9130 Glenoaks Boulevard, Sun Valley, CA 91352, 213-875-1900, Fax: 818-767-4479

Global Arts, John Lane, writer, audiobook producer/consultant 2572 S. Williams St., Denver, CO 80210, 303-698-9310, Fax: 303-698-9310

Marc Graue Recording Services, 3421W. Burbank Blvd., Burbank, CA, 91505, 818-953-8991

Guerrilla Marketing Online, Jay Conrad Levinson and Charles Rubin, Guerrilla Marketing International, P.O. Box 1336, Mill Valley, CA 94942, 800-748-6444;

Guestfinder, online media guest service, www.guestfinder.com

Guthy-Renker Corporation, informercials, 41-550 Eclectic, Palm Desert, CA 92260

Hall Closet Book Company, Ron Hall, P.O. Box 9335, Seattle, WA 9810, 800-895-8915, fax 206-286-0656

Mark Victor Hansen, *Chicken Soup For The Soul™* co-author, P.O. Box 7665, Newport Beach, CA 92658-7665, 800-433-2314, 714-759-9304, Fax: 714-722-6912

Harper Audio and Harper Children's Audio, 10 E. 53rd St., New York, NY 10022, 800-C-Harper, www.harperaudio.com and harperchildrens.com

Harry Fox Agency, music copyright clearance, 711 Third Avenue, New York, NY 10017, 212-370-5330

Keith Hatschek, Passion Press, Box 277, Newark, CA 94560, 800-724-3283, www.passionpress. com

High Windy Audio, P.O. Box 553, Fairview, NC 28730, 800-637-8679

HighBridge Company, audio publisher,

Ingram Book Co., Ingram Audio, 1 Ingram Boulevard, La Vergne, TN 37086, www.ingrambook. com, 800-937-8200

ITA, The International Recording Media Assoc., Charles Van Horn, exec. dir., 152 Nassau St., Suite 204, Princeton, NJ 08542, 609-279-1700, Fax: 609-279-1999

Intermedia Video Products, Douglas Booth, 9200 Deering Ave., Chatsworth, CA 91311, 818-882-3073, Fax: 800-228-2209

Jackson Sound Productions Ltd., duplicator, Linda Cano-Rodriguez, 3301 W. Hampden Ave., Unit C, Englewood, CO 80110, 800-621-6773, 303-761-7940, Fax: 303-789-0557, e-mail: dubs @jacksonsound.com, www.jacksonsound.com

Jeffrey Lant Associates, Dr. Jeffrey Lant, P.O. Box 38-2767 Cambridge, MA 02238, www.world-profit

Jenkins Group, Inc. , *Small Press* and *Information Entrepreneur* magazines.Jerrold Jenkins, co-author with Mardi Link, *Inside the Bestsellers*, 121 E. Front Street, 4th Floor, Traverse City, MI 49684

Jimmy B's Audiobooks, 5225 W. Rosecrans Ave., Hawthorne, CA 90250-6621, 310-643-7640, jimmyb@audiobooks.com

Jack Johnston Seminars, *Male Multiple Orgasms*, 1257 Siskiyou Blvd., #195, Ashland, OR 97520

Arlie Kendall, voice talent, **The Write Stuff**, 25 Apache Rd., Evergreen, CO 80439, 303-670-5077

Dan Kennedy, Empire Communications Corporation,5818 N. 7th St., #103, Phoenix, AZ 85014, 602-269-3111, Fax: 602-269-3113

Kerstetter & Rillo, San Francisco, CA, 415-399-8330

Kirsch's Handbook of Publishing Law, ISBN 0-918226-33-3, Acrobat Books, P.O. Box 870, Venice, CA; Jonathan Kirsch, 310-785-1200

Kliatt, phone/fax 617-237-7577

Knowledge Products, Shirley Cantrell, P.O. Box 305151, Nashville, TN, 37230, orders 800-264-6441, 615-742-3852, Fax: 615-742-3270, crom@edge.net

Lacerta Group Inc., Ali Lotfi, Richmond, VA

Landmark Audiobooks, library leasing program and Audio Adventures rentals nationwide along highways, 4865 Sterling Drive, Boulder, CO 80301, 800-580-2989

Ron and Celeste Lasky, *The Basics of Getting Started in Self-Publishing,* Write on Publications, 2441 Long View Drive, Estes Park, CO 80517, 970 586 8374, Fax: 970-577-0351, e-mail: writeon-pub@aol.com

Library Editions Audio Packaging, Ed Honeycutt, P.O. Box 3704. Albuquerque, NM 87190, 800-876-1909, e-mail: libed4175@aol.com

Library Journal, 245 West 17th Street, NY, NY 10011-5300, 212-463-6819

Library of Congress, Madison Building, Room 401, at 101 Independence Ave., S.E., Washington, DC, www.lcweb.loc.gov

Listening Library Inc., long experience publishing childrens' titles, other subjects. Tim Ditlow, 1 Park Ave., Old Greenwich, CT 06870, 800-243-4504, e-mail: moreinfo@listeninglib.com, listeninglib.com/list lib

Terri Lonier, *Working Solo*®, P.O. Box 190, New Paltz, NY 12561, 800-222-SOLO, Fax: 914-255-2116, e-mail: Lonier@workingsolo.com, www.workingsolo.com

Marantz Recording Equipment, Superscope Technologies, Inc., Niko Karvunidis,1000 Corporate Blvd., Suite D, Aurora, IL 60504, 708-820-4800, Fax: 708-820-8103

Marketing With Newsletters, 2nd editions, Elaine Floyd, Newsletter Resources, 6614 Pernod Ave., St. Louis, MO 63139, 314-647-0400, Fax: 314-647-1609, NLNews@aol.com,

Master Duplicating, Janita Cooper, CEO, 2907 W. Fairmont Dr., Phoenix, AZ 85017, 602-274-9111, Fax: 602-279-6297, e-mail: JCooper@masterdupe.com

John McCabe, P.O. Box 1272, Santa Monica, CA 90406-1272

Media Books, publisher, 560 Sylvan Ave., Englewood Cliffs, NJ 07632, 201-894-8550, Fax: 201-894-1831. Carmen LaRosa, VP and general manager at sales and marketing office, 536 Lawrence St., Port Townsend, WA 98368, 360-379-3009, 3013. E-mail: CarmenLa@localnet.com

Media International Inc., duplicator, 4-color imprinted labels, Duane Lundeen, 6312 Roosevelt Road, Oak Park, IL 60304, 800-200-8701

Media Lab, Inc., CD-ROM creation, digital technology for web, Win/Mac, 400 S. McCaslin Blvd., Louisville, CO 80027, 303-665-0374

Mellex International Corp., cassette shells & packaging, John Cristiano, 150 St. James Ave., Saint James, NY 11780, 516-862-6829, Fax: 516-862-1903

Midwest Book Review, James A. Cox, Editor-in-Chief, Diane C. Donovan, Editor, 278 Orchard Drive, Oregon, WI 53575, www.execpc.com/~mbr/bookwatch

Justin Mitchell, journalist/editor, c/o Audio CP Publishing, 1660 S. Albion, #309, Denver, CO 80222

More Than You Ever Wanted To Know About Mail Order Advertising, Herschell Gordon Lewis, Prentice-Hall, Inc., ISBN 0-13-601039-3

William Morris Agency, Inc. , 1325 Avenue of the Americas, New York, NY 10019

Frank Muller, e-mail: WaveDancer@aol.com

It's a Jungle In There, marketing bookpack for Musicraft, Oregon duplicator, now closed, used with permission

NAPRA (New Age Publishing & Retailing Alliance), P.O. Box 9, Eastsound, WA 98245-0009, 360-376-2702, Fax: 360-376-2704, e-mail: napra@bookwire.com, www.napra.com

The National Association of Independent Publishers Representatives, 111 E. 14th St., Ste. 157, New York, NY 10003, 508-877-5328 or fax 508-788-0208, e-mail: naipr@aol.com

National Public Radio, the *Best of Car Talk®*, www.NPR.org, shameless commerce division

National Speakers Association, 1500 S. Priest Drive, Tempe, AZ 85281, 602-968-2252, Fax: 602-968-0911, www.nsaspeaker.org

Nightingale-Conant Corporation, 7300 Lehigh Ave., Niles, IL 60714, 800-525-9000, 847-647-0306, Fax: 847-647-7145, www.nightingale.com

Nolo Press, 950 Parker Street, Berkeley, CA 94710, 510-549-1976, e-mail: www.nolo.com

Terence O'Kelly, KODAK Recording Products

Para Publishing, *The Self Publishing Manual,* ISBN 1-56860-018-6, Daniel F. Poynter, ninth edition, P.O. Box 8206, Santa Barbara, CA 93118-8206, Order line: 1-800-PARAPUB, Free info kit: 805-968-7277, Fax: 805-968-1379, Fax-on-demand: 805-968-8947 (some free documents), www.parapublishing.com

Penguin Audiobooks, 375 Hudson Street, New York, NY 10014

Penton Overseas, Inc. long established publishers of language tapes, distributor, Hugh Penton or Jean Gonzales, 2470 Impala Drive, Carlsbad, CA 92008-7226, 760-431-0060, 760-431-0060, 800-748-5804, Fax: 760-431-8110, E-mail: penton@cts.com, www.pentonoverseas.com

Personal Power, Anthony Robbins, c/o Audio Rennaisance, Los Angeles, CA

Precise Media, duplicator, Layne Scharton, Pomona, CA 91768

Professional Media Service Corporation, distributor, 19122 South Vermont Ave., Gardena, CA 90248, 800-223-7672, Fax: 800-253-8853, e-mail: Promedia@class.org

Publishers Marketing Association (PMA), Jan Nathan, 627 Aviation Way, Manhattan Beach, CA 90266, 310-372-2732, Fax: 310-374-3342, www.pma-online.org

Publishers Weekly, 249 W. 17th St., N.Y., NY 10011, 800-278-2991

The Publishing Mills, Jessica Kaye, President, 9220 Sunset Blvd., Suite 302, Los Angeles, CA, 90069, 310-858-5385, Fax: 310-858-5391, e-mail: editor@pubmills.com

Quality Books, Inc., library distributor, 1003 W. Pines Road, Oregon, IL 61061-9680, 800-323-4241

R.R. Bowker, 121 Chanlon Road, New Providence, NJ 07974, Publishers of *Literary Market Place* and *Words on Cassette,* 800-521-8110, Fax: 908-665-6688

Radio/TV Interview Report, Bradley Communications, Landsowne PA

Random House AudioBooks, 201 East 50th Street, New York, NY, 10022, 800-726-0600, Fax: 800-659-2436, e-mail: audio@Randomhouse.com, randomhouse.com

The Reader's Chair, Delia White and Steve Gordon, P.O. Box 2626, Hollister, CA 95024, 408-636-1296, Fax: 408-636-1296, e-mail: TRC@ReadersChair.com

ReadersIndex.com, www.ReadersIndex.com

Recorded Books, 270 Skipjack Road, Prince Frederick, MD, 20678, 410-535-5499, Fax: 410-535-5590, e-mail: www.recordedbooks.com

Replication News, Clive Young, editor, Miller Freeman PSN Inc., 460 Park Avenue South, Ninth Floor, New York, NY 10016, 212-378-0400, Fax: 212-378-2160, e-mail: pro@psn.com

Resources for Organizations, Bob Pike, 7620 West 78th Street, Edina, MN 55439,612-829-1954, Fax: 612-829-0260

Rezound International, Inc., distributor specialty in rentals and purchase, 5701 Shingle Creek Parkway #500, Minneapolis, MN 55430, 800-328-1639

Rose Packaging & Design, Inc., Rob & Mary Rose, 6444 S. Quebec St., Bldg. 7, Suite 212, Englewood, CO 80111, 303-773-1003, Fax: 303-773-1041

Sanborn and Assoc., Mark Sanborn, 695 S. Colorado Blvd., #415, Denver, CO 80222, 303-698-9656, Fax: 303-777-3045, e-mail:MarkSpeaks@aol.com

School Library Journal, (Book review dept., or A/V review dept.) 249 W. 17th Street, N.Y. 10011, 212-463-6759, Fax: 212-463-6689, www.sljonline.com

Screen Actors Guild (SAG), 5757 Wilshire Blvd., Los Angeles, CA, 90036-3600, 213-954-1600

Sensible Solutions, Judith Appelbaum, publicity help, see Judith Appelbaum

Howard L. Shenson, deceased, John Wiley & Sons, Inc., 605 Third Avenue, New York, NY 10158-0012

Shiloh Media, Inc., Carol Shapiro, producer/publisher, 100 Belgrave Ave., San Francisco, CA 94117 (living abroad '97-98)

Shorewood Packaging, 2220 Midland Avenue, Unit 50, Scarborough, ONT M1P 3E6, 800-387-5137, 416-292-3990, Fax: 416-292-0480

Simon & Schuster Audio, 1230 Avenue of the Americas, New York, NY 10020, 800-223-2348, 212-698-7184, Fax: 212-698-632-8091

Small Press Association of North America, SPAN, See About Books, Inc., e-mail: abi@about-books.com, www.SPANnet.org

Small Press Center, 20 West 44th Street, New York, NY 10036

Small Press Magazine, Jerrold Jenkins, co-author with Mardi Link, *Inside the Bestsellers*, 121 E. Front Street, 4th Floor, Traverse City, MI 49684

SmartPractice™, Jim and Naomi Rhode, 3400 E. McDowell, Phoenix, AZ 85008-7899, 602-225-9090, Fax: 602-225-0245, www.smartpractice.com

Mark S.A. Smith, co-author *Guerrilla Selling* and *Guerrilla Tradeshow Selling*, The Valence Group, 3530 Cranswood Way, Colorado Springs, CO 80918-6338, 719-522-0833, 800-488-0780, Fax: 719-522-079, e-mail: MSASmith@aol.com, www.RXSelling.com

Sonic Solutions, Yuki Miyamoto, 101 Rowland Way, Novato, CA 94945, 415-893-8021, Fax: 415-893-8008, e-mail: yuki@sonic.com

Sonopress, Inc., duplicator, 1540 Broadway, 28th Floor, New York, NY 10036, 212-782-7668, Fax: 212-782-7650

Sony Disc Manufacturing, Thomas E. Farrington, 3181 N. Fruitridge Ave., Terre Haute, IN 47804

Sony Electronics Inc., Dwuan Watson,1200 N. Arlington Heights Rd., Itasca, IL 60143

Soundelux Audio Publishing, 37 Commercial Boulevard, Novato, CA 94949

Sounds True Audio, Jay Zwicky, Mkg. Mgr., 4135 Aurthur Ave., Louisville, CO 80027, 303-665-3151, Fax: 303-665-5292, e-mail: soundstrue@aol.com, www.puzzlergulch.com/ Sounds_True

Speaking Secrets of The Masters, Speakers Roundtable, Jim Cathcart, P.O. Box 9075, La Jolla, CA 92038

Spoken Word Audios, John Runette, studio, director, editor, Los Angeles, CA, 310-398-9858

Jean Marie Stine, *Writing Successful Self-Help and How To Books*, ISBN 0-471-03739-7, John Wiley & Sons. Available from IFGE, Box 229, Waltham, MA 02254-0029, Orders 617-895-2212 or Fax: 617-899-5703

Tangled Web Audio, *Forebodings: American Classics*, Linda Jones, 1063 King Street West, Suite 133, Hamilton, Ontario, 519-442-5010, Fax: 519-442-2346, tangled@bis.on.ca, www.eidos.ca/tangled/

Tape Specialty, Inc., Steve Feldman, 13411 Saticoy St., North Hollywood, CA 91605, 800-310-0800, Fax: 818-904-0267, e-mail:tsinet@earthlink.net

Telex Communications, Inc., Blake Erickson, 9600 Aldrich Ave., South Minneapolis, MN 55420

Terry's Audiobooks, Terry Pogue, www.idsonline.com/terraflora/audio

Time Warner Audiobooks, Maya Thomas, producer, or Samantha Fahnestock, 1271 Avenue of the Americas, 11th Flr., New York, NY 10020, 212-522-7334, Fax: 212-522-7994, www.pathfinder/twar

Brian Tracy, Brian Tracy International, 462 Stevens Ave., #202, Solana Beach, CA 92075, 619-481-2977, Fax: 619-481-2445

KC Truby, The Lonesome Cowboy will send you a FREE copy of his latest *Business Builder* cassette tape. Phone 307-472-1941, Fax: 307-472-1950, e-mail: kctruby@aol.com. Specify *Knowledge Centered Selling* for a copy of tape to match script.

Tri-Plex, Inc., audio packaging, John Risdon, 245 Fifth Ave., New York, NY 10016

Vermont AudioBooks, RR1, Box 60, Richmond, VT 05477, 800-639-1862, e-mail: vtaudio@together.net

Vinylweld Media Packaging, 2011 W. Hastings, Chicago IL 60608, 800-444-4020, Fax: 312-942-0693

Joe Mister Fire! Vitale, *Cyberwriting,* copywriting, online free reports, Box 300792, Houston, TX 77230-0792, mrfire@blkbox.com

Walt Disney Records/Buena Vista Audio Publishers, 500 S. Buena Vista St., 2230, Burbank, CA 91521

Lilly & Dottie Walters, *Speak and Grow Rich,* P.O. Box 1120 Glendora CA 91740, PO Box 1120, Glendora, CA 91740, 818-335-8069, Fax: 818-335-6127, e-mail: Call4Sprkr@aol.com

Thomas J. Winninger, Winninger Institute for Market Strategy, 3300 Edinborough Way, #701, Minneapolis, MN 55435-5963, 612-896-1900, Fax: 612-896-9784

Wireless catalog, P.O. Box 64422, St. Paul, MN 55164 -0422

World Media Group, duplicator/replicator, Brad Cates, 6737 East 30th Street, Indianapolis, IN 46219, 317-549-8484, Fax: 317-549-8480, e-mail: wmg@indy.net, www.al.com/wmg/

Writer's AudioShop, Elaine Davenport, 204 E. 35th Street, Austin, TX 78705

Writer's Market, Writer's Digest Books, F&W Publications, 1507 Dana Avenue, Cincinnati, OH 45207, 513-531-2222, Fax: 513-531-4744

Joyce Wycoff, Mindmapping®, www.mindlinks.com

Yellow Moon Press, folklore & storytelling, Box 381316, Cambridge, MA 02238, 800-497-4385, Fax: 617-776-8246

You're Good Enough, You're Smart Enough, and Doggone It, People Like You!, Guided Visualizations by Stuart Smalley, Al Franken, ISBN 0-553-47094-9, ©1992 Al Franken, Performance Copyright Bantam Audio Publishing

ZBS Foundation, *Dynotopia,* RR #1, P.O. Box 1201, Fort Edward, NY 12828

John Zobrist, duplicator, Musicraft Multimedia, Woodburn, OR 1-800-637-9493

Orders

Your Company   ORDERS

TITLE: _____   **ORDER DATE:** _____

Name: _____   Ship To: _____
Address: _____   Address: _____
City, State, Zip: _____   City, State, Zip: _____
Phone: _____ Fax: _____
Amount Paid: _____   Credit Card # _____
P.O. # _____ ☐ Check ☐ MO   Expires _____
Signature: _____   Ship Date/Tracking # _____
Notes: _____
_____

Name: _____   Ship To: _____
Address: _____   Address: _____
City, State, Zip: _____   City, State, Zip: _____
Phone: _____ Fax: _____
Amount Paid: _____   Credit Card # _____
P.O. # _____ ☐ Check ☐ MO   Expires _____
Signature: _____   Ship Date/Tracking # _____
Notes: _____
_____

Name: _____   Ship To: _____
Address: _____   Address: _____
City, State, Zip: _____   City, State, Zip: _____
Phone: _____ Fax: _____
Amount Paid: _____   Credit Card # _____
P.O. # _____ ☐ Check ☐ MO   Expires _____
Signature: _____   Ship Date/Tracking # _____
Notes: _____
_____

Name: _____   Ship To: _____
Address: _____   Address: _____
City, State, Zip: _____   City, State, Zip: _____
Phone: _____ Fax: _____
Amount Paid: _____   Credit Card # _____
P.O. # _____ ☐ Check ☐ MO   Expires _____
Signature: _____   Ship Date/Tracking # _____
Notes: _____
_____

Production Schedule

PRODUCTION SCHEDULE FOR _____	Week 1	Week 2	Week 3	Week 4	Week 5	Week 6	Week 7	Week 8	Week 9
Jobs or Actions to Be Accomplished									

Tape Content or Editing Log

EDITING LOG			
TAPE CATALOG FOR:		**Your Company Name**	
TAPE TITLE OR SUBJECT:		*Your Company Advertising Line*	
DATE: **Tape** **of**		Your Company Street Address City, State, Zip	
Machine		(000) 000-0000 • Fax: (000) 000-0000	

Counter	Voice	Technical/Edit	Content

Time Value

	Time	Payoff	Delegate?	Task Total
Preproduction:				
Telephone calls/info gathering				
Meetings/researching				
Determining market				
Selecting packaging and supplier				
Arranging for cover designer				
Writing cover copy				
Writing/reviewing the script				
Gathering source tapes				
Auditioning voice talent				
Negotiating fees, agreements				
Gathering source tapes				
Confirming all's on track				
Production:				
Recording session				
Reviewing session tape				
Transcribing/marking edits				
Reviewing edited tape				
Notes, changes, mark edits				
Soliciting peer review				
Telephone/ meetings				
Choosing music				
Rerecording/editing/reviewing				
Duplication/Packaging:				
Design labels, proof and sign off				
Design cover, proof and sign off				
Order packaging, verify details				
Verify arrival, assembly details				
Meet duplicator to place order				
Listen/approve test cassettes				
Confirm shipping locations				
Other Tasks Not Included above:				

Commentator's Quick Test © 1997 Audio CP Publishing

What do I want to say?

Who do I want to tell?

Why do I want to say it?

Book Pack (Generic Dimensions Only)

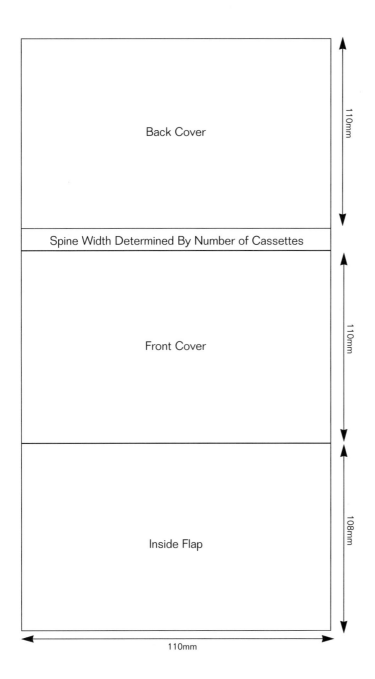

Back Cover

Spine Width Determined By Number of Cassettes

Front Cover

Inside Flap

110mm

110mm

108mm

110mm

Cassette Label, For Direct On Shell Labels

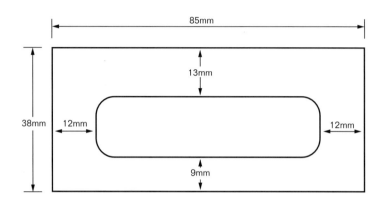

CD Liner

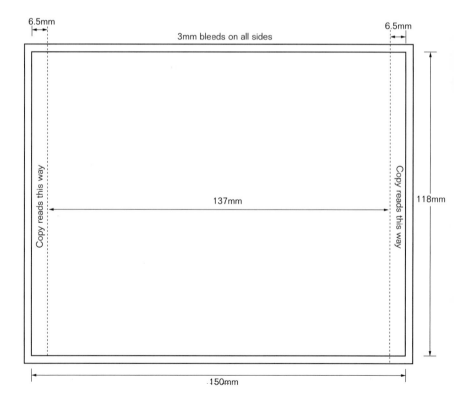

Single J Card, No Extra Flaps

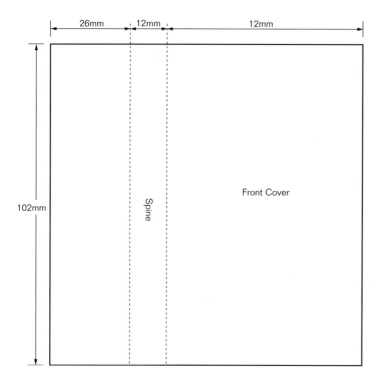

26mm | 12mm | 12mm

102mm

Spine

Front Cover

"O" Cards

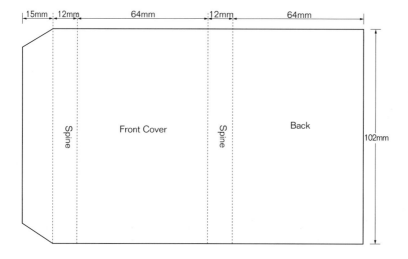

15mm | 12mm | 64mm | 12mm | 64mm

Spine

Front Cover

Spine

Back

102mm

Cassette Label Template at 200%

Index

ORDER ANOTHER COPY

"Words On Tape," the first complete guide to audio success, makes a great gift! Share the secrets you need to know to develop, record, and sell audio products with a friend or colleague. Contact your favorite bookstore or use the handy order form below.

200+ pages • Index • Templates • Resources • Experts. ©1997 •
ISBN 0-9655721-4-5

Ship to:

Name _____

Address_____

City/State/Zip_____

Day Phone_____ Fax_____

E-mail Address _____

☐ Publisher   ☐ Speaker/Trainer   ☐ Other _____

☐ Check ☐ Visa ☐ MC Card #_____

Exp. Date_____ Signature_____

Name as it appears on card: _____

$27.95 US funds+ $3.00 shipping (1-2 books), $1.00 shipping each additional book.

_____ Books X $27.95 $ _____

_____ Shipping X $3.00 $ _____

_____ Shipping X $1.00 $ _____

Order Total $ _____

Order Now! Three Easy Options
Phone: 1-800-582-9392 (orders only)
Fax: 1-800-250-4921 (secure)
Mail: AudioCP Publishing 1660 S. Albion, Suite 309 Denver, CO 80222